SOCIAL RESEARCH & REFLEXIVITY

SOCIAL RESEARCH & REFLEXIVITY

CONTENT, CONSEQUENCES AND CONTEXT

TIM MAY with BETH PERRY

Los Angeles | London | New Delhi
Singapore | Washington DC

SAGE Publications Ltd
1 Oliver's Yard
55 City Road
London EC1Y 1SP

SAGE Publications Inc.
2455 Teller Road
Thousand Oaks, California 91320

SAGE Publications India Pvt Ltd
B 1/I 1 Mohan Cooperative Industrial Area
Mathura Road
New Delhi 110 044

SAGE Publications Asia-Pacific Pte Ltd
33 Pekin Street #02-01
Far East Square
Singapore 048763

Library of Congress Control Number 2010922362

British Library Cataloguing in Publication data

A catalogue record for this book is available from
the British Library

ISBN 978-0-7619-6283-0
ISBN 978-0-7619-6284-7 (pbk)

Typeset by C&M Digitals (P) Ltd, Chennai, India
Printed in India at Replika Press Pvt Ltd
Printed on paper from sustainable resources

CONTENTS

PREFACE

As with the writing of all books, there are sets of circumstances that both enable and constrain their production. What is often needed is a systematic period of time to devote to its production. In my case, this was never to appear as my career took on new challenges in different contexts. While I sought the time, the effort bargain surrounding my work altered and the need to generate large amounts of external income and develop and then maintain an organization, its values, integrity and culture, predominated.

The processes that surround what we do inevitably influence our production at some level and given this, periods of time were taken within my daily practices to write this book. In the end, it was the context and content of those practices and the learning, knowledge and experiences that it generated that has informed the writing of this book. I found myself surrounded by varying expectations and entering into new terrains of activity. Then, in 2001, an opportunity arose to be seconded to the Centre for Sustainable Urban and Regional Futures (SURF). SURF is an interdisciplinary, largely self-funded research centre with its own offices in Central Manchester.

After a few months of my secondment I was asked to run the centre and we set about building it up and obtaining the necessary funding to provide for its reputation and ensure its medium term sustainability. It was hard work. Yet the chance to do something different increased and this experience has taught me a great deal. It was certainly not the same as my past experiences of academic life.

I had to learn about new areas of work and engage in the creation of a distinctive identity that sought to balance applicability with credibility. All of this took place whilst liaising with external clients, working to tight deadlines and producing lengthy research reports in short time periods, whilst actively seeking in our practice to adhere to a set of values concerning the importance of academic work. We sought clarification through journal articles and book chapters as a matter of routine and were highly successful in the game called the 'research assessment exercise'. We designed websites, engaged in dissemination activities according to the idea of knowledge being a public good and sought to balance the attraction of expertise with a cooperative spirit of inquiry. Our own culture of inquiry, therefore, was of key importance to maintaining a sense of value in an ambivalent world.

In many ways I returned to elements of what I was – an agricultural engineer – before I became a social scientist, but with new forms of knowledge, values and experiences. When people speak of those in the public sector having no experience of the private sector – and with that the assumption that they are somehow 'lacking' – I feel no need to be defensive or deferential. I actually find the tendency to be deferential to those in the private sector to be without foundation and this detracts from the important need to sustain the difference and distinctiveness of universities as sites of knowledge production, cooperation and dissemination.

We are engaged, as a matter of the realities that inform our everyday work, with clients in the public and private sectors who find what we do useful and challenging. That means we have to work at being different in both the university sector and in public and commercial life in general. We have to make spaces of reflection in places of expectation. This is important for the future of university life, but it receives little systematic attention and is frequently divorced from the content of academic work.

All in all, a great deal of change has taken place in a short period of time in my public and private lives. Throughout this period I have had the support of my friends at SURF where Vicky Simpson acts as our Centre Manager. Simon Marvin and I have been through many discussions and experiences in running SURF together. I have valued our friendship during this time and during one long evening, he gave me advice that I will never forget. Mike Hodson not only has been a friend and someone with whom I have enjoyed many good discussions over the years, but he also read parts of the book and provided valuable comments on its content.

Calum and Cian, my children, are often scathing about my endeavours and their friends have picked up books and asked: 'What is this all about?' The reply is usually: 'I don't know, ask my Dad'. They know I think the content may matter because we have talked about how knowledge can make a difference. What has made a difference to me, however, is being with them as they grow up and having an increasing feeling of well-being for the type of people that they are becoming and feeling very proud of who they are. Vikki Baker has provided inspiration and support during the process of writing, as well as reading chapters and providing valued advice. Thanks Vikki, not only for this, but for so much more in our lives together.

There are many friends and colleagues that I wish to mention who have influenced the content of this book in different ways. Malcolm Williams and I have worked on a number of projects and enjoyed numerous discussions about methodology, theory and philosophy of science and he has provided valuable feedback on the content of the book. Ken Parsons and I did our PhDs together and have remained good friends since that time. My thanks to you Ken for your support and our many memorable meetings over the years. There are also those who have been generally supportive of my endeavours and I wish to record my thanks to them. They are: Jason Powell, Linda McKie, Paul Taylor, Zygmunt Bauman, Richard Brown, Alan Bryman, Rom Harré, William Outhwaite, Bev Skeggs and Dorothy Smith.

As well as the above, a number of other people were kind enough to comment on previous work that has informed the writing of this book. My thanks therefore go to the following: Alan Scott, Davydd Greenwood, Craig Calhoun, Lisa Adkins, Steve Fuller, Jeff Hearn, Richard Jenkins, Craig Pritchard and Stewart Clegg. My thanks also to Chris Rojek, Mila Steele and Jai Seaman at Sage for being so patient during the process of its production.

Particular thanks are due to Beth Perry. Beth is a friend with whom I have worked on many projects for research councils, universities, the National Health Service and the public and private sectors in general since 2002. Beth is a never-ending source of insight, support and inspiration. We have shared our experiences and understandings during very busy, difficult, but also rewarding times. It made perfect sense to ask Beth to collaborate on the third part of this book, which is informed by extensive empirical work that has been conducted nationally and internationally across the range of SURF's work.

We have interviewed hundreds of people, about universities, innovation, science and society in different countries, who work in national governments, the European Commission, business and industry, regional and local authorities, research foundations and universities. At SURF we have conducted work for universities on their socio-economic role, populated the idea of 'urban knowledge arenas' and contributed to the development of Science Cities; examined the processes and expectations surrounding investments in knowledge and innovation for city-regional socio-economic growth; introduced the idea of 'active intermediaries' into knowledge exchange; interrogated public policy and practice in terms of its relations between governance and economic geography and contributed to developing holistic views of critical infrastructures in city-regional development in an era of climate change and resource constraint.

Despite the reality of many of our experiences in seeking first to puncture the hyperbole surrounding the supposed relations between knowledge, innovation and economic activity and then suggest effective alternatives, we have never given up on the value of knowledge for illuminating and informing these activities, nor upon extensive reflections on the limitations of particular ways of understanding. Nor have we ever given up on our role in learning through utilizing skills that are not taught, nor could ever be, in any module or course. Our experiences could cover another book, as we have sat with those in power who regard understanding as an impediment to their ambitions, as well as with those who are not so powerful, finding such understanding does not always change things. For now, however, the focus has been on producing this one and we hope that within its pages, others will find the confidence, contexts and cultures in and through which they can engage with the world.

We have drawn upon previously published material and a great deal of research that we have conducted within SURF (for more information please see: www.surf.salford.ac.uk). This work has been extensively elaborated upon, broken up into sections and completely abandoned along the way. Nevertheless, it is right that we should acknowledge the editors and publishers of the following:

May, T. (2006) 'Universities: Space, governance and transformation', *Social Epistemology*, 20(3–4): 333–45. May, T. (2006) 'The missing middle in methodology:

Occupational cultures and institutional conditions', *Methodological Innovations Online*, 1 (1). Available online at http://erdt.plymouth.ac.uk/mionline/public_html/viewarticle.php?id=22&layout=html. (May, T. (2005) 'Transformations in academic production: context, content and consequences', *European Journal of Social Theory*, 8 (2): 193–209. May, T. (2005) 'Reflexivity and sociological practice', in M. Williams (ed.), *The Philosophical Foundations of Social Research, Volume 3*. London: Sage. May, T. (2002) 'The discontented epoch: Freedom and security in Bauman's postmodernity', in P. Beilharz (ed.), *Zygmunt Bauman: Volume 3, The Postmodern*. London: Sage. May, T. (2002) 'Trans-formations in principles and practice', in T. May (ed.), *Qualitative Research in Action*. London: Sage. May, T. (2000) 'A future for critique? Positioning, belonging and reflexivity', *European Journal of Social Theory*, 3(2): 157–73. May, T. (1998) 'Reflexivity in the age of reconstructive social science', *International Journal of Social Research Methodology: Theory and Practice*', 1 (1): 7–24. Perry, B. (2008) 'Academic knowledge and urban development: Theory, policy and practice', in T. Yigitcanlar, K. Velibeyoglu and S. Baum (eds), *Knowledge-Based Urban Development*. New York: Information Science Reference (an imprint of IGI Global). Perry, B. and May, T. (2006) 'Excellence, relevance and the university: The "Missing middle" in socio-economic engagement', *Journal of Higher Education in Africa*, 4 (3): 69–92.

INTRODUCTION: MOTIVATIONS FOR A CONTRIBUTION

The writing of this book represents the latest stage in a journey where issues have arisen that are bound to preoccupy those practitioners who reflect upon the basis of their work in terms of its knowledge claims, its purpose, for whom their knowledge is produced and its overall relationship to the culture and organization of their practices.

In working through these issues, there are a series of concerns that have driven my engagement with ideas in the pursuit of clarification. Accompanying this is no expectation of resolution, but orientations in the service of engagement. For me, this is important. As soon as practices within the social sciences are assumed to achieve resolution, rather than clarification for the purpose of generating understanding and informing actions, they have overextended themselves and disappointment is inevitable. Responses on the part of individual social scientists to this state of affairs can range from self-referential indulgence, via denouncement, to celebrations of technicism and theoreticism.

One aim of this book is to examine writings around these issues and their implications for the practice of social scientific research. This is underpinned by a concern with the transformative potential of social scientific insights, based on an understanding of their historical roots, consequences and the contexts and cultures in which they are produced.

Before moving on to this investigation, I would like to reflect on the reasons that have led me to this project. Such things are often hidden away in books where products, rather than dispositions and positions, are focused upon. I hope this discussion informs an understanding of my motivations so that the reader may engage more productively with what follows.

I started working as a university lecturer at the turn of the 1990s following another career. During my time as a student I was confronted by a climate in which critiques of positivism, empiricism, Marxism, action theory, structuralism, malestream social science and modernity circulated in a bewildering manner. Once I had my qualifications and managed to obtain a job, I then deliberately sought, through a series of publications, to engage with some of these debates and take them seriously by being an interpreter of their insights for different audiences.

During this time there was a set of dispositions that I brought to my reading which I have sought to expose to scrutiny. First, history does not carry with it some unfolding towards an end state in which power and conflict are eradicated according to some posited ideal of humanity. Second, autonomy is not based on an isolated individualism, nor will it automatically flourish in a particular set of social arrangements via a conjuncture between self-identity and social context. Beyond these initial orientations, there was no intellectual foil against which to slash at these new ideas; all of which was accompanied by an uncertainty concerning my right to belong to a community of what appeared to be clever folk.

I wanted to be educated and trained in social science to address my evident ignorance and deploy those skills in the service of better understanding which would, in a small way, contribute to an overall improvement in social conditions. Part of this was to understand how differences might constitute, rather than negate, knowledge claims and to recognize how frequently they were suppressed in the name of narrow interests. Power flows without tolerance or recognition of difference, but also increasingly enables an absence of responsibility through indifference in an inverse relationship with positions that actually afford privileges and choices. I thus retained a strong belief that social conditions could be improved, but without allusion to paradigms that shut down the practical difficulty of their achievement via the simple slogan 'this is the solution, now the problem'. Equally, while acts of problematization are important elements in practical social science, they easily lapse into an indulgence that escapes the effort of engagement.

I watched critiques that were originally aimed at positivism and empiricism and which built upon a long legacy of the relativism versus objectivism debate in the philosophy of science move into other terrains. Critiques of explanation, informed by those who seemed to invoke limited understandings of the process of knowledge production within the physical sciences, seemed to be turned upon claims to move beyond particular contexts in any discipline. Therefore, while tempering exaggerated claims that informed the work of some practitioners, the results appeared to undermine engagement in the service of illumination through over-generalization. Whether overtly, or as a result of presuppositions that remained beyond question, the decisions that are made about theory, methods, methodology, ethics and politics are now open to routine scrutiny. None of this sidesteps the fundamental question: how far should this go without undermining the very basis upon which distinctive and insightful knowledge is generated?

It is nothing new. Some have argued that its opening in Western thought began in the late nineteenth century in the writings of Friedrich Nietzsche (Habermas 1992a), while there are those who have written about how social science had inherited terms that, although outdated, remained rooted in practice. These 'standard categories of thought', if generalized to contemporary situations, 'become unwieldy, irrelevant, not convincing ... so now The Modern Age is being succeeded by a *post-modern period*. Perhaps we may call it: The Fourth Epoch'

(Mills 1970 [1959]: 184. Italics added). What is new is that these critiques, whether by design or default, can work in the context of a more general disenchantment regarding any possibility for improving our understanding of and improvement in social relations.

If the epoch which has given us these critiques is concerned with the search for new values, identities and ways of life, perhaps it is not surprising that practitioners range, in reaction to these criticisms, from those who argue that nothing has changed, via those who continue in their work regardless, to those for whom anything less than a total embrace is an act of betrayal. As a result we find calls for a return to an unproblematic scientism – defined as the belief that science is seen as the only form of legitimate knowledge which is to be applied and which unproblematically claims to be the judge of all alternatives – mixing with those which denounce any allusion to scientific evidence in favour of alternative means of representation: for example, fiction and art. For those napping in the cosy slumbers of unreflexive orientations to their work, their practices may be characterized as branches of literary criticism which, in turn, slips into becoming the queen of the sciences. The philosopher-king who once sought to speak in the name of Truth is dead. So do we now hail the queen who speaks in the name of truths?

Polarizations between an unreconstructed scientism and acts of literary deconstruction do little to aid understandings that are generated by a myriad of social scientists during the course of their daily practices. While the idea that one can, without question, claim to speak in the name of a separate and unproblematic reality has been open to question for a long time, so too is the claim to speak in the name of different realities as mediated by alternative modes of representation. The same tendencies are evident in both: that is, seeking to legislate over the constitution and nature of social reality thereby alleviating the need to 'work at' understanding. Placing a priori limits on the practice of the social sciences relieves many of those who pronounce upon a single reality and commit atrocities in the name of their limited ideologies.

In the process of these contestations, scientism becomes confused with science. If the latter mixes with sensitivity to context and a willingness to engage in an understanding of the relationship between justification and application that is not taken to be beyond question, it can engage with considerations that rightly lie beyond the confines of its boundaries. These include the desirability of various courses of actions, as well as recognition of different forms of life and their role in the constitution of social reality. Yet all too often, allusions to context-sensitivity are translated into context-dependence and that carries with it all the connotations of the relativism–objectivism debate (Bernstein 1983). Equally, a more balanced consideration serves to prevent those who deploy science in ways that are nothing more than regurgitations of prejudice and a desire for ever more profit.

There is not only the content of these debates to consider in terms of their implications for practice, but also their transmission and reception in relation to the organizational contexts of social scientific knowledge production and its standing in the public realm. In terms of those contexts, a series of acts of demolition on so-called classic texts can assist in the process of accumulating the reputations that appear to be so central to academic cultures. The project is to expose the presuppositions of those who were once canonized as representatives of a tradition that budding apprentices are expected to emulate in their practice. What is lost is a process of mutual learning, not only because of an absence of context-sensitivity in terms of the period in which people were writing, but also because of the new standards that those who charge themselves with this undertaking invoke. Learning is lost and so too is the inspiration that comes from knowing how those authors rose above their time and place to shape a different understanding.

Instead of the process of learning in supportive and developmental cultures, the tendency is to produce competing academic camps, with those defending established procedures pitted against those who set themselves the task of finding tacit assumptions that represent nothing more than nostalgic yearnings for a bygone age, or a disjuncture between rhetorical claims and actual practice. Academic conferences readily accommodate themselves to this process with different streams representing alternative approaches as if the effort involved in understanding is for others to undertake, not for those who must, by virtue of their practice, expect it of others. We then await the next stage in which those thinkers who have been subject to acts of deconstruction enter a process of resurrection. Careers are forged in this process allowing another set in the intellectual class to beat their keyboards.

Elements of this activity are central to the distinctiveness of scientific endeavour and may be found in other areas of work. They are a vital part of the vibrancy of intellectual work and function as an instrument for sensitizing practitioners to the consequences and assumptions built into their practices. Yet at what point do these issues undermine research activity and add to a process of individualization in academic departments, via the production of particular types of work, and delegitimation in the public realm through self-referential activity? Both the contexts of that work and the standing of disciplines in the public realm enable those practices in the first instance. Is this where an answer to the fundamental question that surrounds reflexivity may be clarified? How far to go? One thing is for sure, this activity constitutes a production line in which knowledge is continually deconstructed. Newer entrants and even established members of disciplines are then even more bewildered as textual exegesis triumphs over clarification. At least the latter has the potential to build a confidence needed to engage in realms where social science meets its publics.

From a pedagogical point of view, the knowledge that is generated may be applied to existing contexts in such a manner that inspiration is permitted little role. Processes of context revision that come from inspiration are replaced by context dependence in ever lengthening reading lists. Does anyone emerge any the wiser? At what point does such activity become counterproductive from the point of view of engagement, inspiration and understanding itself? When does it cease to inform in order to question and even potentially transform and, instead, lead to confusion, paralysis, apathy and inactivity? Meanwhile, the future is left to those who are less preoccupied with deconstructing the past and present.

In the face of these practices it is possible to form the distinct impression that discussions become trapped within ever descending interpretative circles. With the struggles for academic reputations in place, they may be forged via interpretations of interpretations. Yet how are the interpreters authorized to make their interjections in the first place? Would this be something to do with the institutional authority that is bestowed upon them and which enables a distance to be maintained from the practice and products of systematic social investigation? If there is a distance from everyday necessity which, when combined with education and organizational position, allows for certain insights into social relations, how does that relate to practice and how might it be defended according to its more general role in society?

There are important advantages to such distance, particularly when compared with the proximity of those whose practices are driven by the interests of sponsors who make specific demands according to the pursuit of narrow aims. The distance afforded by the university can also easily lead to an indulgence that misses its mark through, for example, assuming that external interests are homogeneous and allowing their free play through an absence of engagement and challenge. The question is not the absence of interest, but whose interests, according to what reasons and with what consequences? What we are talking about here is their nature and influence in relation to the process, product and interpretation of the research itself. Here we find that the limits to reflexivity inhere in a willingness to subject one's own position to critical scrutiny; not, it should be added, as an end point, but as part of a process that is supportive and informs practices according to a collectively understood ethos.

If we add to these observations that the world is not about to stop and listen to such debates, this tells us something about the ways in which dominant modes of organizing social relations will take their revenge on those who perpetuate practices that are indifferent to the conditions of their possibility. Shouting from the sidelines, even with the best of intentions, does not make much difference and is too readily dismissed by those who should stop and listen. When attention is turned to such matters, there is the potential to expose the limits to particular discourses. In this way we may not see them as all encompassing of social relations and instead begin to ask other questions and see spaces of potential for alternatives to be opened up to examination and transformation. In so doing we might then better understand how an analyst may make modest, but insightful claims from their vantage points, in the face of what are taken to be overwhelming social forces. Seeking to work at these issues as ongoing matters can provide the basis for more sustainable and engaged practices.

We are still left with another issue: reconstruction. Engaged, theoretically informed empirical work can be conducted in order to illuminate issues and bring to the attention of a wider audience the dynamics and consequences of social relations, thereby providing for the possibility of things being other than they are via a critique of false necessity. What is at stake is not only how others dominate, but also how we are positioned and position ourselves and with what consequences for our actions, aspirations and understandings. Such an aspiration is consistent with the impulse to match the work of reconstruction alongside the need for deconstruction in order to remain sensitive to the working assumptions that inform practice.

Here we can detect another possible consequence in relation to engagements between social science and social life. If there is a withdrawal from fields of current endeavour, there are plenty of those, unfettered by the latest critiques concerning the quest to uncover realities, who are only too happy to fill them. These are the armies of 'journalists, pundits, politicians, and pop-theorists, who are always more than willing to supply that need' (McCarthy in Hoy and McCarthy 1994: 220).

These issues raise the need for clarification. Contrary to the attitude of those who regard such matters as detracting from 'real' work, a discussion of socio-theoretical writings is required towards this end. The important consideration is, once again, how far to go? Narrow specialisms around adherence to methods of social research, theory, philosophy and methodology are not helpful towards this end. Nor is it helped by increasing struggles for academic recognition accompanied by greater specialization that prevents cross-disciplinary learning. We all deploy, as a condition of our being-in-the-world, sets of assumptions that render it intelligible. However, if a certain form of practice and contemplation – as that which enables research to be undertaken in the first place – lies in a position that at some point in its process is distanced from necessity in order to produce intelligibility, what conditions enable this to happen? I will argue that it is conditions which inhere in the social world which not only have a more systematic expression in social scientific practice, but also provide for its possibility and its value. Understanding these relationships also acts as a check upon exaggerated claims.

Writings on reflexivity tend to be manuals that provide steps for the practitioner to become more reflexive. What is replicated is an individualism that separates content, character and context. There are no easy routes and no self-help books with ten steps to 'becoming reflexive'. Because context matters, it will be necessary to turn to the study of conditions of knowledge production. Not only is this a guard against conflating different forms of reason, but also the complacency that is born in dispositions that have the potential to accompany *all* modes of thought – whatever their claims may be concerning the constitution of social reality. I will argue that understanding such conditions provides for a modesty which informs a greater sense of the value of social research in society.

The background to these discussions centres upon the complacency of empiricism, in the sense that a simple separation between knower and known is posited. Readers of works devoted to reacting to this issue may be forgiven for thinking that the result is a rather inward-looking practice, such that the way in which knowledge is produced is now of more importance than what it tells us about the social world. Here the Janus nature of reflexivity rears its head. This is not assisted by reflexivity having become one of those social scientific buzzwords that is thrown about as if it were a guarantor of good scientific practice and deployed as a means of denigrating the work of others. 'Are you being reflexive enough?' Such a question may be productive if accompanied by a dialogue aimed at understanding the reasons for its appearance, the context of production and the criteria and consequences that underlie its call, but instead it often works in an accusatory fashion and little is learnt as a result.

When caught between the epistemic superiority of a complacent scientism, whose knowledge is instrumentally driven and a self-defeating relativism, so often accompanied by 'end of history' celebrations characteristic of the arrogance of the ebbs and flows of modern day capitalism, where is one to turn? Of course, how and why such questioning manifests itself is variable. For those on short-term employment contracts, questions such as these may seem a luxury where the concern understandably remains with where the next source of funding may come from in order to meet the necessities of everyday life. For others, established in their positions and apparently certain in their knowledge, such questioning may be seen, at best, as a distraction and at worst, destructive of established presuppositions that enable analysis of social life in the first place.

There is no suggestion that those on short-term contracts do not reflect on these issues, or that those established in their positions are not given to such thoughts. It will, however, be suggested that there is a relationship between organizational context and knowledge production – or, more generally, between positioning, belonging and reflexivity – that requires more thought in terms of its implications for practice. In addition, there is a relationship between knowledge, action and power that it is the business of the social scientist to understand. As a result it becomes necessary to understand the limits to reflexivity and action that are implied in abstract discussions of autonomous individuals through an examination of how we are positioned and thus enabled or constrained in particular ways.

Without this in place those who once sought something called an unproblematic 'reality' can turn their attention to past mistakes, while experimenting with new forms of writing. Here the issue lies in the potential for further illumination of social dynamics and conditions to slip from being complimentary to having a substitutory role in relation to practice. Social research moves, by default, from having a reflexive function, to a constitutive one. Different forms of representation are then assumed to take precedence over the results of systematic social investigation and in so doing, the scales are simply reversed.

Fiction can so easily be assumed to become equal to reality, because no one can speak in its name any more, rather than having the potential to be complimentary in its discovery and act as an important source of inspiration. Seeing the relationship in this way does not detract from the questions we should ask of forms of representation: whom do they affect, under what circumstances, for what reasons and with what overall consequences? It should also be recognized that spurs and incentives to action and imagining different possibilities is far from a monopoly of science. It is frequently the art of persuasion, rather than the results of systematic social investigation, that has the potential to produce particular outcomes.

There is also another issue at work in these pages: that is, what are the consequences of the direction of current practices for future generations? What about those who are under pressure to produce results according to the edicts of institutions and sponsors which, after all, pay their wages? In the face of this how can critical interventions provide those persons with the resources to challenge organizations that will continue to commission research? Here we will turn our attention to a major site of knowledge production: universities. If there is something different about the knowledge produced in those contexts, what is it? Some may be positioned to ignore, or reduce the impact of negative interventions in relation to their working practices, but not necessarily the next generation of those who will be employed in these contexts and may now be doctoral students and those on temporary research contracts.

None of this suggests that neatly demarcated boundaries exist, or that there are any easy answers to these questions – far from it. It is to say that a failure to understand the forces that act upon the process of producing research and the conditions under which it is enacted, as well as its relations with the contexts in which social life is conducted, leads to a limited understanding of the place and value of research in social life. Anyone who wishes to change or preserve elements of practice, but does not take these conditions into account, will miss their target. In the productive agonisms that exist between social science and social life, we need to understand much more about how and under what circumstances social scientific practices can engage, without capitulation to the power of social forces that seek to mould its findings in their name.

Not all of these issues are addressed in the book. It is a contribution to clarification. Some issues concern the inevitabilities that surround and inform the practice of social research over which it cannot, and should not, have the last say. Others are attainable. I hope what follows is a positive intervention in contemporary debates to inform and argue for the importance of social research for coming to understand ourselves in better ways. The book also seeks to provide an understanding of how attention to the ways in which social research is organized can open up new possibilities for practice.

What is undertaken here is an engagement for the purpose of trying to generate insights for current and future practices, noting that our futures are influenced by the past. No nostalgic call for a return to the whole and the one is contained herein. Not only is it doubtful that such a state of affairs ever existed, but also it appears as yet another imaginary foil against which those who claim epochal breaks, or no change at all, may sharpen their insights. Assertions such as these tend to hover on the margins of the very thing it is hoped to avoid: an inward-looking practice, as opposed to engagement with the social world that marches on despite such interventions. As a result, this book is about a practice which is neither a celebration of an irresponsible open-endedness, nor that of a narrow and closed universe. Many conditions are given by circumstances outside of the control of sites of practice, but which are nevertheless open to understanding, amelioration, intervention and even transformation.

Content Overview

The aim of this book is to inform the production and reception of a more reflexive, engaged and confident social research practice. By bringing together writings and insights on the relationship between social research and social life in an examination of reflexivity, positioning and belonging, as well as the contexts and cultures of knowledge production that inform and shape the practices of research, the lineage of debates on the relationship between research and practice are charted.

The discussions are intended to have implications for the actual practice of social research, as well as engaging in debates over its future role in society. In the process the aim is to open up alternative possibilities between scientism and relativism, capitulation and withdrawal, advocacy and objectivism, excellence and relevance and expose a series of issues relating to how knowledge production informs an understanding of and makes a contribution to contemporary social relations and issues. The book represents the culmination of work over the past few years, but it is also a part of the work that must always continue in order to ensure a continuing vibrancy through which to generate insights that have the potential to inform improvements in social conditions.

The journey starts with a critical examination of existing accounts of reflexivity. Rather than arrogant gestures from enclosed realms of activity, or denunciations born of unrealistic expectations, we need to learn from mediating between different cultures of inquiry. From some we can take a refusal to posit a polarity between common sense and social scientific understandings and from others the need to do so in order to inform transformation. A more robust reflexivity may then emerge through acts of critique and deconstruction and then reconstruction. Such writings act as a defence of social research and illustrate how reflexive thinking has always been part of a healthy and ongoing debate within the social sciences. What is also highlighted is the need to guard against a hypodermic realism and avoid collapses into self-referentiality or relativism, as well as the absence in such accounts of the need to consider contexts and cultures of knowledge production in informing the potential of reflexivity for practice.

The book then turns to examine the work of those concerned with mediation between social research and social life. Here we see an emphasis on the need for a two-way relationship between the knower and the known, between lay and technical languages and for work that is both relational and transformational.

The aim is to overcome a subject–object relation that initiates the role of the 'expert'. Nevertheless, we also need to recognize the social conditions and contexts that enable scholastic points of view on the world to emerge. Here we see concern for context that is missing from earlier accounts. Individualistic cultures and the cult of the expert, that reduce exceptionality to character without due consideration of contexts and cultures, emerge here and are taken up in later chapters. The relationship between disposition and position, informed by conditions of knowledge production, has the potential to inform forms of reflexivity that inhere within institutions and disciplines in different ways.

In the unfolding of contents of reflexivity, the book then examines modes of representation. Ideological critique and then a critical ethos provide the basis for insights in relation to capabilities and capacities for action, as well as the need to create conditions of possibility, rather than make pronouncements that lead to closure. Here we find a refusal to accept a legislative role for scientific knowledge and instead interpretation emerges in a spirit of inquiry that is about understanding the human condition, without recourse to problematic foundations. Such knowledge only comes with a more nuanced formulation of the self than we find here and this is a theme returned to in later chapters. What emerges from this discussion is the need to translate, or actively mediate, between frames of meaning as a practical activity.

In the second part of the book these issues are built upon to examine forms of epistemic permeability and reflexivity. To move away from romanticized ideals contained within reflexive calls, degrees of epistemic permeability need to be considered based on an understanding of endogenous and referential dimensions. Bringing these together is essential in developing a context-sensitivity that is also context-revising, while taking content and context seriously. The emphasis here is on the role of social research as a mediator, but with attention to the rigours of translation. A layering upon previous arguments can be seen here, as it is argued that further understanding of the relations between reflexivity in social research communities (endogenous) and between these and lifeworld communities (referential) is needed to bring content and consequence together within a practical endeavour. The meeting of these forms of reflexivity, informed by differences in epistemic permeability between disciplines and institutions, is also where cultures of knowledge production and reception come together.

The oscillations between the dimensions of reflexivity are argued to relate to the tensions between positioning and belonging and the abilities to account for action and capabilities to act. Identity and power come into play here and this account requires a formulation of the self that is neither one of annihilation or exaltation. That, in turn, is related to the capability to act. The chapter brings to awareness the contexts in which aspirations are constrained or enabled which, once again, is drawn upon in discussions in later chapters. It is suggested at this point that social research is the systematization of links between self-identity and the enacted environment and as a result is bound to be conflictual when considering the question arising from research findings: 'How do we proceed?'

In the third part, written with Beth Perry, we turn towards the contexts and cultures that create, or indeed prevent, the conditions for a vibrant research practice. All too often this is neglected in discussions of reflexivity that focus upon the individual researcher separate from their work environments. The three chapters move from an understanding of macro, meso and micro issues within cultures of knowledge production and reception that influence the consolidation of a more reflexive and critically engaged practice. We chart changes in the political economy of knowledge relating to the justification, production and application of knowledge across disciplines and institutional settings. Through an examination of theoretical developments, policy frameworks and urban and regional practices, issues around excellence, relevance and reflexivity are considered. With increased demands for relevance, referential reflexivity is surely implied, yet instead we see a mirroring of debates on reflexivity in which relevance quickly turns to relativism, thereby assuming simplistic collapses in different domains of activity. It is their differences that provide for dynamic and insightful encounters. Instead of this consideration, however, a narrow excellence-driven paradigm or calls for 'engagement' tend to predominate.

In this part we focus upon universities as the major site of social research production. It is, of course, not to suggest that other sites of activity do not exist and indeed we have worked in partnership with those in such settings. However, universities as institutions act to mediate external changes and so have profound effects upon degrees of epistemic permeability. Inter- and intra-institutional variability persists as our unfolding journey charts. Nevertheless, a generic tendency can be seen in how universities structurally and culturally act to magnify ambiguities in external environments concerning demands for work that require referential and endogenous reflexivity, relevance and excellence. Shifting values in relation to a market-driven instrumentality and attributed values to particular forms of knowledge lead to differential levels of expectations of and support for different disciplines with varying consequences for the practice of social research.

Without due consideration to degrees of epistemic permeability and the reasons for their existence, a gap between expectations, structures and practices emerges. With so many different expectations in play, greater attention to questions of whether universities are best placed to mediate between research and the lifeworld are required. Without this in place, the distinction of the knowledge produced in universities, from other sites of activity, risks being diminished by partial understandings.

We then continue to build upon insights from earlier chapters by looking at the dynamics of cultural conditions of production in universities. In different ways, these act as inhibitors to reflexivity which requires a supportive context in which to work, as opposed to a celebration of exceptionality through an overblown individualism. Entrepreneurialism also reaches into the university as an imperative that works around and through academic culture to create increasing uncertainty. Academic reactions to changing conditions include mobilizations of discourses of academic freedom and autonomy, without consideration of what conditions and contexts enable such positions to be held.

Such reactions are often coupled with retreats to orthodoxy, disciplinary entrenchment, specialization, talk of transdisciplinarity and enormous variability in reflexive understandings between individuals, their practices and institutional positions. It is the bounded nature of professional knowledge production that appears here, working to reinforce distinctions, polarizations and dichotomies that critical thinkers have sought to expose and break down. In other words, an absence of reflexivity in relation to cultural representations of practice, as well as conditions of knowledge production, may explain why some practices in particular contexts are able to ignore these insights and so enable exogenous factors to remain at endogenous levels. Yet this can provide for the generation of insights in institutional relations between belonging and positioning. The limits to reflexivity therefore inhere in knowing how far to go in questioning the premises of one's own discipline or that of others, without undermining their value.

Through an examination of the above issues, the book moves through an understanding of contents, consequences, contexts and cultures. It provides a set of socio-historical interrogations of the works of those who have been concerned with reflexivity and builds on these to develop ideas on epistemic permeability, positioning and belonging. It then takes these discussions into the major site of knowledge production: the university. These contexts shape the extent to which different forms of reflexivity and practices of social research can emerge.

In the spirit of working towards alternative possibilities, we end with a productive opening, not a conclusion at which we terminate. We seek to populate the 'missing middle' between cultures of knowledge production and knowledge reception without recourse to simplistic slogans that do justice to neither domain. Active intermediaries that maintain and enhance distinctiveness, while also working at translation within a context-sensitive and so revising ethos, are outlined. Rather than collapse spheres of activity in the name of a hypodermic model of knowledge transfer not exchange or allusions to hierarchies of excellence as if relevance necessarily followed, we find no substitution for effort. In creating these spaces of potential, we can see just how social research and social life can enter into a more dynamic and productive encounter within a modest, yet highly significant, set of practices.

PART 1

CONTENT

COMMITMENT, CRITERIA AND CHANGE

In the Introduction I noted that reactions to the call to reflexivity are variable. For some they are unduly philosophical. At best they are of marginal significance to social scientific practice and at worst, destructive. For others these critiques serve as the legislative forums in which what counts as the 'truth' is to be subjected to continued deconstruction in order to expose the myth of a 'modernist dream'. While aspects of these perspectives assist in generating a greater sensitivity to the issues that inform practice, the overall result can be so unhelpful that it tends to polarize debates and achieves little for advancing our understandings of the limits, strengths and role of social research in the constitution and understanding of social relations.

The production of reflexive thoughts on social scientific activity takes place against a background of pre-reflexive assumptions. This may seem like a paradox, but it prevents a paralysis in action. Some set of assumptions is necessary in order to practice in the first instance. They might subsequently be open to revision in order to learn from the ebbs and flows of history and accompanying changes in contextual knowledge. To this extent we have the benefit of hindsight through an open-endedness that subjects ideas and practices to revision, rejection and qualification. After all, ideas and experiences from the past inform the present and future.

Reflexivity is a guard against hypodermic realism: that is, the assumption that there is an unproblematic relationship between the social scientific text and its valid and reliable representation of the 'real' world. It also guards against the assumption that textual openness reflects a fluid world in which choice is equally distributed within and between different populations. Writings on reflexivity exist on a sliding scale from those who seek to represent the real while recognizing such an enterprise must be open to revision through the production of new knowledge, to those for whom such an enterprise is pointless and ultimately, arbitrary.

Within the following histories we will see sets of reasons that drove writers to clarify their relationship to a range of ideas and issues that informed the contexts in which their work was produced (Hughes 1979). By moving beyond a relativism that threatens to collapse into solipsism and the sort of *ad hominem* denunciations that relieves hearers and readers of the need for systematic, relational thought, we can open up a productive dimension and see what those ideas may still offer us in seeking to understand current times. In the process we can admit of a socio-historical dimension to our activities without which social research would have no capacity to produce meaning and insight in its studies. We have much to learn from history in order to improve our current practices, as well as from imagining futures that have the capacity to correct some of the defects of the present.

Overall, this process can set up a continual scrutiny in order to develop ideas and practices for knowing the social world. Degrees of 'fixity' of assumptions are required on the part of the social scientist, without which one would collapse into infinite regress, in order to examine the social world in the first instance. The question is not whether this occurs, but how and with what implications for our understandings? It is a willingness to consider the content and context of social scientific practices and how that relates to its process and product and then refine its insights as a result, that separates lay from social scientific reflexivity. I now turn to an examination of those 'fixities' in different traditions and how they have provided distinct and novel answers to these issues.

Commitment and Criteria

Our brief history could start a very long time ago. In celebration of 'classical rationality', for example, we find a concern with reflection as means for prioritizing a stability which then allows the analyst to cast an objective gaze upon social reality. Reflexivity then emerges as a focus because the dynamics of change inform an increasing need to understand the socio-historical context of knowledge production (Sandywell 1996). Thus, at the end of the eighteenth century, Johann Fichte, writing in the post-Kantian idealist tradition, argued that the 'I' was an activity that was aware by limiting itself through an awareness of a 'non-I'. As he put it: 'All possible consciousness, as something objective for a subject, presupposes an immediate consciousness in which what is subjective and what is objective are simply one and the same. Otherwise, consciousness is simply incomprehensible' (Fichte 1994: 114). George Herbert Mead, working in the pragmatist tradition in the early part of the twentieth century, then wrote: 'Inner consciousness is socially organized by the importation of the social organization of the outer world' (Mead 1964: 141).

What we see in this shift are more socially and historically sensitive approaches to ideas as exemplified in philosophical and social scientific critiques of Cartesian dualism. Our concerns, however, are not just philosophical, but relate to the implications of these changes for an understanding of the place and practice of social research in society.

Commitment

Taking these insights into the realm of methodology, a neo-Kantian view holds that conceptualizations of the world order what would otherwise be chaotic, through the capacity of transcendental reason present within the minds of individual investigators. Kant divided his ideas on reality into the noumenal – those things 'in themselves' that exist independently of human cognition – and the phenomenal – those things that are knowable in relation to human cognition. Because we cannot know all of the reality that we inhabit through cognition, we are led to examine the forms through which reality is represented to us. For Max Weber (1949), the practice of social research must replicate the same qualities that Kant found within the human mind. They cannot simply be about the collection of social facts, but reflexive practices in terms of being 'ideas of ideas' (Albrow 1990: 149). His 'ideal type', which has been the subject of much writing, thereby serves as an analytic instrument for the ordering of empirical reality.

A difference between the social and natural sciences is said to exist because the former produce understandings of the ways in which history and culture are themselves changed by human actions. Therefore, in seeking to understand a dynamic environment, they too will exhibit a conceptual and methodological dynamism. What we then find are Weber's methodological writings combining influences from Wilhelm Dilthey's emphasis on the meaningful 'inner' experiences of people (understanding), together with an analysis of the observed regularities of human behaviour (Weber 1949). In the name of a social science, Weber sought to fuse the intentionality of conduct with an analysis of cause and effect. Meaning could then be understood and explained through reference to the social conditions of action.

An overall concern with the social sciences and the study of the meaning of action meant that it was not possible to turn to law-like generalizations for analytic purposes. Nor was it possible for reflection to turn unproblematically into a social scientific methodology that ruled out reflexivity as an unnecessary preoccupation. Weber shared with the Austrian economists a concern with the idea of choice driven by ultimate values, but without allusion to an abstract model of a rational person that persists in so much social science to this day.

Reference to ultimate values was based upon a methodological individualism that appeared to work as a corrective to the grander claims of Weber's time. Yet what we often see in his work is a mixture of ethical pluralism and reference to the nation as an ultimate value. His works were informed, in various ways, by his political predispositions, philosophical influences, interdisciplinary engagement (at one time he referred to himself as a 'social economist': Holton and Turner 1989) and a refusal to read off human actions according to the dictates of universal explanations (whether based on individual rational calculation or read off from some concept of social totality).

The sum of influences upon Weber constitute a powerful set of ideas that still resonate with contemporary issues. Weber's recognition of the reactions of social research to the changing conditions in which they find themselves provides a core dynamic for the philosophy of social research as it seeks to understand the grounds for the status of disciplines (Williams and May 1996). The relevance of social research lies in refracting the social landscapes it studies because it is a part of those and their corresponding cultural practices. It does not reflect, but mediates through the deployment of particular tools of inquiry. Perhaps Weber was insufficiently aware of this relationship in terms of its implications for research practice, but he was only too aware that disciplines are bound to evolve through a need to reflect changes in their environments (Weber 1949).

Max Weber's understandings of processes of rationalization ultimately reveal a tension between his methodological writings and historical sociology. Ruling out instrumental rationality as sufficient grounds for the explanation of human conduct and allowing for the importance of substantive rationality as a sphere of value choice into which social research should not venture, became an undertaking that led to an emphasis upon voluntarism in the face of the iron cage of modernity. Contingency then unfolds as necessity with the hope of transcendence residing within the isolated subject. As one form of rationality was unfolding 'externally' to mould the subject in its image and so stifle imagination and freedom, it left the other to emerge through an apparently autonomous process of 'internal' choice.

The implications of this line of thought had a particular effect upon Weber. Here was an extraordinary thinker seeking to bring together Kant and Nietzsche with Marx as the significant ghost, who poured scorn upon traditional approaches to morality, knowledge and truth. At this point Goethe appears as the figure that allows Weber to seek an active resolution of these conflicts (Albrow 1990). In subscribing to an ethic of ultimate ends and it being no business of the scientist to enter into political judgements, the search for his own meaning must lie elsewhere. What then appears for Weber is the same fate as he was to leave for the rest of us: that is, an individual matter in the face of the forces of detraditionalization and scientific progress, leading us into further disenchantment. It is at this point that the persona of heroic scientist, rather than scholar whose meanings should be related to a context, gained its hold with particular consequences for Weber's own well-being and intellectual legacy. We can see this in both 'Politics as a vocation' and 'Science as a vocation'. In these essays he alludes to the facts of environments in order that his audiences may see the choices that face them. There is nothing beyond personal responsibility for choice: 'Scientific pleading is meaningless in principle because the various value spheres of the world stand in irreconcilable conflict with each other' (Weber in Gerth and Mills 1970: 147). Then, in discussing differences in age, he writes: 'Age is not decisive; what is decisive is the trained relentlessness in viewing the realities of life, and the ability to face such realities and measure up to them inwardly' (Weber in Gerth and Mills 1970: 126–7). We end up with an ethic of responsibility deriving from the inevitability of individual choice given the impersonality of social forces. Behind and moving through these forces stand politics and the threat of violence with the accompanying demand that social scientists make a clear differentiation between facts and values in their work.

In 'Science as a vocation' Weber wrote of the value of commitment, as well as the need for intellectual integrity. This is over eighty years before the philosopher Bernard Williams (2002) was to extol such virtues as a source of hope for the future and a means of counterattack against those who preferred irony to the demands of the production of truth. Yet if we end up with a radical situatedness in which these matters become the sole province of the individual, how can the social sciences be sustainable, cultural practices? Culture and context become secondary to a space in which the individual is left to face these inevitable burdens alone.

A resulting tension between an ethic of responsibility for the production of accurate accounts and the ethic of conviction that motivates us to do so in the first place, while subsuming our own substantive values, is individualized. Yet how is this to be reconciled with a continual need to seek new ways of understanding social life within the unfolding of history (Weber 1949)? The dialectic of individual transcendence with its utopian ideals and empathic understanding may be just too great a burden to place upon our shoulders without supportive cultures of inquiry.

With the above noted in this unfolding journey, we can take from Weber matters of continued importance. There is the issue of there being no universalistic standpoint upon which to base the foundations of a social scientific methodology. Instead there are only particular perspectives making choices problematic, if not impossible. The Kantian separation of art, morality and science was placed in question by Weber and his studies on rationality. Subsequent postmodernist writings have sought to de-differentiate these spheres or to blur their boundaries, the basis and consequence of which can be seen in the debates that took place between Jean-François Lyotard and Jürgen Habermas (see Holub 1991) and the accompanying interventions of Richard Rorty (1992).

It is at this point that the tragedy which Charles Turner (1990) highlights in Weber's writings is so apparent: between that of needing to hold onto one's convictions in order to maintain dignity, while also recognizing the existence of so many others such that their realization is far removed from any likely reality. Yet the 'Weberian move away from an (ironic) "totalising perspective" refuses to substitute for an ethical "totality" a series of postmodern partial standpoints. For a standpoint worth adopting is one which … never abandons its secret desire to be the only one worth adopting' (C. Turner 1990: 115). Weber exposes the illusion that a general standpoint can act as final arbitrator *and* that it is not necessary to cease our investigations at the partiality of different viewpoints. Instead, as a matter of practical importance, we can learn from mediating between different cultures of inquiry (Hall 1999).

We also have the importance of the context of knowledge production, as well as reception. It is clear that Weber was sophisticated in his understanding of, for example, the consequences of the material relations between commerce and the university (Tribe 1994), but there is a need to go further if we are to productively deploy his legacy for contemporary understandings. We can do this by taking a strategic, rather than strictly methodological position, in Weber's writings on value freedom (J. Scott 1997). By taking the latter we end up in a situation in which the fact-value dichotomy becomes so entrenched it does not take us forward in terms of understanding, while also being indefensible at the level of practice.

If reflexivity works in the service of research to deploy ontological, epistemological and methodological fixities – often to define the difference between science and common sense – we set limits on reflexive thought that do not enable us to see the relations between what is produced and how it is received in the public domain. Simply asserting that one sphere of activity is value laden while the other is not, undermines the productive potential of social science where its findings are contestable in the public domain. They are contested because they are invested with meaning and its product often assumes that there is a separation to be made between knowledge and action. Introducing history into this relationship allows us to move from the idea of an ontological or logical separation between facts and values to one of 'natural proximity' (Pels 2003). What is allowed for is a greater reflexive vigilance in understanding their relationship in practice which allows us to see the value of respective knowledges in social life.

Criteria for Doing

For Alfred Schutz, Weber failed to recognize the episodic nature of human conduct and hence that causal adequacy was bound by sociological and historical understanding (Schutz 1973). For Schutz the meaning is the event, or an act is a meaningful process. From this point of view *verstehen* (see Outhwaite 1986) is not a method for doing social research, but what social scientists should study, for it represents the 'experiential form in which common sense thinking takes cognisance of the social cultural world' (Schutz 1979: 29).

The mediation of first and second order constructs should be a topic of reflexive concern. A common-sense stock of knowledge orientates people to apply meaning to their own actions, those of others and the events that they encounter. The lifeworld exhibits the basis for a primary experience that enables people to orientate their actions through taking its self-evidence, or pre-reflexive constitution, for granted: 'I find myself always within an historically given world which, as a world of nature as well as a sociocultural world, had existed before my birth and which will continue to exist after my death' (Schutz 1970: 163–4).

The generation of social scientific knowledge (second order) should concern itself with the explication of Husserl's 'natural attitude' by rendering apparent the 'taken-for-granted' in everyday life. It follows that social phenomena are constituted as meaningful before the researcher appears on the scene. These basic 'meaning structures' are then analytically rearranged by social research with the consequence that it does not accurately reflect social relations. To guard against this, Schutz argued that social scientific constructs must satisfy the 'postulate of adequacy' by being compatible 'with the constructs of everyday life' (Schutz 1979: 35).

Schutz presents a clear argument for the study of 'lay' reflexivity. This is not a subjective state of affairs, but an intersubjective one that represents a process of acculturation as manifested through publicly available forms of communication, including language. In order to adequately grasp the meanings used in everyday life the 'postulate of adequacy' should be followed: 'Compliance with this postulate warrants the consistency of the constructs of the social scientist with the constructs of common-sense experience of the social reality' (Schutz 1970: 279).

Although moving the analytic focus of social research towards a representation of everyday life and meaning production, Schutz leaves an important issue to one side. Recalling Heidegger's insights, interpretative procedures produce meanings that are oriented only to the context in which they are produced. Therefore, this may be interpreted as suggesting that the 'truth' of these procedures cannot be established outside of these contexts. Social research is then destined to become a relative and descriptive endeavour. However, at this point a Kantian element in Schutz's work appears in terms of the discovery of the organizing principles of our 'being-in-the-world' that 'consists in spelling out the transcendental conditions of the meaningful world as we know it' (Bauman 1978: 183).

Despite the critique of Max Weber, the social sciences retain their role in thinking through 'ideas about ideas'. We can see this in the criteria for the 'postulate of logical consistency' such that:

> the objective validity of thought objects constructed by the social scientist and their strictly logical character is one of the most important features by which scientific thought objects are distinguished from the thought objects constructed by common-sense thinking in daily life which they have to supersede. (Schutz 1970: 278)

While an intriguing formulation, we are still left with a tension: that is, between the form of justification within the social scientific community and its intelligibility to common-sense reasoning. An action-oriented social theory with an emphasis upon common-sense reasoning appears as a solution to this issue. In the unfolding of social thought, Alan Dawe (1970) originally held this to be part of the social action, rather than social system, end of social theory. He was to correct this dichotomy with a more productive understanding of the relations between social scientific production and reception when he noted that both perspectives begin with human action (Dawe 1979). Instead of a separation between the two, they capture an ambivalence that represents an existential feature of social life as expressed between impersonality and freedom of choice: 'Thus dualism of social experience is central to our very existence in modern society. It is ... central to all the forms of thought and work which articulate our experience of that society' (Dawe 1979: 365).

With Weber the resultant issues tended to become an individual matter. What now emerges is not a construct of the social sciences, but a relationship inherent to social life that varies according to circumstance. In being reflected back into the domain of social research and then mediated from there via reasons and consequences into the public domain, we have a vibrancy and relevance of insights, if not an acceptability according to universal rules of scientific method. If we take this view, we are left with a productive legacy when the strictly methodological interpretation of Schutz's work moves aside for a more nuanced view. Schutz left social science with a critique of the 'intellectualist bias' in knowledge construction (O'Neill 1972) that became apparent in the work of many scholars (see Berger and Luckmann 1967; Strydom 2000).

Ambivalence within everyday life is catered for through many techniques that enable sufficient consistency to allow for a degree of predictability. Yet the articulation in social scientific work of experiences of seeking to regain such control in daily life are often mediated through the lenses of work that claim to be reflexive, but may be nothing more than the disguised regurgitation of positivism. Thus, we see a celebration of fluidity through social studies, but upon examination of the justifications for the process through which the work was conducted, a falling back upon established and detached ways of seeing and constituting social reality. The confidence to retort with anything other than either a totally 'detached' paradigm or the allusion to the account being but one interpretation among many others is often apparent.

With respect to these issues, Alfred Schutz had a much more sophisticated understanding of the relationship between common-sense and social scientific understandings than subsequent interpretations have allowed (O'Neill 1995). Stepping outside not only the strictly methodological literature, but also the socio-theoretical literature that seeks its place through castigation of 'other' perspectives, we find a number of productive elements in Schutz's work for the purposes of our study. For instance, moving away from narrow interpretations of the postulate of adequacy, we can take from it an emphasis upon how scientific reasoning is also dependent upon the 'common-sense communicative competence of the community of scientists in general and the larger lay society in which they live and work' (O'Neill 1995: 152). A normative orientation towards the search for the truth informs a community of scientific inquirers that draws from a wider view of value orientations. Therefore, in terms of theory: 'coherence, simplicity, and elegance determine theory selection as much as the preservation of otherwise well-confirmed theories of predictive power and instrumental potential' (Habermas 2003: 223).

To examine these relations requires not only an understanding of changes over time, but also the creation of 'mediating institutions' between social scientific and lay understandings of knowledge and its implications for action. A public discussion of the role and value of these mediating institutions is significant. In its absence, researchers are left to fall back upon institutional positions and justifications separate from any discussion of mediation. How the domains of science and common sense interact and inform each other is of primary consideration, not the assumption that each is unproblematically separate. We need to find a language that not only translates between institutional and individual discourses, but also between scientific and common-sense ones (O'Neill 1995: 152).

I started this section with the differences between Schutz and Weber. Yet if we take the latter's idea of authority in terms of the position of the social scientist and the ethic of conviction and place that alongside how expertise is increasingly placed in question in contemporary times and the need for mediating institutions and discourses, it allows us to examine the contemporary importance of the relationship between knowledge, expertise and democracy (S. Turner 2003). Once again, neither allusion to simple dichotomies or separations between social thinkers will get us far in understanding this in terms of the role and practice of research.

Doing as Criteria

Schutz's emphasis upon common sense was to take social science in new directions with the emphasis upon 'science' without positivism. Harold Garfinkel was then to take this turn in the most novel way according to some primary issues. First, what is the status of the actor's accounts of their actions, in particular when these conflict with the accounts offered by social scientists? Second, people share knowledge, but how does this relate to a theory of action which seeks to generalize beyond the particularity of social settings? Third, people are not manipulated by forces beyond their control, but make strategic choices that shape their environments. These three gaps that he identified in Parsonian systems theory are referred to as the problems of 'rationality', 'intersubjectivity' and 'reflexivity' (Heritage 1984: 23). In addressing these issues ethnomethodology was to provide a unique perspective.

The tools of inquiry for this purpose were noted by Garfinkel in his dissertation:

At least two important theoretical developments stem from the researches of Max Weber. One development, already well worked, seeks to arrive at a generalized social system by uniting a theory that treats the structuring of experience with another theory designed to answer the question, 'What is man?' Speaking loosely, a synthesis is attempted between the facts of social structure and the facts of personality. The other development, not yet adequately exploited, seeks a generalized social system built solely from the analysis of experience structures. (quoted in Heritage 1984: 9)

Seeking the means to analyse these 'experience structures' led Garfinkel (1967) to refuse to differentiate between everyday theorizing in social life and social science. This is where the concept of 'indexicality' comes in. Indexicality is taken from Charles Peirce's semiology and in ethnomethodological parlance, this states that everyday language and actions cannot be understood without being situated within the social context in which they are uttered and produced because meanings will vary from context to context. Schutz's Kantian influence is thereby overcome. To address this, social scientists produce metaphors in order to theorize as to how objects are constructed in the social world. Nevertheless, these do not reflect the situated and practical manner in which the process of recognition and production takes place in everyday life. Researchers are called upon to build analytic apparatuses that 'will provide for how it is that any activities, which members do in such a way as to be recognizable as such to members, are done, and done recognizably' (Sacks 1974: 218).

The social scientists' use of abstract theoretical 'categories' results in a disjuncture between the 'concreteness' of everyday activities and their social scientific representation. The overall result is that 'real society' comes into being only 'as the achieved results of administering the policies and methods of formal, constructive analysis' (Garfinkel 1991: 13). To accurately represent meaning-production within the lifeworld, its context-dependence must be recognized not as an analytic impediment, but as the starting *and* finishing point of social analysis.

Meaning within the lifeworld is now sought in the situated and practical aspects of everyday life without reference to what has been termed as a 'phenomenological residua' in social thought (Coulter 1979). Both the setting in which action takes place and the account of that action are fused in the routine, reflexive monitoring of conduct undertaken by actors within the lifeworld. Further, reasons given for actions are not viewed against the background of a normative order that is 'internalised' by actors (Heritage 1984). Instead, following Winch's (1990) interpretations of the social scientific implications of the work of the later Wittgenstein, they are determined through the study of publicly available linguistic forms. Words become the tools through which intersubjective understanding is achieved and thus the proper topic and not resource, for social research.

The idea of reflexivity, as the basis of order within the lifeworld, is given through accurate descriptions of accounting procedures used by 'members' within social settings:

> The central recommendation is that the activities whereby members produce and manage settings of organized everyday affairs are identical with members' procedures for making those settings 'account-able'. The 'reflexive' or 'incarnate' character of accounting practices and accounts makes up the crux of that recommendation. (Garfinkel 1967: 1)

Reflexivity contributes to social order and is displayed through situated and public activities that are open to analysis.

A number of consequences for the study of social life now follow. First, all that is accountable by lay actors becomes rational. Second, indifference in the process of studying formal structures is maintained by abstaining from all judgements of their 'adequacy, value, importance, necessity, practicality, success, or consequentiality' (Garfinkel and Sacks 1986: 166). Third, the hermeneutic implications of a meeting between the language games of ethnomethodologists and lay actors are sidelined in favour of meticulous description in the manner suggested above. Fourth, the issue between language as a medium for the expression of interests and motives by people differentially positioned within discourses and language as a topic for uncovering the methods through which ordered activity is generated, is found in favour of the latter. Finally, but by no means exhaustively, the idea of knowing and being in the social world is reduced to a study of language use.

When it comes to an understanding of the relations between social scientific and lay discourse, we are left with an issue. Is there a collapse between an understanding of reflexivity in actions *and* the ability of actors to reflect upon those actions? A key question arises: 'if, and in what way, the "reflexivity" of actions implies the "reflexivity" of actors, or what kind of "reflective capabilities" are implied in the ethnomethodological perspective?' (Czyzewski 1994: 166). Actors within the lifeworld appear to be denied the potential not only to reflect upon their actions, but also to change the conditions under and through which their actions takes place.

What of the reflexivity of the investigator in this process? The impression is of an analyst who seems capable of freeing themselves from their own language games without concern for the process or consequence of mediation between frames of meaning. What is eradicated is a consideration of the relations between production and reception of social scientific knowledge. Such considerations are side-stepped in favour of a collapse: 'If it is possible to lay bare the constitutive ordering of the world that experimental subjects owe to their own interpretive rules, then the process of translation between them and the observer can be done away with' (Habermas 1990: 110).

Objectivist accounts are set up as the protagonist to the reflexive but what guarantees, the ethnomethodologist would ask, are given by being generally reflexive? To regard reflexivity as being the property of particular positions, texts or social researchers allows it to operate on the basis of being exclusive. Yet from the point of view of ethnomethodology, reflexivity is mundane and uninteresting and so it questions the 'epistemological hubris that seems to accompany self-consciously reflexive claims'. Its study of 'constitutive reflexivity proposes no unreflexive counterpart' and instead is part of the 'infrastructure of objective accounting' (Lynch 2000: 47).

Processes of purification and institutionalization within social scientific communities now leads to a terminal point: the expunging of all residues that once provided for radical insights. In a consideration of the ethnomethodological legacy, Mervin Pollner refers to endogenous and radical reflexivity. The former refers to the constituting social reality in terms of 'how what members do in, to,

and about social reality' (Pollner 1991: 372). The latter, on the other hand, refers
to how social reality, in general, is constituted. The object of its practices thus
includes the presuppositions that are employed by social inquirers in their construction of social reality. For him, the central legacy of ethnomethodology lies
in its emphasis upon radical reflexivity.

A greater emphasis upon endogenous reflexivity in the unfolding of this tradition
has led to radical reflexivity being downplayed. Relations between the general
and particular are not considered. Above all, it is about 'unsettling' and not simply the generation of meticulous descriptions via methodological prescriptions. It
generates 'an insecurity regarding basic assumptions, discourse and practices used
in describing reality'. Further, 'Because it is the antithesis of "settling down" it is
not surprising that radical reflexivity is abandoned' (Pollner 1991: 370) as a community of inquiry is constituted that seeks a scientism, albeit in a different form,
for its legitimacy. This may also be the consequence of the blurring of the boundaries between conversation analysis (CA) and ethnomethodology with the
emphasis upon the former being an 'increasingly detailed explication of endogenous processes' (Pollner 1991: 373). To this extent there appears, in the history
of this tradition, to be differences between Harold Garfinkel and Harvey Sacks
on the topic of radical reflexivity.

Ethnomethodology sought to overcome the scholastic point of view in the
study of social life (Garfinkel 1991). It aimed to guard against writings on reflexivity becoming a means of privileging particular positions by reminding us about
the mundanity of reflexivity in everyday life (Lynch 2000). By attending to the
ways in which everyday life is produced through the work of interpretation by
lay actors, there is a key challenge to the idea that the social world is unintelligible
until the work of the social scientist is completed. As a study in the legacy of
Winch for social science concludes: 'Everyday understanding might not be the last
word, but it certainly ought to be the first' (Hutchinson et al. 2008: 138).

What we see in the relations between research and social life is not eradicated
by reliance upon either scientism or naturalistic description. Both act as affirmations of end points by either collapsing the differences between social scientific
discourse and everyday life, or by assuming one is superior to the other. Instead
we need to see understanding as a task and not something eradicated by a reflexive situationalism or some free-floating universalism. Such a task may come with
a commitment to social change.

Commitment to Change

Alvin Gouldner took aim at ethnomethodology as a form of 'micro-anarchism' that
delighted in exposing the fragility of the social order. It appeals to those who
wished to engage in a 'non-violent revolt' against the status quo because they could
not, or would not, challenge dominant social structures (Gouldner 1971: 394–5).

His aim was more concerned with social change and the inevitable, pre-reflexive assumptions of social scientists.

Social scientists normalize 'unpermitted worlds' that threaten stability and order. Accommodation to this state of affairs is enacted in several ways. First, via allusions to value neutrality that enable an existential distance to be maintained from the implications of one's work and the subjects of investigation. Second, it is ignored via technicist allusions that deny its significance through sole attention to the rigour of method or rule it out via the adoption of particular methodologies (Gouldner 1971: 484–8). Both of these moves, as Jürgen Habermas (1989) argues, are symptomatic of the empiricist legacy in our apparent post-empiricist age.

Gouldner expressed caution about the possibilities for his call to reflexivity given how it might be translated into practice. He did not want it to become: 'just another topic for panel meetings at professional conventions' or 'another burbling little stream of technical reports' that focus upon the 'profession's origins, educational characteristics, patterns of productivity, political preferences, communication networks, nor even about its fads, foibles, and phonies' (Gouldner 1971: 489). To guard against this predisposition towards 'administrative de-politicisation' (May 2006) that is so characteristic of associations that seek to represent particular academic specialisms in terms of some narrow idea of detached professionalism and the preservation of hierarchies, a 'radical' project was required.

The term 'radical' is deployed because knowledge production should be linked to the investigator's position within the world. Further, the knowledge produced should seek to transform, as well as know the world, while the body of knowledge should pass through the researcher as a total person. These translate into issues that concern not 'how to *work* but how to *live*' (Gouldner 1971: 489. Original italics). Attention to the conduct of social researchers, therefore, is a necessary, but not sufficient condition for maturation: 'What is needed is a new *praxis* that transforms the person' (Gouldner 1971: 494. Original italics).

We are left with the following implications for a reflexive practice. Understanding is to be directed toward how the researcher's praxis and their role and social position relate to the product and process of their work. It seeks to deepen self-awareness of the production of valid and reliable 'bits of information', strengthen a commitment to the value of this awareness and generate a willingness to be open to 'hostile information'. It is not about the object of study, as such, but the mode of study in terms of the relationship that is established between being a social scientist and a person in the world (Gouldner 1971: 494).

We now enter the realm of the personal and its relationship to the process and product of social research. Taking formal logic, along with the evidential basis for the adoption of a theory, or its openness and resistance to falsification as sufficient reason, brackets an understanding of the experiential basis of theoretical adherence. It is not suggested, in any way, that we replace evidence with the particularity of experience, but it is to accept that the behaviour of the social scientist is not 'shaped solely by a willing conformity to the morality of scientific method' (Gouldner 1971: 30). What, then, are the factors that shape such behaviour?

What is not open to scrutiny is the relationship between a social scientist and a theory as being 'intuitively convincing'. An alignment between the background assumptions of the social scientist and those of the theory occurs such that 'psychic closure' or 'consensual validation' is achieved (Gouldner 1971: 30). Here Gouldner is drawing upon the work of Michael Polanyi. He is getting at articulation, never being able to reach finitude, expressing the 'ineffable': 'something that I know and can describe even less precisely than usual, or even only vaguely' (Polanyi 1962: 88). The 'internal', as represented by the biography of the researcher and the 'external', represented by the work of theory, become aligned through elements that are obscured in each. These background assumptions range from those that are general and orientate in such a way that the unfamiliar becomes meaningful, through to assumptions as applied to those within a single domain: 'they are, in effect, the metaphysics of a domain' (Gouldner 1971: 31). As to whether theories must rest upon such assumptions, or if researchers should or should not be influenced by them, these matters are held to be for philosophers of science and 'methodological moralists', respectively. That they influence practice is an empirical matter (Gouldner 1971: 32).

Background assumptions are characterized by the absence of explicit criteria to assess their utility and when it comes to domain assumptions, they rest upon sentiments. This is not to say that they are directly related, for when sentiments are at variance with those things taught within the culture we may find open rebellion and 'adopting or seeking new domain assumptions more consonant with the feelings they actually have' (Gouldner 1971: 39). It is not to suggest that this is commonplace because it may be easier to live with older assumptions; feelings of inadequacy may result from such disjuncture such that it is individualized and turned into an expression of personal pathology, or it may be articulated among trusted others where it finds understanding within supportive cultures of inquiry.

Whatever the outcome, such tensions may be expressed in terms of the relations between what is called 'role reality' and 'personal reality'. Role reality is what is expected to be learnt and known by a competent practitioner, while personal reality relates to the imputations made about the social world separate from the obligations attendant upon systematic thought and evaluation. What may result from this tension is a subjecting of the latter to 'systematic doubt' such that they sink into 'subsidiary awareness', but nevertheless remain of consequence for practice (Gouldner 1971: 41–5). A resultant conflation of personal and role reality enables the particular to be read as the general; the point being that cultures generate different personal realities and so exhibit differences in the process and product of theory construction (Gouldner 1975: 309).

While the history of social science has been written as a difference in view between Weber and Gouldner, the latter still speaks of a tragedy in the practice of social research totally reminiscent of the former. While both emphasize that disciplinary preoccupations can become a form of escape, rather than engagement with the issues of the time, their 'solutions' are not the same. The struggle between scientific demands and personal impulses is overcome for one by a refusal to be assimilated to something that is ultimately unbearable and illegitimate. There is an escape from tragedy when it is recognized that the practitioner:

> need not allow themselves to be assimilated to their cultural masks ... when they insist that it is they who are the measure, and they who do the measuring ... in confining work to the requirements of a demanding and unfulfillable paradigm [they are] sacrificing unexpressed parts of themselves ... in a wager that this sacrifice is 'best for science'. (Gouldner 1975: 320–1)

There are a limited number of solutions for how to link a person with the expectations surrounding their role. While Gouldner outlines some of these and makes no assumption regarding a final resting place, he is clear that those who jump the gap without knowing where they will end up are to be applauded for providing models for those who are left just 'dawdling at the edge' (Gouldner 1975: 322).

Gouldner takes reflexivity into new terrains by linking the personal and cultural with the particular and general. Yet some have interpreted his concerns about 'dawdling at the edge' as confusion between a call to reflexivity and his own intellectual memoirs (O'Neill 1972: 216). For the purposes of this discussion, however, despite his call for blending the inculcated gaze of the social scientist that allows for the constitution of the social world as an object of investigation with subjective experiences, what we end up with is a call that relies upon authenticity at the individual level. While he and Weber were to converge and diverge on issues, we may end up in the same place. Although attention to the conduct of social scientists is necessary in order to understand the differences between good and poor practice, it is not a sufficient condition for maturation. Gouldner's call displays a disjuncture between professional rhetoric, practice transformation and conditions of production. As a result it has a tendency to become nothing more than an act of celebration or impeachment: 'Hooray for myself. Down with the others!' (Pels 2003: 167).

Taking this legacy forward into our unfolding history allows us to examine another tradition that sought to take up the issues of how positioning and belonging relate to knowledge production. This is where feminisms enter the terrain of our investigations.

Feminisms and Transformation

The insights of feminisms are central to the investigation of reflexivity. They examine the separation between subject and object (another way of expressing

Gouldner's personal and role reality within a community of researchers) not from a position of disinterest from which the researcher works, but that interest itself comes from 'being engaged' (Hartsock 1987).

What this places in question are simple and unsustainable ideas of bias being constituted in terms of possessing 'interests'. At one level this is undertaken through a general comparison of the differences between men and women: an 'abstract masculinity' compared to the 'connectedness and continuities' between women living in everyday life exemplified through the exercise of empathy and an 'ethic of care' (see Larrabee 1993). As I mentioned earlier, despite methodologically and theoretically sophisticated arguments to the contrary, so many researchers are still caught in simple separations between facts and values through an over-extension of domains of practice. Even though these remain disguised behind the dances of textual sophistications and theoretical exegesis, their persistence is evident in the justifications used about practice and the forms of expertise constituted to pronounce upon various phenomena.

The dominance and persistence of these ways of thinking leads to an absence of understanding of how people are embedded within the social milieux that they inhabit, how they shape and are influenced by actions. Scientific abstraction can gloss over experience in everyday life, the result of which is the production of a 'third version' of events that is explicable neither in terms of the subjectivity of the analyst, nor that of the subject herself. Borrowing from the theoretical and empirical labours of non-feminists exacerbated this problem and was to demonstrate the limits of conventional approaches that glossed over important elements in social life: for example, the unseen and yet fundamental efforts involved in emotional labour, relational work with significant and generalized others and the whole politics of reproduction without which production would be unthinkable. These are the invisible workings of societies and an absence of their understanding leads to questions about the modes through which partial understandings of the social world are constructed and passed off as universal truths.

Dorothy Smith (1988, 1993, 1999), who draws upon various sources including Schutz, Garfinkel and Marx, takes the absence of women's experiences in social scientific accounts as symptomatic of 'relations of ruling' which occur through processes of social construction: 'They are relations that coordinate people's activities across and beyond local sites of everyday experience' (Smith 2002: 45). The creation of a sphere in which women can make links between experiences and the images and ideas through which they can make sense of them – the dimension between knowledge production and reception – is thereby limited. The point is to create this sphere of reflection by employing the ontological exclusion of women in the service of improvements in scientific insights.

Women are not constituted as subjects, but the 'other'; they become the objects, rather than the subjects, of social scientific discourses. Women are not seen as possessing 'an autonomous source of knowledge, experience, relevance and imagination' (Smith 1988: 51). Such exclusion is deployed productively because an analytic focus upon the differences in men's and women's situations gives 'a scientific advantage to those who can make use of the differences' (S. Harding 1991: 120). A 'strong objectivity' thereby emerges in which thinking from women's lives can uncover those processes and structures which, from a male point of view, appear natural but from a feminist standpoint position require explanation. A resultant focus upon macro tendencies 'permits a more robust notion of reflexivity than is currently available in the sociology of knowledge or the philosophy of science' (S. Harding 1991: 149).

Captured here are the relations between the particular, expressed in terms of women's experiences and the general, as that which roots those experiences through social location and resultant knowledge within a more general theory of social processes concerning class, race, gender and sexuality. The otherwise problematic relations between experience and representation via social scientific work that ended up sequestrating those experiences, as Garfinkel and Schutz argued, is thereby resolved through an objective vantage point from women's lives as the 'other'.

Whereas conventional epistemology speaks of knowledge as if it were a free-floating voice, this approach takes the underlying social epistemology that is implied in any theory of knowledge. It then examines the significance of the gap that lies between an understanding from the point of view of oppressed and dominated groups and the dominant conceptual schemes that ride over such experiences in the name of a 'weak' objective social science. The result is a 'standpoint' that, unlike a perspective, is socially mediated and requires *both* science and politics to achieve (S. Harding 1991: 276, footnote).

In terms of the relations between facts and values and how those impinge upon practice, a distinction is made between constitutive and contextual values. The former refer to those values that inform the 'rules determining what constitutes acceptable scientific practice or scientific method'. Contextual values, on the other hand, 'belong to the social and cultural environment in which science is done' (Longino 1990: 4). Instead of assuming a simple distinction, as with the idea of natural proximity, they exist in a dynamic interaction that is actually required by the process and practice of scientific inquiry.

This dynamic works to both protect and challenge scientific claims exhibiting the same ambivalence that is characteristic of the world which is studied. Claims to autonomy are frequently based upon the separation of facts and values as acts of purifying ambivalence in the name of defending scientific activity and certainty. However, as is possible with more productive readings of Weber and Schutz, to see this as a strictly epistemological matter precludes the social dimension to scientific activity. To admit of a social dimension to knowledge is often seen to rule out allusion to certainty and permanence. Is this a great loss? Given that 'no epistemological theory has been able to guarantee the attainment of those ideals, this seems a minor loss' (Longino 1990: 232).

There is no need to be content with a 'weak' reflexivity that creates an artificial isolation of research communities from larger social forces. They are 'disabled by their lack of any mechanism for identifying the cultural values and interests of the researchers, which form part of the evidence for the results of research in both the natural and social sciences' (S. Harding 1991: 162). The result is a tendency towards judgemental relativism and weak objectivity and while there are allusions to not wishing to harm subjects and note cultural biases, these concerns still 'remain at the level of desire rather than competent enactment' (S. Harding 1991:163). By taking account of social situations and cultural particularities in terms of relations between other work that is of importance, an 'oppositional theory' may be developed which takes on board experiences and examines the causal tendencies that are part of natural and social life.

During the process of social investigation it is necessary to take these insights on board and translate them into research practice. The process of research itself is not regarded as being valid by virtue of being constituted by the reflexive attitude of the investigator's point of view. Research becomes a dialogic process whereby the views of research participants are incorporated into the findings (J. Cook and Fonow 1990). Rooting actual experiences within institutional relations not only brings to light similarities in experiences, but also demonstrates disjunctures between personality and culture that demand analytic attention, as opposed to being glossed over in favour of formulaic neatness as determined by the isolated and lone researcher.

A process of 'explication' arises in which relevance derives from the subject's 'lived actualities' and not from:

> an abstract space with relevances determined by notions such as the cumulation of a body of scientific knowledge … The discovery of an objectively existing social process is thus, through its capacity to generate bases of experience, seen *from such bases of experience*. The aim is to disclose the social process from within as it is lived. (D. Smith 1988: 176–7. Original italics)

The feminist analyst takes the ambivalence that arises from seeking to answer the questions 'Who am I?' and 'How do others see me?' An absence of connectivity due to occupying contradictory social locations (inside and outside) is then turned into an analytic advantage. What is retained is a scientific viewpoint *for* women without collapsing into the issues associated with identity politics in which knowledge is accessible only to particular groups which then not only acts as a reason for celebration, but also functions as exclusion.

The overall result so easily slips into a celebration of situatedness in which a particular ethic takes the place of epistemology and borders on individualism in which the opportunity to learn from others and engage in understanding so easily departs. Yet does this still privilege a 'view from nowhere' that is characteristic of weak objectivism? The issue of judgement of relevance still remains. Wealth and power divide women as much as men, so does this evade, as oppose to seek to resolve, issues associated with the relations between research and everyday life?

In seeking answers to these issues we can see a change in thought in Sandra Harding's work in *Feminism and Methodology* to *Whose Science? Whose Knowledge?* (Harding 1987, 1991). What emerges are the following points of clarification. First, in considering gender differences, it is an examination of the causes of differences that is the unifying principle *between* different women. In the pursuit of this aim a common factor emerges: 'it is the same group of white, European, bourgeois men who have legitimated and brought into being for the rest of us life worlds different from theirs' (S. Harding 1986: 175). This, in turn, contributes to an 'intellectual participatory democracy' into which the results of feminist research are fed and discussed:

> To enact or operationalize the directive of strong objectivity is to value the Other's perspective and to pass over in thought into the social condition that creates it – not in order to stay there, to 'go native' or merge the self with the Other, but in order to look back at the self in all its cultural particularity from a more distant, critical, objectifying location. (S. Harding 1991: 151)

This represents the need to recognize and investigate, rather than deny, the relations between subject and object. Contained within this call is also the need to avoid an adherence to a 'truth ideal' that is nothing more than attempts by powerful groups to legitimize how social relations are to be organized, as well as determine the form of interactions with nature (S. Harding 2006). Overall this is held to be a common project that involves a critical reflexivity through attention to history in the collective constitution of women as 'other'. A dialogic approach to scientific activity then acts as a check upon the privileging of social scientific accounts according to one standpoint as an assumed 'universal'. The aim is to create a forum through which the lost voices of women may be recovered in terms of making links between women's experiences in a more public, rather than private, forum. This activity of empowerment overcomes the tendency to see women as other. In the process, women's reflexivity within everyday experiences is revealed, rather than concealed in the partial perspectives of male 'scientific' findings.

An emphasis upon the epistemological advantages of ontological exclusion is certainly a novel move, taking us from the apparent certainties of early modernity to its later, ontological phase. At the same time it could be read as yet another means of gaining access to a universal truth that downplays difference via a denial of relativism which has posed critical issues within feminist thought itself (Haraway 1991; Murray 1997; Soper 1997; Spelman 1990). To speak in the name 'of' requires some unifying factors among women. As noted, a 'unifying principle' among different women may be a common group of men as rulers, but critiques emerged from within feminism itself on the basis that such ideas still rested upon the idea of 'woman' as somehow universal and thus, in the process, questioned the ontological basis upon which these perspectives were constructed.

Judith Butler writes of performativity in relation to both gender and sex as being different from performance because it does not presuppose a subject or a standpoint rooted in ontology. Taking performative speech acts, as those things that bring something into being as a result of being named, along with the insights of Michel Foucault, it follows that discourse brings into being the subject, not the subject who produces discourse. In this way performativity is *that aspect of discourse that has the capacity to produce what it names*' (Butler 1994: 33. Original italics). The opportunities for women to access understandings that bring together their experiences with explanations for those in relation to positions in a social field beyond discourses, is thereby diminished through being constituted by discourses.

Symbolic systems are held to be unstable and hence open to revision. With subject consciousness and its relation to that beyond discourse blocked, is engagement in the name of improvement also then blocked? With the subject positioned by objects within an object culture, narratives from everyday life become but one element, as opposed to *the* element in contemporary culture (Lash 1999). What emerges is a radicalized ontology in which it is no longer possible to speak of 'woman' but 'women'. Associating ontology with a necessary commitment to essentialism provides for celebrations of indeterminacy, fragmentation and relativism. A degree of stability or even a common 'foe' from which to base an engaged research practice aimed at change by recognizing the social nature of scientific knowledge production, now moves aside for an emphasis upon difference: 'if we … say no to modernity and its regulatory shackles in an effort to rehabilitate a utopia of the past, then I think we miss the chance to understand how the analysis of sexuality is pervasively structured by sexual difference' (Butler 1999: 20).

Disrupting what is taken to be the exclusionary effects of performativity in order to produce a more inclusionary society is a clear aim of Judith Butler's work. The normative judgements for this purpose are not apparent and we are left with a position that it not so much for consensus, but against non-consensus. In terms of the implications for the role of social research in society, we see a clear tendency towards privileging the local, specific and discrete, over matters concerned with articulation and contextualization (Fraser in Benhabib et al. 1995). The overall effect is to theorize a social openness but the implications for an engaged practice are far less clear.

The issue of agency and the ability to exercise reflexivity in an approach that sees identity as bound up within a relational approach to language has been raised in respect to ethnomethodology. We have reflexivity in action, but what about reflexivity upon actions? If we take identity as an effect of language, what happens about the relationship between social scientific findings and lay knowledge in terms of any transformative potential for improving women's lives that results from such interaction? The overall effect easily slips into a detachment between analysis and social location (McNay 2008). Yet a concern with the relationship between openness and engagement can be seen in an interview in which Judith Butler speaks of the need to produce feminist alternatives to those such as Catharine MacKinnon in the public sphere, but without undermining or demonizing existing work (Butler 1994). Such a move requires that the focus upon how subjects are constituted becomes one goal among others within a normative framework:

> there are questions of social and economic justice which are not primarily concerned with questions of subject-formation. To this end it is crucial to re-think the domain of power-relations, and to develop a way of adjudicating political norms without forgetting that such an adjudication will also always be a struggle for power. (Butler 1995: 141)

How do you undertake such work without displacing the very terms of reference that have constituted the uniqueness and power of feminist approaches to knowing the social world? A productive ambivalence that informs intellectual practice is so easily side-stepped in favour of ever increasing retreats into theoretical neatness. The institutionalization of such activities is a social process, but a perspective that focuses upon discourse deconstruction to the exclusion of a focus on the institutional arrangements under which knowledge production, dissemination and reception takes place is not politically well equipped to defend itself, except in the most reified places far removed from the lives of those whom it is intended to assist. It can easily become not the discipline of feminism conducted in the name of women, but the disciplining of feminism itself (Messer-Davidow 2002). We find that the history of an intellectual and political struggle to enable women's studies to be recognized within educational institutions runs the danger of being assumed by those who now enjoy the benefits afforded by earlier resistance and struggle.

What is at risk if engagement with social processes, that is said to characterize feminist practice aimed at social change, is abandoned? As Mary Maynard (1998) points out, feminist approaches to research may not reflect new methods of social investigation as such, but new questions pursued for different purposes. Here the practice and dissemination of research findings is explicitly designed to improve the position of women in different societies and groups through contributing to dialogic communities that are designed to enhance understanding. In the need to recognize, but not reify, difference and in the name of improving women's position within societies, writers have noted the need for a balance between the potential arrogant complacency of universalism and the nihilism of perspectivism (J. Martin 1994).

The social character of knowledge and the efforts involved in mediating between constitutive and contextual values can so easily be lost, leaving not the work of understanding, but instead those who shout across chasms informed by a positioning and process that has long since ceased to be an object of investigation taken forward into practice. By taking an alternative route, feminist research can build upon findings concerning women's positions and experiences within the social world (Walby 1997). That route is not achieved by 'flattening out' an understanding of conflict and diversity between and within women's experiences (Segal 1999), nor from regarding agency as arising from the indeterminacy of symbolic structures (McNay 2000, 2008).

Summary

Opening up the practice of social research to reflexive scrutiny has a number of consequences. At the experiential level of the researcher, a tension will be felt between the centrality of their experiences, measured against the aggregate of social values and practices they seek to understand. Feelings of inconsequentiality may result as individuality is absorbed within totality. For Weber this existed as a tension between an ethic of commitment and an ethic of responsibility: that is, a belief in the value of science and a commitment to represent that which is discovered. Although his work has been interpreted as erecting walls between the integrity of science and arbitrary values, it is equally plausible to suggest that it resulted from the effort to construct a sphere in which 'affirmation was possible and, most important, where bureaucratic and scientific rationality were impossible' (Wolin 2004: 380).

In the absence of supportive and open cultures of inquiry, all this so easily becomes unproductive, as opposed to a productive tension taken forward in practice. Expressions of individual inadequacy result in an age in which social problems are increasingly individualized. Pushing too far in this direction sees individuals or groups of individuals opting for particular schools of thought, thinkers or methods because such allegiances provide a relief from this basic tension or, alternatively, there is a reflexive turn inwards on scientific constitution that does little to help in understanding the relations between social research and social life.

Each of the above insights in this chapter has contributed to greater sensitivity in relation to these issues. At the same time each, in their different ways, quietly seeks closure of a more general consideration of the role and future of social research in social life. Max Weber and Alfred Schutz are both thinkers whose work has passed through so many hands. A return to their insights shows, as would be expected, both strengths and limitations. Similarly, with Harold Garfinkel we find an emphasis upon reflexivity that should alert us to unrealistic claims for the benefits of its various practices, along with a caution against collapsing spheres of activity whose differences constitute their vibrancy and insight.

We have much to thank the writers discussed in this chapter for showing us the social nature of knowledge production. However, there are limits to this endeavour when deployed in the service of reflexivity. It is plausible to suggest that precisely because the physical sciences are not so consciously reflexive, they are 'normal' sciences in the Kuhnian sense of the word. How often can people explicate the reasons for their actions when they may be intuitive? Herein lie certain limits. So too do limits lie in the celebration of context over content. If production is reducible to an explanation of context, what might we then say about why some practices, ideas and findings get taken up elsewhere? Context can help us with understanding knowledge production, but content is also a key component of explanatory adequacy and the efforts aimed at achieving practical understandings in everyday life in terms of knowledge reception. An understanding of both pro-duction and reception enables us to examine the natural proximity of social science and social life and the interactions between constitutive and contextual values.

In terms of social research, this requires us to examine what it sees and the manner in which it is constructed, while considering its wider place within social relations. Accompanying this is recognition that 'practical' interventions in the organization of social life are central to its endeavours and vital to its future. Limits also need to be recognized. While Alvin Gouldner rightly introduced the topic of feeling to its prac-tice, this can hover on the edges of an individualist and idealist conception 'straight out of nineteenth century Romanticism' (Dawe 1973: 51). The point of taking on board the role of experience in practice is also to hold a place for a practice whose value lies in its ability to provide insights that inform and also question our common understandings. The feelings and experiences of the researcher are the starting point to this process, but they are certainly not the finishing point.

Similarly, to allude, albeit in a disguised fashion, to a sense of belonging between the researcher and researched that is unproblematically regurgitated as a condition of interpretative adequacy and thus the authenticity of findings, elides an under-standing of the different ways of understanding that come with any attempt aimed at explanation. This is the point that Dorothy Smith was making not only about feminist-inspired social research, but also about the translation and contes-tation of ideas between contexts and groups.

I chose here to concentrate on particular ideas within the diverse body of thought that constitutes feminisms. The reasons are that these authors explicitly seek to retain engagement with social and political issues, alongside recognition of the limitations of science and its reconstitution. Here we find several impulses characterizing the poles of reflexivity. First, the continual process of deconstruction in order to remain sensitive to working assumptions and their effects on research practice. Second, reconstruction in order to inform engagement via improved prac-tice and third, a concern with the dissemination and interpretation of such knowl-edge and its implications for actions. Overall, therefore, deconstruction is performed in the name of reconstruction (Harding and Hintikka 1983).

We can also observe that an absence of reflexivity in research practice can be symptomatic of a politics that takes organic belonging as unproblematic and any questioning of those relations as an act that automatically debunks supposedly self-evident truths. Institutions are said to bear the problems of reflexivity, not people. Reflexivity is de-bunking as the automatic critique of the self-evident.

Knowing one's place according to a strong tradition is what constitutes a viable society and is the political and social solution to the problem of reflexivity. When dealing with the issue of reflexivity in this manner, however, we can terminate in some sinister 'solutions' to these 'problems' (Dahl 1999).

At another level we must ask: once the adherence to a technicality in method is unsettled, what takes its place? Reflexivity might work as a sensitizing device bringing into view those elements of research that remain hidden by the limitations of such approaches, but when it works to produce yet another social scientific hierarchy through which to judge the adequacy of results about the social world, it easily slips into undermining, as opposed to positively contributing to, dialogue and representation.

Such an outcome can easily occur within environments in which there is no shortage of those willing to occupy this space and who are far less reserved in their pronouncements of how the world should be. Both a narrow technicism and the repeated inventions of reflexive adequacy can work to produce an image of good and bad social science, leaving those less reserved about such matters to participate in the public realm in which judgements, formulations and policies are routinely made. Here, I am reminded of a colleague and friend, well known in social research, who rang me up to ask what an editorial board was asking about when they requested him to be 'more reflexive' in his article. He wanted to talk about the world, not the word. They wanted to reverse the equation in the name of something whose justifications had no sense at all of this relation.

Reflexive thinking can be part of a healthy and ongoing debate within the social sciences that should not only enable clarification and improvements in precision, but also aim to question the conventions upon which practices are based in order that pre-reflexive assumptions are open to critical scrutiny; all of which may be conducted in the name of obtaining greater insight into the dynamics of social life. However, there is a basic tension in these aims, for the very act of raising such issues may itself threaten established procedures and beliefs. The core question then becomes: how far do you go? David Silverman recounts a story to illustrate his resistance to taking reflexive questioning too far:

> Many years ago, I remember a research student who used to make visiting speakers flounder by asking them: 'how would you apply your own analysis to the text you have just presented?' As they wriggled, I wriggled too – not from intellectual difficulty but rather from distaste for this sort of wordplay which appeared to make a not very articulate student into a profound thinker. (Silverman 1997: 240)

Reflexive questioning should not only involve an examination of the grounds upon which we may claim to know the social world, but also point to the limitations of our knowledge. In this sense it acts as a corrective to the instrumentalism informed by the desire to control, rather than understand, the social world. Academic commentators do not enjoy a monopoly on reflexive questioning and also find themselves increasingly subject to the very forces which may act to counter reflexivity. In our apparent methodologically post-positivist/empiricist/ modernist age, the quiet revenge of instrumentality marches onwards.

We will return to the issues associated with the contexts of knowledge production later in the book. With the above issues in mind I now turn to a more in-depth understanding of mediation and social research. Here we find not only a one-way relation of contributing to an improvement in social research practice, but also a relation in which practice itself becomes the object of reflection, critique and change.

MEDIATION AND RESEARCH

2

A great deal of writing has been devoted to the idea of producing more reflexive accounts in research practice. All this takes place against the backdrop of the incurable nature of reflexivity in an age characterized by increasing individualization and detraditionalization. As the charge was once made of being a positivist, to be an unreflexive practitioner can work to signify someone who is inadequate, incomplete and worst of all, outdated. As will be clear from my discussions so far, I am seeking clarity in this literature in the service of engagement.

It is possible to gain the distinct impression in relation to a number of writings that concern with clarification for engagement is at a premium. There is a lot of material out there which seems to be conducted in the name of theoreticism or technicism where limits are constituted only by the opinions of significant others within limited communities. At what point in this process does creativity fall into indulgence? Yet toleration of differences informing divisions of labour in social research is required for a responsible social science to flourish and develop. That means not celebrating expertise by placing knowledge beyond question, but recognizing limits and being prepared to enter into a dialogue concerning implications for actual practice with those who are neither the objects of social research, nor the passive recipients of findings from laboratory-based studies of objects.

The considerations that inform the circumstances for this to take place lie beyond the confines of social research practice and concern the natural sciences and humanities, contextual values, cultures and material relations. Knowing limits is as important as understanding strengths: we cannot know one without the other. With these points in mind, I continue this journey informed by writings concerned with mediation between social science and social life.

Hermeneutic Mediation

How do we understand the relations that mediate between the practice of social science and social life? To examine this question some authors have turned to hermeneutics in order to see how social science stands in a 'reflexive social relation to its subject matter, human social action' (Giddens in Giddens and

Pierson 1998: 40). It is simply not possible to make social scientific statements that refer to 'sensory observations' in theoretically neutral ways (Giddens 1976: 135).

To side-step this issue via meticulous descriptions of everyday life, or pre-occupations with the technicality of methods, does not relieve us of the need for reflexive inquiry in the engagements that occur between social research and social life. Exhaustive descriptions of meaning in use through bracketing accounts of intelligibility, in other words, do not remove the need for interpretive accounts of context and content in order to sharpen our insights. Indeed, the very practicality and relevance of research for social life lies within a domain which is not abandoned via a slavish adherence to method or theory.

What is not implied in the above is the abandonment of methodological rigour, but instead a more inclusive process of understanding. As a result a general concern is opened up with how what is knowable by the sciences is brought into the contexts of mutual agreement in which we exist. Hermeneutics steps in at this point with its concerns about human knowing and doing. It 'not only accounts for the procedures applied by science but also gives an account of the questions that are prior to the application of every science' (Gadamer 1981: 137). Hermeneutic scrutiny falls upon a learning process as mediated by comparative contrast:

> The process of learning a paradigm or language-game as the expression of a form of life is also a process of learning what a paradigm is not: that is to say, learning to mediate it with other, rejected, alternatives, by contrast to which the claims of the paradigm in question are clarified. (Giddens 1976: 144)

Alvin Gouldner placed emphasis upon the position of the knower in an active process of knowledge production. While acknowledging this as a desirable standpoint, it does not absolve the social analyst from the need to establish criteria relevant to judging the substantive validity of a claim to knowledge. In Gouldner's writings, however, 'one searches in vain … for a sustained discussion of this issue'. As a result Gouldner's call to reflexivity is seen to be subject to the same 'self-defeating circularity characteristic of ventures into the sociology of knowledge' (Giddens 1987: 268–9).

In terms of taking on board this possible outcome, reflexive inquiry within the social scientific community is exhibited in the relationships that exist between lay and technical languages. Alfred Schutz argued these were one way. Here it is argued there is a constant movement between the two with consequences for everyday practice and the practice of social science: 'It would not be at all unusual to find a coroner who had read Durkheim' (Giddens 1990: 42). It also follows that within everyday practice the 'objective' causal conditions which influence human conduct can, in principle, be recognized by people and thus incorporated into their actions in such a way as to have transformative consequences.

Expressed in these terms the practice of social research can be seen as a 'double hermeneutic'. This characterization refers to the ways in which lay and professional concepts become implicated in a continual slippage between frames of meaning (Giddens 1984: 374). As a community of social researchers is not able to lay claim to an unproblematic and separate identification of a social mechanism or set of circumstances that give rise to actions in a manner that cannot then be incorporated into those actions, the 'revelatory' nature of their expertise instead gives rise to an 'interpretive' mode. Set against the backdrop of a huge increase in information it follows that: 'No one can become an expert, in the sense of the possession either of full expert knowledge or of the appropriate formal credentials, in more than a few small sectors of the immensely complicated knowledge systems that now exist' (Giddens 1990: 144).

The backdrop is 'reflexive modernization'. The term refers to susceptibility, in both material relations with nature and social activity, 'to chronic revision in the light of new information or knowledge' (Giddens 1991: 20). A continual generation of knowledge results in the undermining of the Enlightenment claim for certainty leading to the era of 'late modernity'; an era that is not transcended by postmodernity, but is better able to understand the conditions of its own existence. In terms of ontological security, this has ramifications for 'trust' and 'risk' in everyday human relations (Giddens 1990), where the latter has been taken as a defining characteristic of the modern age (Beck 1992). The age is one in which: 'You have to construct and invent your intersubjectivity in order to be an individual' (Beck in Beck and Beck-Gernsheim 2002: 212).

So what of the role of research and its claims to expertise? People have reasons for actions, even if those reasons are further illuminated by virtue of reading an account of those actions. To be informed that our actions result from external circumstances will be disconcerting. Yet before one is tempted to lay claim to any explanatory superiority, based upon the expertise that constitutes a research study that has access to an objective reality separate from its perception, it is held that there is no knowledge that cannot be incorporated into lay understandings: 'objections to such findings may thus have a very sound basis. Reification is by no means purely characteristic of lay thought' (Giddens 1984: 284).

If research reports have the potential to be taken on board in such a manner, how does this happen? Social investigations contribute to knowledge and cannot escape from the duty of making 'intelligibility, intelligible' (Giddens 1976: 40). In understanding this process, the following are now opened up as a legitimate part of social scientific knowledge production: the forms of communication and styles deployed in report writing; an ethnographic component of all research as the condition of entry into knowing what is already known by lay people; a concern to guard against the non-conflation of methodology with ontological reality (for example, using institutional analysis and assuming that governs face-to-face interactions) and a sensitivity to the time–space constitution of social life (Giddens 1984: Chapter 6).

The spirit of this work is relational and transformational with society being viewed as the accomplishment of skilled agents (Bhaskar 1989). The opacity of the social world also derives from the following: the unacknowledged conditions of actions; the routine deployment of tacit skills; relations between the unconscious and cognition and the effects of the unintended consequences of actions. What we see here is a move beyond an aggregation hypothesis (the macro as the sum total of micro events) to one of unintended consequences in which the capability and knowledgeability of social actors is seen as bounded (Knorr-Cetina 1981: 1988). Accompanying this is an emphasis upon a Heideggerian inspired ontology of potentials in human action. Three emphases, in particular, then arise that hold open sets of possibilities for circumstances to be otherwise.

First, there is 'dialectic of control' at work such that whatever knowledge and control is lost through increasing processes of abstraction may be reappropriated within everyday life activities. Second, a 'duality of structure' exists such that structure does not exist outside of social practices, but is constituted in the moments of their performance and third, the development of an understanding of how the movement from reflexivity within actions to reflexivity upon actions occurs. While these work to avoid deterministic connotations in the construction of a theoretical framework, the last of these specifically concerns relations between the production and reception of social scientific knowledge.

That move places this work at odds with particular variants of ethnomethodology, despite there being a clear debt to that tradition (May and Powell 2008: Chapter 5). Different forms of reflexivity are at work. One form is associated with the understandings people have of themselves as agents with others having to 'accept these actions and understandings' (Giddens 1999: 203). An emphasis upon the tacit awareness of the social skills that people possess leads to the observation that: 'a great deal of social research just writes out the area of practical consciousness' (Giddens in Giddens and Pierson 1998: 83). Such reflexivity also includes discursive consciousness: what actors are able to say about the conditions under and through which their actions are performed. That may follow from either intentional or unintentional conduct from which, having either performed the act or being confronted by the implications of one's actions, 'means being able to put things into words' (Giddens 1984: 45). We may characterize these forms in terms of a tacit awareness of how to get 'on' in social action and how to account 'for' that action.

References to reflexivity are also found in terms of being 'social' or 'high'. Returning to the conditions under and through which we act, these refer to general changes in society whereby information becomes constitutive of what people do and the reasons they give for their actions. Here we have a high level of generality expressed in terms of 'a condition of life in modern societies' (Giddens 1999: 203). A connection may be established here with institutional reflexivity considered as a historical phenomenon enabling a distance to be achieved from daily life. A more calculative attitude may then be adopted towards the social world which, when linked with a theory of action, possesses a transformative capacity. Social agency depends solely upon the capability of actors to 'make a difference' in the production of definite outcomes, regardless of whether or not they intend (are aware) that these outcomes occur. Since 'to make a difference' is to transform some aspect of a process or event, understandings of objective features of the social world can be incorporated into actions and the reasons given for those actions. The results of social research, therefore, can become a source of such potential. Incontestable scientific truths characteristic of traditional societies, now give way to contestable truth claims within a dialogic public sphere within late modernity.

In considering the relationship between social research and social life in this manner, we need to return from the institutional level to the connections between the social self and late modernity. An emphasis is then found upon ego-psychology in which the unconscious is viewed as a kind of 'security system' to be activated at times when self-esteem is threatened and anxiety seeks to be avoided. Nevertheless, while admitting of the need to address the unconscious in social theory, it is practical consciousness that is regarded as the 'cognitive and emotive anchor of the feelings of *ontological security*' (Giddens 1991: 36. Original italics). The tacit knowledge upon which people routinely draw in the course of their conduct thereby provides for the maintenance of the unconscious within what is an over-arching emphasis upon the existential.

Introducing this emphasis means that it sits rather uneasily alongside the idea of late modernity being characterized in terms of 'discontinuity' whereby tradition, order and control increasingly give way to flux and uncertainty. In the intersections between the self and modernity, there is a clear concern with 'ontological security' – defined as continuity in self-identity and constancy in material and social environments (Giddens 1990: 92). In an age of globalization, decisions that affect daily lives stretch increasingly away, in time and space, from the immediate social environment. Processes of decentring and increased envelopment exist side by side whereby everyday life becomes 'detraditionalized and individualized but also *palpably globalized*' (Beck and Beck-Gernsheim 2002: 151. Original italics). The overall result is a 'disembedding of mechanisms': 'Few people anywhere in the world can any longer be unaware of the fact that their local activities are influenced, and sometimes even determined, by remote events and agencies' (Giddens in Beck et al. 1994: 57).

Disembedding coexists within a shrinking sphere of certainty giving rise to 'reflexive modernization'. Social scientific knowledge is part of this process. Bearing in mind the nature of reflexivity and the dialectic of control, knowledge is then subject to greater normalization within everyday practice. It does not operate in a revelatory manner based upon object-distance from human relations, but instead is co-opted into the constitution of those relations and is thus also potentially transformative. From the point of view of knowledge reception we then find that: '"Openness to criticism" among social scientists inevitably implies "openness to utilization" on the part of others' (Giddens 1989: 290).

In terms of the individual the

> reflexive project of the self is energised against a backdrop of moral impoverishment. Small wonder then that in such circumstances the newly constituted sphere of pure relationships may come to bear a heavy burden as an area of experience generating a morally rewarding milieu for individual life development. (Giddens 1991:169)

Yet in turning towards science to seek certainty, a body of knowledge is found that is open to continual revision. In the face of a mixture of uncertainty and a need for ontological security, it is not surprising to find humanism manifested in terms of modernity not being some Weberian iron cage, but a state necessitating a 'protective cocoon' for the 'self' (Burkitt 1992).

In traditional societies the amount of individual skill, in terms of action over a given environment, could be argued to have been greater despite the collective conquest we now claim over nature – even if the associated risks of such actions have now increased (Beck 1992). In relation to combating climate change, for example: 'What hope is there that, as collective humanity, we will be able to control the forces we have unleashed?' (Giddens 2009: 228). Increasing uncertainty is then manifest in a turn from tradition to expertise in which the latter, in comparison to lay knowledge, implies an imbalance between the two in respect to a given field of action. With the relations between self and modernity, reflexivity and the dialectic of control in mind, expertise and tradition are then compared according to the following dynamics. First, expertise is disembedding and trans-local. Second, it proceeds according to scepticism rather than formulaic truths. Third, the accumulation of expert knowledge concerns increasing specialization. Fourth, trust in experts is not readily derived from esoteric wisdom, and finally, 'expertise interacts with growing institutional reflexivity, such that there are regular processes of loss and re-appropriation of everyday skills and knowledge' (Giddens 1996: 38–9).

Now we seem to have both a characterization of modernity in terms of the protection of the self and recognition that expertise is constituted in terms of the universalism of doubt, or minimally propositional truths open to continual revision, while also having a position to pronounce upon given fields of action. From the point of view of knowledge production, to give oneself over to context would mean undermining the impersonal nature of knowledge constitution as expressed in these terms; all of which takes place against the backdrop of the continual possibility of utilizing social scientific knowledge without due recognition of its source. Just what, then, might be the basis for legitimizing social research as an activity?

Legitimation, as a mode of according consent to the activity of others who are seen to possess knowledge and skills by those who are subordinate to power, might be too strong a term. However, acting according to a belief in the impartiality of knowledge within a given community appears closer to what is referred to as 'authoritative centres'. These are based on impersonal principles and seek to influence or regulate knowledge-claims, as well as being open to innovation. To that extent they cut across and even undermine the rational-legal procedures that Weber argued characterized bureaucracy: the mobility implied in expertise does not simply bow down to the idea of stability embodied in the duty of the official (Giddens 1996: 39).

There is quite a mixture here. In terms of the spirit in which this book is written, we may first observe that this is a general theoretical orientation which in terms of its immediate implications for practice works more as a sensitizing device, than a body of work intended to inform practice. Within the philosophy of science we may refer here to the under-determination of theories through reference to criteria that are non-empirical (Hesse 1974). Therefore, an argument is maintained whereby socio-theoretical development stretches away from social research as an endeavour that cannot possess empirical referents. In addition, there is an emphasis upon the ordering of institutions across time and space, the reproduction of systems as organized regularities within social practices and sensitivity to the relations between knowledge and social reproduction within conditions of reflexive modernization. Each of these relates to what is actually changing in social relations within the unfolding of history. We also find an important relation between social research and social life in terms of its impact, via knowledge reception, upon social practices.

While the above raise general issues, they are held to be central to the 'self-understanding' of the social sciences in the contemporary era (Giddens in Held and Thompson 1989). Although a separation between how relations are and how we seek to know those relations is understandable, to maintain this separation in such a way as if one can legislate from a theoretical vantage point about the inadequacies or limitations of modes of understanding, whether from a so-called modern or postmodern point of view, should be held in check. We may have various forms of reflexivity from which to choose, but the assumption of co-optation of expert by lay knowledge rests upon an assumed ontology of potentials. An unproductive abstraction then results when seeking to understand the relations between the production and reception of social scientific knowledge. Therefore, this is particularly important when seeking to understand, from a hermeneutic point of view, the relations between the sense and reference of a text in terms of the internal structure of its meaning within particular social contexts *and* the possible worlds that are disclosed as a result (Ricoeur 1981).

Take a few examples. First, the idea of research findings, as with social structure being instantiated in human action, does not allow for the possibility that reflexivity upon actions may be born in encountering objective constraints that are not immediately amenable to change at the level of agency. In such times the ability to reflect *upon* actions, as opposed to *within* actions may be enhanced, but the capability to effect change as a result remains a different, although not unrelated, matter. Second, while an initial stage may be reached in which reflexivity upon actions has an effect upon an understanding of actions, it is also the case that such an initial condition can lead to the production of subsequent actions such that those initial spheres of reflexive action become diminished over time. Third, to hold on to both a reflexive modernization and ontological security thesis at the same time seems to curtail, rather than guide, empirical inquiry. The result leaves embedded and embodied understandings, adaptations and actions at a local level closed by theoretical fiat. Fourth, it may be argued that in order to understand social science, we need to reflexively understand the relations between its practice, the constitution of its objects of inquiry and how those interpretations feed back, or not, into its understandings, as well as those of the lay community.

In respect to this latter point the production of social scientific findings meets an epistemology of reception: that is, how such information is translated and how it relates to practical activities. As opposed to viewing this as a topic, we find an overdrawing of the demarcation between expert and lay knowledge, with the paradoxical result that the dynamic dimensions of production-transmission-reception in scientific practices are relatively neglected. What we are dealing with is not so much a double hermeneutic, but multiple hermeneutics that may imply a transformative capacity in the sense of power 'to', but it may equally be a relationship in terms of knowledge as power 'over'. This would help us better understand why: 'Increasing freedom for some regularly goes along with, or is even the cause of, greater oppression for others' (Giddens in Beck et al. 1994: 187). The idea of 'trust' in expert systems thus needs to be replaced by a more complex understanding of the relations between the social scientific and lifeworld communities if we are to better understand the mediated nature of social science in respect to social life (Wynne 1996).

The reflexive modernization thesis states that as modernity unfolds alongside an increasing knowledge of the social conditions and situations in which we find ourselves, an increasing optimism concerning improvements in the human condition occurs. A reflexivity concerning modernity, on the other hand, leads equally to a more pessimistic account in which the world appears as a juggernaut out of control for there is no implied connectivity between circumstances, their understanding and transformation. From the point of view of a practice whose existence depends upon engagement with the social world as a necessary condition of its understanding, it is not necessary to exercise a choice in relation to either of these perspectives. However, they may well inform the predispositions, or background assumptions, of its practitioners and to that extent are of core interest. Equally, they may be of interest in order to correct the technicism that would presuppose that they are resolved through the correct application of method.

We have here a similar outcome for the practice of theoretical understandings and a social research practice that seeks to understand the social world through engagement via the application of methodological rigour: degrees of ambivalence. Within each, justification may be readily invoked in different ways in order to reduce this outcome. A community of scholars may agree, consciously or otherwise, concerning the application of a method and a similar community may all come together to celebrate the work of a particular school of thought or scholar. In both cases this may occur without concern for the justification–application continuum. Surely, however, justification is a matter of interpretation? If we are to better understand the place of social research in society, we need to see how and under what circumstances an interpretation is appropriated by those whom it concerns? Equally, we need to consider how such interpretations are mediated, or not, by others in positions of power whose selectivity has an effect on its understanding and dissemination in the public realm.

Democratically speaking, to allude to a public sphere in terms of a deliberative ideal is important as a regulatory principle, but this should not happen in a way that shuts down investigation of this important area of interest. After all, to understand these processes is also to feed into the reconstructions for the justifications for social research practice and so open it up to improved understandings of its place in society. What must be avoided in the process are conflations between different justifications for the assertion of a finding according to a community of scholars who have particular practices and who invoke certain standards and justifications, constituted among wider communities about what is regarded as 'true' knowledge when applied to the social world. In this way we can better understand their interactions and effects.

Existential Analytics: Positions and Dispositions

In examining the production of social scientific knowledge, it is clear that the academic field as a site of production, as Alfred Schutz recognized, constitutes a particular way of viewing the world. At this point we should ask, how does this occur, under what circumstances and with what effects? In turning to these questions it is important to examine the works of Pierre Bourdieu. Here was a social scientist whose interests and practices were routinely informed by empirical engagement, while also being placed in the camp of 'grand theorist'.

Pierre Bourdieu's call to reflexivity took him beyond not only phenomenologically inspired accounts, but also those of Alvin Gouldner and Anthony Giddens. The reason for this move may be found in a need to understand the 'intellectualist bias' in research production (Wacquant 1992: 39. Original italics). The social world is viewed as a 'spectacle' and as a result, problems arise through missing the subtleties of everyday actions, as well as ignoring an explanation of the conditions that have given rise to the natural attitude. Therefore, while descriptions of the taken-for-granted are important, they do not contain 'the principles of their own interpretation'. In relation to power, for example: 'Interactions between a physician, an intern, and a nurse … are undergirded by hierarchical relations of power that are not always visible during the directly observable interaction' (Bourdieu in Bourdieu and Wacquant 1992: 73).

When examining the mediation of lay and professional concepts, authors have focused upon 'the *social* origins and coordinates (class, gender, ethnicity, etc) of the individual researcher' (Wacquant 1992: 39. Original italics). In order that this is not an end in itself that leads to a psychological reductionism without implications for cultures of knowledge production, the position of the researcher within the academic 'field', constituted as a set of objective relations with others, requires examination. In addition, how researchers define themselves, in particular through their difference from and distance to others with whom they compete in the academic field, are key elements that brings together the disposition *and* position of the individual practitioner without a lapse into individualism. What is encompassed here is not knowledge as such, but a 'relation to knowledge' expressed through knowing how to construct an object of analysis in ways that are recognized by others in the field (Bourdieu 2004).

It follows that social researchers should submit to critique their ways of thinking about the world: that is, the ways in which they retire to think about that world (and hence from acting in that world) and how they construct actions in that world. Presuppositions, built into concepts, methods of analysis and the practical manner in which research is conducted, should not be subject to some intellectual introspection, but a 'sociology of sociology' (Bourdieu 1990). Such a call to reflexivity moves into the relations between content and context and so 'extends beyond the experiencing subject to encompass the organizational and cognitive structure of the discipline' (Wacquant 1992: 40). Why? To:

> *produce more science, not less.* It is not designed to discourage scientific ambition but to help make it more realistic. By helping the progress of science and thus the growth of knowledge about the social world, *reflexivity makes possible a more responsible politics*, both inside and outside of academia. (Bourdieu in Bourdieu and Wacquant 1992: 194. Original italics)

A clear intent to work with reflexivity to produce an improved science exists alongside the wish to deploy science to improve social conditions. Not surprisingly, perhaps, no credence is given to the 'usual somewhat fatuous discourse about "neutrality"' (Bourdieu 1993: 11), such that interest and truth are seen as either opposites or in some tension. We need an interest in producing the truth in the first instance among a particular community. There are parallels here with the view that for something to be objective, it must be justifiable in a manner that is independent of one individual, leading to an intersubjective understanding through a culture of testability as a precondition of scientific status (Popper 1968).

When it comes to the practices of a scientific community that informs such a culture, there is a tension: between the necessary interest which aims at the production of truth and an excavation of the conditions that give rise to classificatory practices that frame ways of seeing the world. The latter is related to a particular position, while the scholastic point of view suspends practical intent in what, following Husserl, is a 'neutralizing disposition' (Bourdieu 1998a: 128). A condition of entry into the academic field is an attitude in which the necessities of life are suspended in order to constitute contemplation as an end in itself. A commitment to understand the relations between classificatory practices and social and economic conditions – key to which is understanding how practical urgency is constituted, along with its reasons and effects – finds itself the object of contemplation by those for whom both temporal emergency and perhaps even economic necessity, is bracketed.

In analysing objects of analysis in this way we find the application of a particular vision of social practices that becomes constituted in an entirely different way from the practices themselves. Here we find parallels with the insights of Georg Simmel. Simmel noted how human thought was always synthesizing 'the given into units that serve as subject matter of the sciences' (Simmel 1964: 5). One example he used was the Gothic style whose existence cannot be shown, but instead is seen in 'particular works of art which along with individual elements, also contain stylistic elements' (Simmel 1964: 5). It is impossible enough to track the detail of the behaviour of individual units, but that is not of primary concern. If we were interested in the behaviour of the Greeks and Persians in the battle of Marathon, a 'true' account of historical cognition would take place only if it included the behaviour of all those individuals who were involved. Yet even that may not be a solution, for our concern focuses upon the collective and its consequences and that is a different issue. To speak of the histories of cities, political territories and the feminist movement is abstract, but it is also a fact of our existence. To scientifically analyse characteristics of the individual is also to separate out innumerable influences that stretch away in time and space which are just as 'real'. To end at the individual is thereby to eliminate all knowable reality: 'It relegates it into the infinite and looks for it in the realm of the inscrutable' (Simmel 1964: 7).

The importance of distance now moves into the terrain of Simmel's reflections. Differences in cognition come from a 'number of heterogeneous objects of cognition that are nevertheless recognized as equally definitive and consistent. The principle may be expressed by the symbol of different *distances* between such a complex of phenomena and the human mind' (Simmel 1964: 7. Original italics). The perspectives are each correct in their own way and at one level we may see the individual as differentiated from others, but as the distance increases so the individual disappears and a picture of society emerges that 'has its own possibilities of being recognized or missed' (Simmel 1964: 8).

Distance constitutes a way of seeing that marks out the distinction and value of scientific work on an intensive–extensive continuum. That same distance also allows modes of knowledge production to become implicated in relations of dominance. Social problems are easily reflected as issues for social research when 'preconstructed objects … impose themselves as scientific objects' (Bourdieu et al., 1991: 249). Matters of knowledge reception – how it might be deployed, dialogically, in addressing relations of power – are then bracketed and with that the very conditions of possibility for things to be otherwise. The break that allows for objectification in the scholastic mode, therefore, is also a disconnection that stops an understanding of the relations between modes of thought and social conditions.

Scholastic fallacies are seen to fall into three domains: ethics, aesthetics and knowledge (Bourdieu 2000: Chapter 2). The latter consists in conflating practical with theoretical reason (Bourdieu 1998a). The social presuppositions of the scholastic point of view are now objects of reflexive scrutiny. To be woken from 'scholastic slumbers' is an exercise in epistemological questioning, not denunciation, in which the tools deployed for understanding the classificatory schemas and social conditions within the social world are turned back onto the modes through which it is not only contemplated, but also constituted and represented. An objective distance from necessity is what Weber called a 'stylization of life' that enables a focus upon modes of representation via the gaze of the scholastic mode of thought.

The tools deployed in research are now used to study the conditions of its constitution in order to improve, not undermine, its insights. Distance and time produce the conditions that enable an unhastening of science whose calling is to 'give us the close-up, the slow motion replay and the still frame rather than the hellish image blitz of the MTV model of entertainment' (Pels 2003: 219). Time and power are linked as ingredients producing this distance from necessity. Yet this bracketing of time is double-edged because it also informs a scholastic illusion:

> itself correlative with the tendency to transform the privation linked to exclusion from the world of practice into a cognitive privilege, with the myth of the 'impartial spectator', or the 'outsider' according to Simmel, who are exclusive beneficiaries of access to the point of view on points of view which opens perspectives on the game as a game. (Bourdieu 2000: 224)

Conditions of relative stability in which there is a connection between disposition and position tend not to be objects of reflexive scrutiny; hence the inclusion of Part 3 in this investigation. There is no suggestion here of unthinking complicity, but an analysis that examines degrees of integration (Bourdieu 2000: 160). Yet here we find investments that are often the objects of denial in celebrations of limited notions of autonomy, or are not understood because misrecognition is characteristic of the scholastic illusion whose universe is informed by the search for and conferring of distinction. The combination of disposition and position that provides for the constitution of social reality as an object of analysis, therefore, is double-edged because the advantage of distance has a cost for the insights it generates into practical reason. For here we find cultures of inquiry 'characterized by the suspension and removal of economic necessity and by objective and subjective distance from practical urgencies, which is the basis of objective and subjective distance from groups subjected to those determinisms' (Bourdieu 1986: 54). Under such conditions, how is a 'point of view on the points of view' then attained in order to provide for insights into social relations?

In Pierre Bourdieu's work an interrogation of this question takes place via the deployment of a reflexivity that avoids issues associated with the philosophy of the subject through the application of those tools of social inquiry that are normally reserved for the social realm, rather than the realm of its scientific constitution. The overall purpose is to explore the conditions under which objectivity becomes possible, as well as expose the practices that prevent it being opened up to critical inquiry and instead remain based upon limited and ultimately, untenable modes of operation. While this appears to be a self-defeating critique conducted within particular communities that are predisposed to reflexive scrutiny, it actually strengthens practices by revealing value through the distinctiveness of its insights. The tools of inquiry for an examination of the social world – habitus, capital and field (see May and Powell 2008: Chapter 6) – examine modes of production and reception in terms of social reproduction, without resort to either voluntarism or determinism, thereby opening up spaces of possible transformation.

Here we can detect a consistency at the point where other approaches to reflexivity fall silent. It is possible to gain the distinct impression from writings on reflexivity that they are topics for others, or blunt instruments with which to castigate for a failure to live up to unattainable ends, as opposed to being for the actual practice of social research in all of its dimensions. Here we find a challenge to the narrow aloofness of scientific practice via an examination of the presuppositions built into the 'oxymoron of *epistemic doxa*' (Bourdieu 1998a: 129. Original italics). An understanding of the demarcation of fields of activity in order to specify their differences and so their exceptionality is also apparent: 'The unanalysed element in every theoretical analysis (whether subjectivist or objectivist) is the theorist's subjective relation to the social world and the objective (social) relation presupposed by this subjective relation' (Bourdieu 1992a: 29).

If interests within the field of scientific practice constitute the basis of true knowledge about that world that is not available elsewhere, then those interests must also work at the social conditions of their practice in order to obtain a distance from that world as an object of knowledge. A 'genuine epistemology' is then 'built on knowledge of the social conditions under which scientific schemata actually function' and so reflexivity is no guarantee of autonomy because the latter 'does not come without the social conditions of autonomy; and these conditions cannot be obtained on an individual basis' (Bourdieu in Bourdieu and Wacquant 1992: 178, 183).

Approaches that smuggle in the philosopher-king characteristic of the Enlightenment 'view from nowhere' are rejected. At the level of practice we may find a tendency, given by statistical regularity, according to a distance that Simmel (1964) regards as equally real, but it is false to then take this as a rule about social reality. Doing this moves us from what is an observed regularity that can be taken as a guide to further investigation and/or orientation in general to instead seeing the resulting knowledge as a 'fit' governing action in the social world. Quoting from Paul Ziff, an American philosopher and artist, Bourdieu notes: 'To argue that there must be rules in the natural language is like arguing that roads must be red if they correspond to red lines on a map' (Bourdieu 1992a: 40).

Overextending insights are characteristic of the exercise of scholastic reasoning where claims to expertise and the associated recognition that follows within the field abound. The idea that universal rules are embedded in particular societies and individuals conform to these ignores the possibility that human beings are free agents and thus prioritizes determinism over voluntarism within claims to illegitimate generalization. Here, too, another way is often open to illegitimate overextension: that is, deriving an explanation of behaviour according to some posited mechanism of unconscious regulation, thereby replacing practical action with the theoretical model of the analyst. The analyst may then lay claim to being a 'stage manager' of social relations which, in its extreme manifestation, is 'a dream of power' (Bourdieu 1992a: 31) whereby a congruence between the underlying structures of actions and the patterns of analysis used by the analyst is assumed.

A congruence of this type is based upon a misunderstanding. An acceptance of the relations between position and disposition needs to be exposed to reflexive scrutiny and built back into the practice of science in order to better itself. To reduce scientific activity to interests alone fails to see how fields of production not only are competitive, but also require a sharing of information and knowledge in order to acquire recognition for efforts from others. A resulting ambivalence thus occurs between conflicting expectations of competition for excellence and cooperation via the desire for recognition. Nevertheless, this is not a 'collective finalism' characteristic of the functionalism of Merton (1976), but the result of socially constituted dispositions that inform degrees of disinterestedness.

We may see facets of this in studies of education and reproduction. These have a bearing upon the intellectual field itself:

> If the sociology of the system of education and the intellectual world seems to me to be fundamental, this is because it also contributes to our knowledge of the subject of cognition by introducing us, more directly than all

reflexive analyses, to the unthought categories of thought which limit the thinkable and predetermine what is actually thought: I need merely refer to the universe of prejudice, repression and omission that every successful education makes you accept, and makes you remain unaware of, tracing out that magic circle of powerless complacency in which the elite schools imprison their elect. (Bourdieu 1990: 178)

Whether via rules, unconscious motivation, or structural-functionalist routes, the experience of the observer remains absent due to a failure to grasp the 'dialectic of objective structures and incorporated structures which operates in every practical action'. History becomes reduced to:

a 'process without a subject', simply replacing the 'creative subject' of subjectivism with an automaton driven by the dead laws of a history of nature. This emanatist vision ... reduces historical agents to the role of 'supports' (*Träger*) of the structure and reduces their actions to mere epiphenomenal manifestations of the structure's own power to develop itself and to determine and overdetermine other structures. (Bourdieu 1992a: 41. Original italics)

We might expect at this point what we encountered in Chapter 1 to be smuggled into the intellectual armoury: a move towards an unmediated grasp of social relations entailing a drift towards phenomenology and from there to ethnomethodology. Nevertheless, this collapses the differences between a scholastic and practical point of view by assuming that a description of the processes of comprehension are simply reflected in the 'insights' of the former. It collapses theoretical and practical reason in a methodological attempt to break down the real issues that lie between thinking and being. Such a move sidesteps something inevitable: a conceptual scheme is imposed on practical actions through scientific work. The issue here, however, is that these are matters of the world, not the words of the analyst. As Karl Marx put it: 'Their resolution is by no means, therefore, the task only of the understanding, but is a *real* task of life, a task which *philosophy* was unable to accomplish precisely because it saw there a *purely* theoretical problem' (Marx 1963: 87. Original italics).

To avoid 'the things of logic' becoming the 'logic of things' it is necessary to get behind the strategies to the practical sense that is part of the feel for the game within fields. For this reason Pierre Bourdieu deploys 'habitus' (as a system of dispositions), as well as practical sense and strategy in an 'effort to escape from structuralist objectivism without relapsing into subjectivism' (Bourdieu 1990: 61). It also explains his own movement from philosophy to sociology in order to produce a better science and escape the imperialism of philosophy (Bourdieu 2007) and explains an antipathy for committing reflective notes to philosophical asides, or playing the game of seeking to be both philosopher and social scientist which 'announces a lack of ethical and scientific rigour' (Bourdieu 2004: 106).

In order to guard against these collapses between fields, we might recognize that reflexive acts of problematizing social research precepts and processes must be continual in order to strengthen its insights. Such practices, conducted at the level of a social research community, can assist practitioners in freeing themselves from the idea that they do not have any illusions, 'especially about themselves' (Bourdieu in Bourdieu and Wacquant 1992: 195). Internal critique plays a key role. Yet to remain vibrant and relevant to its day, research must consider not only the ways in which it views the social world, but also the social world itself and its place and purpose within social relations more generally. Without this in place it commits the fallacy of internalism that plagues reflexivity: that is, ways of seeing and modes of constructing objects as if they were bounded within particular communities, as opposed to being bound up with what is viewed and the conditions under which they are viewed.

Calls to reflexivity which do not take account of this are idealistic in their aspirations and unrealistic in what they can contribute to improved practice. They add to individualistic cultures that are so characteristic of academic departments in which, paradoxically, problems of practice are readily reduced to individual inadequacies in the struggles for recognition via *ad hominem* denunciations. Here we see the assumption that creativity should be linked with the single act of the individual, enabling the perpetuation of limited understandings that celebrate an exceptionality solely reducible to character without due consideration to context and culture. Therefore, when processes are spoken of as 'socially constructed' with the inevitable focus upon the 'how', let not the issue that is of the world be forgotten: the social construction of what (Hacking 1999)?

From the above it is argued that: 'An adequate science of society must encompass both objective regularities and the process of internalization of objectivity' (Wacquant 1992: 13). It differs from both linguistic *and* structuralist approaches to knowing the social world for they bracket history and an explanation of the conditions under which utterances are produced and heard. In order to understand these conditions, Bourdieu's fields, while ultimately dependent upon the actions of those within them, can also be analysed separately from those actions. In terms of social transformation, therefore: 'This structure, which governs the strategies aimed at transforming it, is itself always at stake' (Bourdieu 1993: 73).

Linking this into our previous discussions concerning relations that are not reducible to mental properties allows the researcher to analyse the constitution of the social world in a different way. Structure, while ultimately reliant upon agency in terms of reproduction, can also exist in the sense of being relatively enduring, separate from the actions of those who seek to transform it. Linguistic utterances are not free-floating separate from power, but are linked to institutional conditions that provide the utterance with authority (Bourdieu 1992b). In the relations between choice, necessity and social change there is no denial of freedom of action, it merely approaches it in a different manner.

The idea of autonomous fields – frequently assumed within the presuppositions of scholastic doxa – is replaced by a more nuanced and realistic appraisal ('regulated liberty') of the role of reflexivity in terms of the mediation of social relations with the realm of social research production:

> It is through the illusion of freedom from social determinants (an illusion which I have said a hundred times is the specific determination of intellectuals) that social determinations win the freedom to exercise their full power … Freedom is not something given: it is something you conquer – collectively. (Bourdieu 1990: 15)

A 'constructivist structuralism' provides for an empirical examination of the interplay between the subjective and objective features of social life, without abandoning the major contribution of the structuralist legacy to social science: that is, 'the *relational* mode of thinking … which identifies the real, not with substances but with relations' (Bourdieu 1989: 15–16. Original italics).

The gaps between social research practice and theoretical development, including those that disguise themselves as methodological reflections, have, through the history of the social sciences, been attempted to be filled by moves of varying types. Between scholastic and practical reason we have seen these attempts range from collapse to separation, each of which have contained varying degrees of celebration. Ultimately there is a tension, but it is a tension of the world. The work of reflexivity is to challenge the supposed privilege of the knowing subject: 'It is thus possible to renounce the absolutism of classical objectivism without falling into relativism' (Bourdieu 2000: 120).

Pierre Bourdieu recognized this tension and did not seek its resolution, but clarification in the service of greater illumination: 'Because the truth of the social world is the object of struggles in the social world … the struggle for the truth of the social world is necessarily endless' (Bourdieu 2004: 115). Philosophical problems are turned into matters of practical politics in the service of science. A resulting 'realpolitik of reason' had as its aim the intention of working 'towards social conditions permitting rational dialogue' (Bourdieu 1999: 226).

Here is a formulation whose tools of inquiry are not only deployed in an outwardly focused manner, but also taken back into the domain in which the inquiry is constituted in the service of better understandings about the world. Overall, a series of probabilities, not determinations, enables the reproduction of society that does not translate into a fate, but a likely outcome from which an individual may escape. An 'empirical existential analytics' (Dreyfus and Rabinow 1993) does not give itself over to those theories of resistance that celebrate the inventiveness of agency when, in fact, it has no repercussions for transformations in social conditions.

While Bourdieu was different among leading theorists in his methodological preoccupations and deriving his ideas from extensive empirical work, what remains of 'the local ways in which a habitus reproduces dominant beliefs, values, and norms through the exercise of symbolic power' (Cicourel 1993: 111)? That form of analysis is filled by processual approaches to the study of social life that focus upon the role of practical reasoning in daily interaction. However, what is missing is due regard to how structures, in terms of an ontology of already existing properties, are implicated in daily life. Thus, in returning to the issues concerned with social transformation, we can say that structural theories tends towards abstraction and determinism in respect to phenomena such as class, whereas processual theories overlook the institutional contexts of locally produced verbal and non-verbal interactions.

That is important. If we are to take these insights forward in a pragmatic attempt to improve social research, we are faced with a dilemma in our estimation of actions aimed at betterment. It matters because if we are to understand and improve social science through an analysis of the conditions under and through which it is practised, the tools we use must be as good as we are able to make them with all the fallibilities that come from actions at given times when subsequently submitted to historical analysis. It matters because if a reflexive project is to overcome the symbolic power that informs social life, it needs to face the same problems that academic feminism has faced in its attempts to become something more than a status group whose internal logic forgets the reasons for its original constitution: improvement in women's lives. The ultimate test is 'success in identifying the conditions of existence and of coming into being of less oppressive forms of social and intellectual community' (Lovell 2000: 44).

What we face here is the extent to which this reflexive analysis is sensitive enough not only to read off social practices according to reproduction of domination through misrecognition, but also to enable a greater recognition of the moments in which truth is spoken to power in order to open up those spaces. There should be caution in saturating social life with the effects of power in all its dimensions. While we might agree with Pierre Bourdieu (1993) that, for example, the refusal of a formalist aesthetics to take account of social context in its pre-occupations with form demonstrates a lack of awareness of the conditions of its possibility, it does not then follow that the practices of art do not contain utopian moments that link other forms of resistance to socially produced classifications schemas (Fowler 1997).

Pierre Bourdieu does tend to read artistic practices in terms of a repression of material determinations (2000: 20). While this corrects the exaggerated claims made by those who have taken the cultural turn in contemporary relations several steps past idealism by ignoring the social conditions of production and often exalting the subject as somehow self-expressive, it can end up severing production from reception as a pragmatic issue in the world. To express this in another way, the analysis leads to a separation between scientific and practical reason in those situations where a pre-existing affinity may be apparent. Instead of this, Bourdieu's methodological writings urge a separation:

In order to produce a science of artistic production, we … have to construct a sociological analysis against, if necessary, the self-understandings of the artists. In order to liberate the self-understandings of the artistic agents, however, we have to analyse reflexively the historical origins of the conceptual framework that we apply. (Robbins 2000: 190)

We hit a number of issues here. First, because Bourdieu applies his own analysis to his works, it can appear that he is placing himself beyond criticism. To perform an act of understanding in this sense is also to render something intelligible from the point of view of it being necessary in a set of social relations. As taking that point of view in respect to practical reason is to commit the fallacy of situatedness through exhausting explanation at the individual level, so too does performing reflexivity through self-analysis lead to justifications for actions. It is best to leave that to others with all the frustrations that can mean for the inevitable offence it causes to what are situated accounts of motivation. Second, he cares about science and to that extent, is a rationalist. It may be, however, that in his denunciations of philosophy, a more productive division of labour is possible performed by those who are not so orientated in the way he suggests, but are nevertheless concerned. Richard Shusterman's (1999) essay is written in this spirit because a revisionist theory works for both discursive and institutional change. Perhaps this was too risky for him to adopt because it took its challenge to scientific orthodoxy too far. Yet if it has the potential to show up the effects of experiments in changes in the intellectual field and so better understand the relations between social science and society, it may be a price worth paying.

Overall, we are dealing here with the relations between the discursive and institutional. A focus on the latter tends to commit his writings to a dominant ideology thesis, while a focus on the former fails to see how symbolic power is implicated in reproduction. It seems that there are a number of reactions to this: some social scientists determine the inevitability of existing systems and so place hope in a state of permanent suspension; there are also those who see social containment as providing a cushion for the subject; there are those who seek to etch out the spaces of inventiveness in otherwise deterministic social universes to examine the limitations of the system; there are also those for whom reproduction, for that is what we are talking about as a condition of our social existence, rests within the lifeworld and thus, presumably, in transformations in those existing states.

Maybe Bourdieu did not give enough over to inventiveness via transgressions in the struggles for symbolic capital, but he did recognize a fundamental tension that needs to be the object of reflexive vigilance within a community of scholars: between the constitution of the scientific gaze and the practical sense necessary to get on in daily activities. The latter, when challenged, frequently turns to justifications around necessity rather than contingency and in so doing forgets history and the relationalism necessary for social action in the first place. The former can readily turn into arrogance by confusing its findings with that of practical sense thereby giving itself over to either relativism through the supposition of reflection, or objectivism via unproblematized understandings of its place and constitution within society as a whole.

Summary

Reasons for calls to reflexivity can start as topics for examining issues concerned with social scientific representations of everyday life. We can then move on to examine arguments that the deployment of reflexivity should be in the service of producing better accounts of social life. For this reason I turned to the works of Anthony Giddens and Pierre Bourdieu.

A focus upon the productive nature of reflexivity does not detract from the evident potential of calls to produce an inward-looking practice that should actually be conducted in the name of finally looking outwards: for example, to those modes of closure in the social world, how they are achieved, under what conditions, utilizing what resources and with what consequences? Without such questions in place, calls to reflexivity that seek to inform social research practice – a vital role – will move from the regulative, in the sense of informing and seeking to shape practice, to the constitutive in which they speak in the name of reality *or* realities. By focusing upon the process of knowing to the exclusion of a place in the social world, conditions of production and what is discovered about the world, this is the outcome.

As mentioned in Chapter 1, there is a division of practice between theoretical developments, philosophy of science, methodology and methods which cannot, whatever the grander claims might involve, be legislated out of sight. There is also a need to understand the different scales of activity about which we are speaking, as well as the positions from which they emanate. The issues concern the consequences of this division of labour in terms of the warranted and non-warranted claims of research and theory in terms of its place and practice in the world of which it is a part. Smuggled into the development of theoretical armouries are statements about the world and its characteristics and properties. Reflexive critiques can bypass research practices and when they hit their mark, produce an uncertainty and so a lack of engagement with social issues. An engaged practice needs to encompass 'the logical possibility of error about, misdescription and misrecognition of one's own state of awareness' as a 'condition of any reflexive intelligence' (Bhaskar 1989: 91–2).

While Pierre Bourdieu left us with issues about the movement from pre-reflexive doxa to reflexivity upon actions – a subject to which I will return in Part 2 of the book – it cannot be doubted that his aim was to produce a better social science or that his legacy generated profound insights into our existences and the conditions for their realization. Nevertheless, another route for reflexivity now presents itself. Arguments for the incommensurability of forms of life may proceed on the basis that any attempt at explanation involving scientific comparison renders injustice to the particularity of world views. Now we encounter the final twist in this tale of reflexivity.

The final twist comes in an alignment of the linguistic and postmodern turns in social thought, with the result that demonstrations of reflexive adequacy at the level of the knower became the ultimate forum of concern. That arena, however, is not constituted in the name of prior reflexive calls. Attempts to refer to the known via any act of comparison may now be regarded as at best misguided and at worst, acts of injustice towards the particularity of world views.

REPRESENTATION IN QUESTION?

3

In Chapters 1 and 2, approaches to the issue of the relationship between the basis of research accounts of social phenomena and representations of the social world have been examined. In the process no approach could be said to have adopted a picture theory of reality such that the relation between research production and representation of the social world is held to be unproblematic. Such defences, in both the physical and social sciences, are rare. However, it does not follow that the role of research in producing valuable knowledge in society is then diminished. More immediately, this carries consequences for both the internal intellectual content of disciplines and their implications for understanding and informing actions.

In this chapter I am concerned with critiques that not only question past certainties, but also move into entirely different terrains in their formulations. The elements which make up these writings include a de-centring of the subject and a tendency towards anti-representationalism informed by anti-foundationalism. The underlying belief may be expressed in terms of the view that science should not be regarded as a reservoir of true knowledge, or a guarantor of social progress. Ultimately, it is a set of practices that rest upon ideas that cannot be scientifically proven, while those who have been its victims have now become its critics (Seidman 2008).

When problematizing the practice of research in this manner, the result is to turn attention to the mode of representation itself. Here we find a range of thinkers – Jean Baudrillard, Zygmunt Bauman, Judith Butler, Michel de Certeau, Hélène Cixous, Gilles Deleuze, Jacques Derrida, Michel Foucault, Julia Kristeva, Luce Irigaray, Jean François Lyotard and Richard Rorty, to name a few – who have added to this critique. We find some affinities with radical constructivism which does not deny ontological reality as such, simply that it cannot be known. The best one can hope for is a 'corroborative objectivity' that is rooted within the subjective experiences of the particularity of lifeworlds (von Glasersfeld 1991). The relation between research production and the representation of the social world according to the universal concepts of validity and reliability have been subjected, by these writers, to sustained critique.

Take Anthony Giddens' call to reflexivity from this vantage point. Here we can detect a universalizing desire that does not render justice to the particularity of world views. Why? Because there is seen to exist an assumption that there can be a mediation between language games under the banner of a scientific metalanguage. Furthermore, consider his emphasis upon the knowledgeability of agents. Writers sympathetic to postmodernist thought have regarded such conceptualizations as 'a caricature based on modernist ideology in which the agent is reflexive, able to monitor his/her actions, skilled and knowledgeable at all times' (Mêstrović 1998: 78).

Reflexive calls of this type provide for a confident relativism. Affinities are evident with a sense of reflexivity that aims to reveal the problems inherent in any attempt to ground accounts of the social world. The play of postmodernism is now the end, with critique a means of demonstrating the paradoxes apparent in any act of textual representation. Methodologically speaking, inconsistency is an inherent feature of practice and attention turns to the author who should be situated in terms of the textual production of their accounts (Clifford and Marcus 1986; Hertz 1997).

To be reflexive in the final twist entails an assault upon studies of the social world through seeking to expose the partiality of accounts in terms of their restriction not only to time and place, but also to the biography of authors. The turn towards reflexivity at the level of the production of social scientific accounts is now complete. If authors are *really* (sic) reflexive, they would recognize the futility of any attempt to 'mirror' reality. Postmodernism thus appeals to those researchers, as with characterizations of postmodern women and men in general, who choose to 'revel in the pursuit of new and untested experience, are willingly seduced by offers of adventure, and on the whole prefer keeping options open to all fixity of commitment' (Bauman 1997: 13).

The significance of this work lies in the ways in which it has added to a questioning of the basis upon which scientific practices rest. The problem in working through its implications for a more reflexive practice, however, lies in the way in which terms are often used to classify diverse thinkers. Under this general heading we find those who study the modes of ordering of knowledges (Foucault) and those who celebrate the free-play of floating signifiers within incommensurable language games (Lyotard), which includes those who state that their work is designed to provoke rather than clarify (Baudrillard). Issues are further compounded by Michel Foucault's scepticism that history possesses any such breaks and Jean Baudrillard's contention that he was not a postmodernist (Gane 1990).

Politically and philosophically, these writings seek to activate differences, alongside a focus upon the textual construction of reality in order to expose aspirations to universal knowledge via the supposed transparency of face-to-face talk. They run along a reactive range from the apparent tyranny of the desire for consensus to a tendential flattening via processes of ordering of social relations that invoke normative integration through binary oppositions. In the case of a feminist deconstructive practice, we find a refusal to invert the masculine/feminine hierarchy as standpoint feminism is assumed to suggest. Instead, a process of undermining what is held to be the male-centred nature of methodology takes place from 'within' language which is heterogeneous and thus not capable of picturing reality. Together with an attention to the 'positioning' of the researcher, this is said to provide for the deconstruction of taken-for-granted oppositions without apparent allusion to metanarratives: culture/nature; reason/emotion; subject/object (Young 1990: Appendix).

A clear tendency in methodological writings to take the words that are written about social life as the central topics for considering the social construction of reality is apparent. In terms of ethnography, for example: 'In a discursive rather than a visual paradigm, the dominant metaphors for ethnography shift away from the observing eye and toward expressive speech (and gesture). The writers "voice" pervades and situates the analysis, and objective distancing rhetoric is renounced' (Clifford 1986: 12). A questioning of the authority of the author is one of the central tenets of such approaches that are said to open up practice to alternative interpretations without relying upon past guarantees.

Inspired by the work of Jacques Derrida, one person has written that this approach 'refuses to view methodology simply as a set of technical procedures with which to manipulate data. Rather, methodology can be opened up to readers intrigued by its deep assumptions and its empirical findings but otherwise daunted by its densely technical and figural findings' (Agger 1991: 29–30). A space is opened up in which researchers are able to consider how language and reality are inextricably linked within the particularity of world views with the outcome, in the words of one advocate, becoming the continual substitutability of terms and of texts that 'makes conclusions undecidable ... Because infinite substitution cannot be a self-confirming process, the expanse that it opens up also seems to be bottomless' (Platt 1989: 649).

The implications are to move reflexivity to a self-referential focus in the face of 'undecidability'. Nevertheless, this is not a familiar terrain. There is no map from which to navigate and there is no landscape; there are only multiple maps and numerous terrains to navigate; 'the map precedes the terrain' (Baudrillard 1988: 166). In resisting methodological closure which would represent the denial of otherness, the injunction becomes to 'wage war on totality ... be witnesses to the unpresentable' and 'activate the differences' (Lyotard 1993: 46).

It is not my wish to rehearse the range of these arguments. There are those who would dismiss social research out of hand as nothing more than an attempt to capture a domain – the social – that no longer exists and would claim that any act of representation is illegitimate. I want to focus upon particular arguments that represent a challenge and add to a productive, reflexive understanding of the place and practice of research in contemporary societies.

Ideology Critique

When it comes to the transformative potential of social research we find, within the tradition of ideology critique, the concept of an 'ideal' state being invoked as that which exists outside of ideological mechanisms that produce distortions of reality in the first instance. Alienation, as the consequence of the capitalist labour process expropriating what is regarded as essential to human endeavours, namely the productive capacities of labour, is a central guiding light in this endeavour. With the process of the objectification of labour, Karl Marx could thus write that: 'The worker therefore only feels himself outside his work, and in his work feel outside himself' (Marx 1981: 66).

We can trace this approach via the tradition of 'critical theory'. Under the auspices of its second director, Max Horkheimer (1895–1973), the Institute for Social Research at Frankfurt sought to recover the failed promise of Marxism (Jay 1973; Wiggershaus 1995). A historical sensitivity to change via a concern with detailed, empirical and multidisciplinary work in a number of areas, together with recognition of the social basis of the human character, then emerged (Horkheimer 1993). However, while there was an evident pragmatism in this work, such that the reduction of suffering and the promotion of happiness served as regulative ideals in the process of social discovery, in order that this remained a 'critical' endeavour, recognition of contingency was balanced against allusions to a 'whole'.

Without allusions to a 'whole' in place, the contingent would be empiricist in orientation and reflect that which was held to be ideologically distorted in the first place. It would reproduce dominant power relations. Hence, at the level of knowledge production, a reflexive vigilance is required that informs an attitude that is aware of the conditions of its own production: a 'critical attitude' is one that cannot assume that facts of existence are 'extrinsic in the same degree as they are for the savant or for members of other professions who all think like little savants' (Horkheimer 1972: 209).

The 'whole' tempers the empiricism of contingency within an inhuman society in which people are stratified according to the systemic imperatives of capitalism. A critical endeavour rests upon a dialectic process that ultimately regards endemic conflict as resulting from a disjuncture between reason and rationality:

> Critical thought has a concept of man as in conflict with himself until this opposition is removed. If activity governed by reason is proper to man, then existent social practice, which forms the individual's life down to its least details, is inhuman, and this inhumanity affects everything that goes on in the society. (Horkheimer 1972: 210)

In the historical unfolding of this rich body of conceptual and empirical work, the concept of the 'totality' becomes such that the determinative powers of the economic system overwhelm struggles aimed at the achievement of meaningful change. A Weberian-inspired Marxism then replicates, albeit in a different manner, the iron cage of modernity whose breaking resides in a general allusion to a macro, rational system and self-determining subject. A pessimism enters into the analyses of the unfolding of capitalism that becomes a journey towards a new kind of barbarism: 'The individual is wholly devalued in relation to the economic powers, which at the same time press the control of society over nature to hitherto unsuspected heights … The flood of detailed information and candy-floss entertainment simultaneously instructs and stultifies mankind' (Adorno and Horkheimer 1979: xiv–xv).

Allusions to a state in which reason may predominate over exploitative forms of (ir)rationality is the way out. Liberation from manipulation, propaganda and indoctrination, is the end. The means towards that end state? A society that is 'rational and free to the extent to which it is organised, sustained, and reproduced by an essentially new historical subject' (Marcuse 1968: 197). In the meantime:

> the productive apparatus tends to become totalitarian to the extent to which it determines not only the socially needed occupations, skills, and attitudes, but also individual needs and aspirations. It thus obliterates the opposition between the private and public existence, between individual and social needs. (Marcuse 1968: 13)

Sensitivity to historical contingency through empirical work is tempered by allusions to subject-centred reason within the deployment of interdisciplinary and multi-method approaches to the study of social relations. In the end, however, we end up as witness to the submission of the subject to a system that is so all-encompassing as to prevent any form of effective resistance aimed at its transformation (Habermas 1992a).

As this tradition unfolded, Hegelian allusions accompanied by the idealizations of the whole, such as those found in Marcuse, came to be questioned. Metaphysical ideas of 'spirit' could not serve as a basis for 'science'. Developments of critical theory in the works of Jürgen Habermas (1984, 1987) involved the development of communicative reason within a post-metaphysical turn (Habermas 1992b, 2003). The ethos, however, was to remain the same: 'Critical methodology … is concerned with careful explication of what *is* in order to ultimately liberate us from the destiny of what *has been* (Morrow 1994: 320. Original italics).

With Louis Althusser's (1969) structuralist Marxism, we find a changing relation between the real and the apparently distorting effects of ideology. The argument takes the form that ideology becomes both 'real' and 'imaginary' between people. Given the existence of the latter, it cannot be employed as a political tool aimed at transformation for it encompasses the very manner in which consciousness is constituted under prevailing economic conditions. In what becomes, in comparison to the above, an 'anti-humanist' formulation of ideology critique, the real is said to exist outside of the consciousness of the subject.

The individual is not considered to be pre-social and is formulated as an agent of an abstract system. Knowledge and action, as elements in Karl Marx's praxis philosophy, become separated. Ultimately, agency is subservient to a highly abstract analysis of the structures of modes of production. The price for abandoning the legacy of humanist Marxism and with that the idea of political 'will', thereby becomes determinism, despite Althusser's clear concerns to overcome such a legacy.

An Althusserian legacy provided for a number of departures and affirmations. First, classical Marxism was connected with other non-Marxist elements, including linguistics and psychoanalysis to provide fertile ground for subsequent work. Second, it added to the belief in the autonomy of social and natural sciences as having definable, objective objects of analysis. Third, it released Marxism from a series of false promises in relation to, for example, the inevitable reaching of end points in history. Fourth, historical materialism became an open programme of research aiming at reductionism and determinism and opening up avenues of investigation with cultural and political practice (Elliott 1993).

Interpretive Analytics

Michel Foucault realized 'how the Frankfurt people had tried ahead of time to assert things that I too had been working on for years to sustain' (1991a: 117). Yet he took on a legacy that is still apparent in the idea of an individual who is in some sense 'pre-social'. This is the requirement for a point of recognition that exists in the subject between ideology, the conditions of exploitation and their systemic reproduction: 'At the root of the problem is Althusser's invocation of an "individual" who is pre-ideological and indeed must be pre-ideological if Althusser's most fundamental thesis (that ideology is the process by which individuals are constituted as subject) is correct' (Barrett 1991: 106).

No matter how the epoch in which we live is characterized, certain questions will continue to pre-occupy us. They are: what can we know? What should we do? What can we hope for? Considering the legacy of Immanuel Kant, from whom these questions are derived, Michel Foucault regarded his own work as 'an event in the order of knowledge' (Foucault 1992: 345). He suggests that modernity should be seen as an 'attitude'; a way of relating to reality that represents not only a way of acting, but also of belonging. The task of analysis should then concentrate not on whether we live in particular times, but how this attitude has always struggled with the forces of 'countermodernity' (Foucault 1984).

In his essay on Kant's 'What is Enlightenment (*Was ist Aufklärung?*)', he writes of a 'critical ontology of ourselves' (Foucault 1984: 50) through a critique of what we do, say and think. From the Enlightenment onwards social thought moved away from an analysis of representations towards an analytic, expressed as the 'attempt to show on what grounds representation and analysis of representations are possible and to what extent they are legitimate' (Dreyfus and Rabinow 1982: 28). People now appear as both the subject and object of knowledge: those who know and are known. Yet instead of a recognition of the limitations of knowledge, the legislator was born as one who pronounces upon knowledge: 'Modernity begins with the incredible and ultimately unworkable idea of a being who is sovereign precisely by virtue of being enslaved, a being whose finitude allows him to take the place of God' (Dreyfus and Rabinow 1982: 29).

Michel Foucault, influenced by Nietzsche and seeking to overcome the limitations of Cartesian thought, as well as the historicism of Hegel, is clear about what his form of critique is not: neither a theory, doctrine, or body of knowledge that accumulates over time. Instead, it is 'an ethos, a philosophical life in which the critique of what we are is at one and the same time the historical analysis of the limits that are imposed on us and an experiment with the possibility of going beyond them' (Foucault 1984: 50). What is the motivation for this work? 'How can the growth of capabilities be disconnected from the intensification of power relations?' (1984: 48).

No 'gesture of rejection' is found in this ethos. It moves beyond the 'outside-inside alternative' in the name of a critique that 'consists of analyzing and reflecting upon limits' (Foucault 1984: 45). The purpose is 'to transform the critique conducted in the form of necessary limitation into a practical critique that takes the form of a possible transgression' (1984: 45). The mode is genealogical in form:

> it will not deduce from the form of what we are what it is impossible for us to do and to know; but it will separate out, from the contingency that has made us what we are, the possibility of no longer being, doing, or thinking what we are, do, or think. (Foucault 1984: 46)

If an ideal remains, it lies in the possibility of setting oneself free without falling back on subject-centred reason. In examining the internal modes of the ordering of truth, but not in the name of a truth that lies beyond it, possibilities for transgression are opened up (Visker 1995).

Explanation with reference to intention or reference to the subject as a site of reason out of context might suffice, but this would return to subject-centred reason. Similarly, reference to the rules of discourses might suffice for analytic purposes, but what of the relation between such analysis and subsequent actions when rules are seen to determine actions? In terms of his recognition of such possibilities, power/knowledge relate to one another, while power exists in a state of 'agonism' with freedom, thereby making ideas of individuality a 'political' problem and so subject to struggle and potential transformation: 'We are prisoners of certain conceptions about ourselves ... We have to liberate our own subjectivity, our relations to ourselves' (Foucault 1989a: 298). The idea of 'governing' thereby appears in terms of how the 'possible field of action of others' (Foucault

1982b: 221) is structured. The exercise of power presupposes a free subject: where there is no choice in actions, there is no power. A slave is not in a power relationship, but one of physical constraint (Foucault 1982b).

Michel Foucault locates the opportunities for autonomy within recognition of an historically located relation between the self and the world in which we act. Without a transcendental vantage point from which to critique existing social relations in the name of a postulated ideal (autonomous self), this translates into an examination of those present modes of organizing social relations in terms of their potential for the creation of autonomy: 'History is the concrete body of becoming; with its moments of intensity, its lapses, its extended periods of fever-ish agitation, its fainting spells; and only the metaphysician would seek its soul in the distant ideality of the origin' (Foucault 1997: 373).

A pragmatic, nominalist account is provided that regards power as not simply repressive, but also productive. To this extent Foucault's work is not a denial of truth, but an examination of the historical conditions for the possibility of its emergence. Historical work examines the extent to which discourses are selective: they are as significant for what they leave out, as well as what they include. Describing the consequences of such selectivity in terms of the appearance of par-ticular statements – their 'conditions of existence' – opens up the possibility for alternative modes of organizing social relations and our relations to ourselves via a his-tory cleansed of what is termed 'transcendental narcissism' (Foucault 1989b: 203).

A refusal to engage in the search for origins through speaking in the name of objects beyond discourses, or idealized ideas of subjectivity, may be apparent in an approach to research practice that is externalist in orientation. Yet if this 'cheerful positivist' sought to avoid the label of being a structuralist – 'certain half-witted "commentators" persist in labelling me a "structuralist"' (Foucault 1992: xiv) – and the anthropologism of historical analysis, then validity and meaning must exist in some kind of relation for there to be a reflexive recognition of how the analyst and the objects of analysis may be implicated in co-production. From the point of view of research practice, this issue is not side-stepped through allusion to philosophy moving from a concern with the distinction between what is true and false to one of examining our relationship to truth.

The refusal to engage in pronouncements that lead to closure and thus the pos-sibility of an alternative relation to ourselves is apparent throughout Foucault's work. Here we do not allude to the content of practices of freedom, but their conditions of possibility. One of these would be the achievement of consensus as a regulatory principle. Yet in avoiding such ideals: 'The farther I would go is to say that perhaps one must not be for consensuality, but one must be against non-consensuality' (Foucault 1984: 379). Normative allusions to the values of a 'we' in order to conduct analysis in the first instance is taken to be an act of closure that limits the possibility of the formation of a 'we' that results from the analysis. That becomes only a temporary 'we' due to us being subjects in history with its ebbs and flows (Foucault 1984: 381–90).

If a methodological injunction follows, if that is not too harsh an expectation, it is one of 'event analysis'. That may appear to possess phenomenological connotations due to a focus upon the direct experience of the world by individuals within it. Not surprisingly, Foucault does not follow this path and refuses to see his methods as ones that draw upon either an underlying anthropological invariant or structural analysis. Rationalization becomes both instrumental and relative (Foucault in Burchell et al. 1991: 79) in order to discover how the true and false are brought into being within particular domains. Singularity is emphasized to breach self-evidence and avoid a processual analysis that refers for its explanatory basis to constants: an anthropological invariant rooted in the capacity of an individualized human reason. Absolutes, as means of evaluating practices, vanish and instead the emphasis is upon: 'how forms of rationality inscribe themselves in practices or systems of practices, and what role they play within them, because it's true that "practices" don't exist without a certain regime of rationality' (Foucault in Burchell et al. 1991: 79).

Two axes of analysis emerge. First, 'codification', as an ensemble of rules and procedures for ways of acting. Second, the ways in which truth and falsity are brought into being through the constitution of a domain of objects that enables that distinction to be made and to justify those ways of acting. This means analyzing a plurality of causes in terms of a focus upon the following: 'connections, encounters, supports, blockages, plays of forces, strategies and so on which at a given moment establish what subsequently counts as being self-evident, universal and necessary' (Foucault in Burchell et al. 1991: 76).

What we can take from Foucault is the insight that critical social scientific knowledge, conceived of in post-Cartesian fashion, cannot embark on its practice on the presupposition of an essence to humanity. The idea of coming to know ourselves differently and viewing the possibilities for transformation is about interpreting ourselves differently. A social scientific critique cannot begin from the point of view that current conditions are not good, but instead 'consists in seeing what kind of self evidence (évidences), liberties, acquired and non-reflective modes of thought, the practices we accept rest on' (Foucault 1982a: 33). The desire for curiosity is met by the production of texts in order to open up otherness to the reader. To that extent, his hope was that his 'books become true after they have been written – not before' (Foucault 1989a: 301). A refusal to legislate therefore means placing in the public domain alternative interpretations to open up different possibilities for how we live together.

Underlying, occasionally informing and perhaps even illuminating these trends is the movement from the Cartesian dream, via Hegel, to Nietzsche's scepticism. In moving from epistemology to historicism, we end up with no discernible means to speak of progress towards an ideal or even human betterment in some form. The abandonment of freedom and truth, as ideals, leads us to permanent imprisonment in power relations in which history simply supplants one set of configurations for another with no discernible means for judging their relative merits.

The implications are clear. Truth lies in the future and it will always do so to protect against the complacencies of the present via simple allusions to those things against which we should guard! Such abandonment, however, leads to a paradox. A high price is paid for those who seek betterment without allusion to simple guarantees and instead see it as a continual project assisted by forms of illumination that seek clarification, not resolution. While repudiating ideas of the 'good', they are often smuggled in at some point to address this issue (Taylor 1992). Therefore, 'in rescuing us from the supposed illusion that the issues of the deep self are somehow inescapable, what is Foucault laying open for us, if not a truth which frees us for self-making?' (Taylor 1986: 99).

For Foucault these issues are symptomatic of a movement away from an analysis of representations towards an analytic that seeks to demonstrate the grounds upon which representation is based. Historically speaking, this was a particular reaction informed by a set of social changes in Europe that, in turn, influenced those such as Descartes. Descartes was a writer:

> exposed in person to the consequences of Henry IV's murder, and to the Thirty Years' War that followed, in which Protestants and Catholic armies sought to prove theological supremacy by force of arms ... People at large were left in bewilderment, sensing that matters were now out of hand. (Toulmin 1992: 69)

The resulting 'quest for certainty' led to a shift from an understanding of 'argumentation' in Renaissance humanism, towards a concern with 'proofs' and universal logic as if they were a guarantee against the ambivalences that are of the world.

In contemporary times, one way of seeking defence against the claims of universal logic lies in the differential capacity of individuals to live up to the promise of Reason which flattens, rather than celebrates, their differences. We can see this in Foucault's writing where, for example, he is not 'for' consensus, but 'against' non-consensus. Thus, an emphasis on differences, fuelled by a turn towards aesthetics as the last refuge for its expression, is evident in Foucault's later works. However, the idea of making one's life a 'work of art' is in clear danger of becoming an individualistic focus that does not ask questions concerning under what conditions this form of life would be possible (Flax 1991)? An over-emphasis upon this aspect reproduces individualism, albeit on different grounds, that renders 'violence' to the actual and potential human desire to understand each other across cultures and traditions of thought.

To fetishize difference as a process through which the subject can make gains in self-consciousness in relationship to the 'other' is highly problematic. Jacques Derrida alerted us to the metaphysical desire to constitute the essence of identity through the exclusion of the 'other' as embodying the negative that enforces the positive attributes of that identity. Stabilizations are not natural and are based upon that which is unstable. It is because of this that politics and ethics are possible (Derrida 1996). We then become interested in the extent to which the 'other' is denied the capacity to constitute an identity, which would include whole groups constituted by the power to exclude.

From Legislation to Interpretation

Expressions of concern with those changes that informed Descartes' time now inform reflections upon a contemporary world that exists in constant flux. Whereas there was a belief that a rationally organized, science-based world would produce outcomes that could be universalized, what we now see is this vision disappearing 'as the disenchantments accumulate' (Bauman 1989: 123). As the apparent disenchantments in science are fading, openness to alternative modes of interpretation in the hope that the future is not simply written in the name of the past and present, increases.

A society that has shut down the possibility of such acts of interpretation is not able to renew itself in order to survive. Acts of interpretation are not the sole province of social research and so in these times it is to literature, music and art in general that writers have turned for their inspiration. Here, as elsewhere, the same questions arise: to what extent is an interpretation of art if not accurate, then at least a contribution to human betterment by advancing an understanding of history and contemporary conditions and practices that can be carried forward into the future?

Those of a modernist persuasion could adopt an avant-garde position in much the same way as science is constituted: its consumers occupy a pre-enlightened state that will be transformed by the production and dissemination of its insights. This strategy has been supplanted. A modernist strategy of waging war against reality in the name of progress has apparently given way to the futility of measuring 'progressive' and 'regressive' artistic achievements. While the avant garde could speak of outdated tastes among those whose potential was yet to be fulfilled, in their strivings for betterment they lived with the paradox that success was always a sign of failure and defeat a vindication of their chosen path.

Demise came from two factors. First, despite a distrust of the masses, it was the market that saw the potential in their work. Those who could afford it were able to prove their good taste to others by displaying, as Pierre Bourdieu (1986) demonstrated, their distance from the uncultured. Commodification was the name of the game and the seduction of consumption for the pursuit of status its manifestation. It is palimpsest identities that become the norm, where we find:

> the art of forgetting is an asset no less, if no more, important that the art of memorizing, in which forgetting rather than learning is the condition of continuous fitness, in which ever new things and people enter and exit without much rhyme or reason the field of vision of the stationary camera of attention, and where the memory itself is like video-tape, always ready

to be wiped clean in order to admit new images, and boasting a life-long
guarantee only thanks to that wondrous ability of endless self-effacing.
(Bauman 1997: 25)

Second, the process of permanent acceleration was bound to terminate given the
continual striving for transgression: holes were dug; silent piano compositions
'produced', along with empty pages of unwritten poems. As a result, for Zygmunt
Bauman, the avant-garde arts proved to be *modern in their intention, yet postmodern
in their consequences'* (Bauman 1997: 100. Original italics).

What meanings one may, or may not, derive from contemporary culture is
considered by Michel Foucault in relation to the inherent pluralism that is contained in its reception. The pluralism that accompanies the reception of different
music, for example, can actually serve to isolate different styles and musicians. In
their striving to give 'voice to the unrepresentable' (Lyotard 1993), artists are
perpetually making rules with the result that they are caught in heroic efforts, 'to
give voice to the ineffable, and a tangible shape to the invisible' (Bauman 1997:
105). Relieved of the burden of representation, contemporary art, as Jean
Baudrillard argues (Gane 1991), adds to life. Artistic and non-artistic reality collapse and for Zygmunt Bauman this makes it, contra Jürgen Habermas, into a
subversive force that is continually experimenting; only this time it is not speaking
in the name of reality.

Following Foucault's distinction, Bauman argues that postmodern artists
undertake two kinds of critique: a general analytic of truth and an ontology of
the present. Once relieved of a method of production/interpretation, both the
artist and viewer/listener then engage in a process of meaning production
which, in bringing together questions of objective truth and subjective ground-
ing of reality, opens up infinite possibilities, 'free from the tyranny of consensus' (Bauman 1997: 111). As he approvingly quotes Foucault: 'A critique is not
a matter of saying that things are not right as they are. It is a matter of point-
ing out on what kinds of assumptions, what kinds of familiar, unchallenged,
unconsidered modes of thought the practices that we accept rest' (Bauman
1997: 111).

If art has the potential to liberate us from consensus in the fusion of the subjective and objective, one must ask, remembering the above Kantian questions, what
is the relation between truth and fiction? Going back to the idea of modernity
being an 'attitude', it is with the attitude we take towards what is said or believed,
rather than a correspondence theory of reality, that Zygmunt Bauman approaches
the question of truth. Yet in pursuing Richard Rorty's (1979) pragmatist idea of
an expedient of truth in this context, one element is missing in the assessment of
the trust and confidence that is necessary to approve of a belief: the 'disputational' function of truth. Truth, being bound up with power, is about having the
authority to speak of beliefs. As we sit at the other end of the modern era from
Kant, the self-confidence of reason is said to be failing.

As with ideology critique, we find that a positivist-inspired quest for certainty is doomed to fail when what is reproduced is nothing more than a reduction to a cognitive platform for individuals in an alienated world. However, while Bauman might wish to avoid the 'aristocratic radicalism' of this tradition (Beilharz 2000), he is not giving up on the possibility that not all of us are seduced by a world in which the price of everything is known, but not its value. The error in seeking to supplant positivism with yet other forms of scientism is not to question the 'supreme authority of the reality-object' (Bauman 1999: 131). Such dissatisfaction often represents not so much a critique of philosophical reflections upon reality, but reality itself and 'with the praxis of suppressed subjectivity and denigrated privacy rather than with the philosophers' epistemological neglect of the subject' (Bauman 1999: 131).

In this reality the truth of intellectual ideas becomes relevant through the extent to which they are allocated time in the public realm. What counts are 'their repercussions, the amount of media time and space devoted to them – and this depends first and foremost on their selling/rating potential' (Bauman 1995: 239). In considering the disputational function of truth, he then asks: 'what is there for the truth-theorists to do?' The answer lies in disputes about other philosopher's theories of truth. As the hope to spread the word of philosophy to the masses diminishes and ideas are dependent on marketization for their dissemination, so philosophy turned inwards. Attention is now upon the truth of truths! 'The task of philosophical reason seems to be shifting from legislating about the correct way of separating truth from untruth to legislating about the correct way of translating between separate language games, each generating and sustaining its own truths' (Bauman 1997: 117). While the philosophers fiddle, what is the counterculture to the technicism of modernity that promotes 'reconciliation with contingency of life and the polyphony of truths' (Bauman 1997: 119)?

As the world becomes an increasingly uncertain place, can we turn towards fiction in order to cling to any remnants of certainty? We are less likely to find ideas of freedom underpinned by universal reason and instead find a foothold in shifting sands. However, it is not living with differences which challenges understanding and turns people towards fiction for answers, for differences have always been with us, but a weakness in the institutionalization of differences. In this sense for the novel to expose the fragility of social order is not a revelation because discontents are born of an excess of freedom over security: 'It is the infinity of chances that has filled the place left empty in the wake of the disappearing act of the Supreme Office' (Bauman 2000: 61).

The modern novel exposed the contingency of what appeared to be an ordered reality, but the work of fiction in contemporary times abandons such claims and becomes the 'factory' of truth. 'Rejoicing in multitude', their truth is seen to have an endorsing or disputational function. In Heideggerian terms, if their concealment blurs the distinction between truth and falsity within being, so new forms of fiction place this process of social construction on display. As a result:

the truths born in and through the work of artistic fiction may – just may – fill in the gap in human existence left by the kind of reality which does everything possible to render the search for meaning redundant and irrelevant to its own self-perpetuation as well as a goal unworthy of life-efforts. (Bauman 1997: 126)

It is with this characterization of science, conceived of in terms of its own self-belief and hermetically sealed off from the world it seeks to comprehend and seeing the limits imposed by the 'garrison commanders' as those which cannot be transgressed, that Zygmunt Bauman takes issue. While changes may be clearly detected from his earlier writings, the spirit was clear:

The price the theory which subjects itself to the test of authentication pays for pulling down the barrier dividing the 'experimenter' and his 'objects', for dissolving the difference in status between them, is likely to be considered exorbitant by a science concerned more with certainty than with the significance of its results. (Bauman 1976: 109)

Over time he turns to other forms of representation in the pursuit of a strategy that, while containing some form of legislative intent, is one that is aimed at 'the authority of interpretation' (Bauman 1987: 197). This is about reading the meaning of communities 'properly' without the assumptions of the universalities of truth, taste and judgement lying behind it. What remains is no mean task as it concerns interpreting 'the meanings for the benefit of those who are not of the community which stands behind the meanings; to mediate the communication between ... "communities of meaning"' (Bauman 1987: 197).

Within such a spirit he approaches other forms of representation. If impermanence and undecidability are features of the contemporary landscape, a turn to art, music and literature holds out, if not the promise, at least the hope of escaping from a world saturated by the market. The poet's mission is not to call upon the obvious and self-evident. If they do so they become, following Milan Kundera, 'false poets'. Instead, they should 'pierce the walls of the obvious and self-evident, of that prevailing ideological fashion of the day whose commonality is taken for the proof its sense' (Bauman 2000: 203). Literature and social science, however, have not become one. It is about the spirit in which they are conducted and their mutual recognition of the role that each has in understanding the human condition: 'Each activity has its own techniques and modes of proceeding and its own criteria of propriety, which set them apart from each other' (Bauman 2007: 315). They may compare their differences and engage in rivalry, but their goals are not incommensurate. They both share the goal of 'piercing the curtain' of prejudgement to lay open the 'endless labour of reinterpretation' and to that extent they are '"objectively" in competition' (Bauman 2007: 315).

Summary

Despite criticisms that his work lacked a normative dimension (Fraser 1989), the orientation for Michel Foucault's approach is clear. In answer to a question concerning 'power as evil', he spoke of the need to resist domination in everyday life: 'The problem is … to know how you are to avoid these practices – where power cannot play and where it is not evil in itself' (Foucault 1991c: 18). The issue translates into how one-sided states of domination can be avoided in order to promote a two-sided relation of dialogue (Falzon 1998). Foucault's interventions were practically motivated. The journey for these investigations being from how we are constituted as objects of knowledge, to how we are constituted as subjects of our own knowledge. It is here, however, that we find important limitations in respect to his theories of the subject – ideas that he was developing prior to his death.

The shutting down of alternatives through not experiencing 'otherness', that exists as a matter of course in history and dialogue, might presuppose a certain willingness to be open to the possibilities that the 'other' offers. If this is to be meaningful, in the sense of an encounter that recognizes the facticity of the existence of alternative modes of being and organizing, this also means being exposed to a certain risk. In relation to human rights and debates conducted between those of different cultural backgrounds:

> all the participants intuitively know full well that a consensus based on insight is not possible if the relations between the participants in communication are not symmetrical – that is, relations of mutual recognition, of reciprocal perspective-taking, a shared willingness to look at one's own traditions through the eyes of a stranger, to learn from one another, and so on. (Habermas 2003: 291)

As our past and present testifies to, othering can lead not to tolerance and respect, but to violence and expulsion. What is clear is that a concern with this outcome was accommodated within Foucault's disposition to be curious and find the familiar strange, accompanied by an ethical commitment to otherness through a refusal to legislate concerning historical investigations. For this to be possible without resort to the romanticism of the exceptional individual, as we found in Weber, also means being positioned in such a way as to be relatively insulated in order to be curious in a systematic manner.

Taking Foucault's work seriously means that it is necessary to comprehend rationales for resistance in order to distinguish between different 'levels of power'. In the process, a differentiation and demarcation of the *effects* of discourse is enabled. Foucault left us with the view of both subject and object being the effect of discourse. Not only is an account of the conditions of possibility that give rise to such discourses then absent (Dews 1995), but also a more nuanced formulation of the self is required to illuminate the relations between reflection, communication, social conditions and transformation. In other words, where do the limits to appropriation of discourse lie and with what implications for social dynamics? How, within particular contexts, do people think of themselves in ways that are contrary to dominant expectations? A study conducted along these lines informs the transition from a 'critique conducted in the form of necessary limitation into a practical critique that takes the form of a possible transgression' (Foucault 1984: 45).

We are then led to the possibility of change, rather than descriptions disguised as explanations of continuity. Nevertheless, for whom, with what effects and through mobilizing what resources and to achieve what ends? These are the questions which should interrogate such thinking. If there is no act of interrogation concerning interpretation, we will see only acts that seek to constitute social reality, rather than provide the possibility for its dynamic transformation. The supposed play of discursive openness is routinely closed in the reality of practices in everyday life and to that extent is also open to revision as much through the illumination of omission in this process, as those things that are brought into the frames of interpretation and deliberation.

To assume that the end of critique is some consensual state of affairs runs the danger of the constitution of complacency. By default, this disguises non-consensuality in a celebration of finality (Foucault 1984). A critical ethos must be seen as a necessary, but not sufficient condition, to guard against 'power as evil'. This appears as a process without end. The potential for critical theory, considered genealogically, is its ability not only to 'reveal reality', but also to 'deconstruct necessity' (Hoy 1998). What is at stake is not only how we are dominated by others, but also how we dominate ourselves. Here we find ambivalence between immanent and transcendent critique. Foucault (1984) perhaps had this in mind when he spoke of consensus as not being a regulatory principle in his work, but a 'critical principle'.

For those who have taken a different path from Foucault, the implications can be to move reflexivity to a self-referential focus in the face of 'undecidability'. The result is that reflections within a limited terrain do not reach out in a dialogue and are closed off. The knowledge generated is held to be relative to time and place. Reflexivity cannot be the act of a community for whom a focus upon the role of writing enables a better representation; this is seen as a modernist dream to attain transparency between language and reality.

Here we find a tendency to celebrate contingency as the inevitable outcome of contemporary conditions. In this way it is possible to understand why it might be suggested that those who wrench culture from the economy in their reflections, might be privileged enough in the first place to enjoy a life free from everyday concerns with money. Methodologically speaking, however, we have a clear favouring of multiple interpretations. Indeed, the very idea of representation is taken as the focus of attack. The aim is then to avoid the idea of representation altogether in the name of producing a kind of cooperative story-making enterprise (Tyler 1986).

The final twist in the unfolding turns of critiques of the so-called truth-making enterprise is informed by an alignment between the central role assigned to language and texts in the constitution of reality. What was a topic of reflexivity in order to be transcended, or recognized and worked through, easily slips into defining the limits of what is seen as possible. In other words, relations between the knower and the known are no longer to be confronted as issues in the path towards better understanding or imagination, but become celebrated as inevitability and then define the limits of what can be known (Lawson 1986). A call to the interpretive can easily lapse into allowing the legislative in through the back door. Yet in a world without apparent complacencies of modernist foundations, this is a process without end in which conversations are assumed to be edifying, even confessional.

For those concerned with the transformative potential of social scientific insights, ambivalence between modernist confidence and postmodernist nihilism all too easily leads to fatalism (Stones 1996). In examining contemporary conditions while also possessing increased scepticism regarding the potential for change that lies within some transcendental truth, there is a long list of writers who have turned to a critique of the social and physical sciences without allusion to the complacencies of relativist social constructionism. Rooting this within a tension between democracy and science, Sandra Harding (2006) notes that while the marginalized require a language with which to engage with contemporary forms of exploitation, 'it is equally important to insist that the dominant groups find a more widely beneficial substitute for their rhetoric about the truth ideal' (2006: 144).

Among those who are dominant, we can count the 'truth-producers': that is, those academics and intellectuals who speak in the name of a state of affairs, process or event as if speaking from a privileged vantage point that is beyond the grasp of ordinary folk. Being positioned and positioning oneself in this way means producing an account from an unproblematized standpoint that refuses to see the grounds upon which it is enabled. It is frequently exemplified by an unreflexive attitude that reproduces a view of reality as if there were no other account available that has any legitimacy. Arrogance is manifest and frequently accompanied by a deficit model in relation to the audience who, if they possessed such expertise, would automatically draw the same conclusions. Such thinking informs hypodermic practices in the public understanding of science, as well as those texts that celebrate obscurity over clarity. The result is an assumed one-way relation between the production and reception of knowledge such that the public are taken to be deficient in their understandings (Irwin and Michael 2003).

Now we discover a conflation between cultural postmodernism with its celebration of free-floating signifiers in a vortex of symbolism, with recognition that existing social arrangements may be plural, but at the same time there are meanings and practices that are fixed and have real consequences in terms of their effects on people's lives. Caution has to be exercised in separating the cultural from the economic and which end up producing theories that are regulative, not constitutive, of the relationship between our attempts to understand the world and the world itself. The effect is one of abstraction and the same claim to be speaking in the name of *reality*, only this time of *realities*. There should be no anguish that comes from recognition of uncertainty. However, there is a need to recognize that there are those who may or may not share such anxieties, but they are shaping the world around us in their image as we seem to move from tragedy to farce (Žižek 2009). They are doing so through their exclusion of alternatives and their increasing monopolization of public understandings of events, processes, things and people.

We may characterize research practice in terms of its contribution to alternative interpretations and so to the possibilities for transformation. As Zygmunt Bauman rightly points out, there are differences between literature and social science, but they should not be exaggerated. The reproduction of sterility in either positivism or antipositivist accounts does not leave the reader with any need to rethink the reality that they inhabit, for it is about their adjustment to reality: expressed as a need for cognitive realignment or so-called descriptions without presuppositions of making that happen in everyday life. Such blocking out in order to produce is apparent among artists, intellectuals and those in general who reflect upon transformations and their effects. Assumed certainties easily bypass the practicalities of living with ambivalence and give way to a celebration of radical situatedness as if the fact of our being, as positioned, were not open to interpretation and transformation. A practice without epistemology or thick descriptions gives way to literature that does not claim to help us interpret issues, but delights in dramatization. In recognizing complexity, we can bring different elements together and enable the visual and literary to play their role: for example, in how we can not only imagine, but also represent, different futures (Byrne 1998).

Inspiration can come from those things that take a part of reality and twist, turn and extend it into hitherto unimagined realms: 'Inspirational value is typically *not* produced by the operations of a method, a science, a discipline, or a profession. It is produced by the individual brush strokes of unprofessional prophets and demiurges' (Rorty 1998: 133). The author of fiction or a work of art is 'interested' in some sense and so there is no claim to a 'view from nowhere', as reality and its form of representation blur. Nevertheless, we should also remind ourselves that there is a long history here:

> Just as social science has entertained the prospect of turning itself into literature, so literature could sometimes imagine itself as a form of social science. There was a strong component in romantic aesthetics recognising critical self-consciousness and epistemological uncertainty as the defining feature of a modern literature. (Simpson 2002: 118)

What is so fundamental to bear in mind in considering the implications of these various critiques of representation is the target itself: is it acts of representation performed by philosophers, social theorists and researchers, or any act of representation? Away from what have been termed by Jürgen Habermas (1992a) its 'performative contradiction', one should recognize that the art of provocation is alive and well. At a productive level for the practice of research we should see these as sensitizing, not total critiques. Those tempted to take the various texts of these writers separate from their deeds, will certainly over-extend their insights.

We are dealing here with a productive tension between knowledge and imagination. As Gilles Deleuze and Félix Guattari have put it:

> philosophy wants to save the infinite by giving it consistency: it lays out a plane of immanence that, through the action of conceptual personae, take events or consistent concepts to infinity. Science, on the other hand, relinquishes the infinite in order to gain reference: it lays out a plane of simply undefined coordinates that each time, through the action of particular observers, defines states of affairs, functions, or referential propositions. Art wants to create the finite that restores the infinite: it lays out a plane of compositions that, in turn, through the action of aesthetic figures, bears monuments or composite sensations. (Deleuze and Guattari 1994: 197)

With knowledge and imagination one seeks to speak in the name of that which cannot be exhausted and the other speaks in the name of that which has not yet been brought into being; one is potentially irresponsible in its saturation of the possible through procedural closure, while the other is irresponsible in its denial of the real in its leap from the actual; one is about comprehensibility in context and the other about the expulsion of context to unleash the realm of the possible. In this process social science can act as translator within and between traditions in the name of greater understanding. In so doing, we need to recognize that: *'there are changeable ratios in the grammar of reason, motive and cause which depend upon the degree of reflexivity in individuals and the openness of their institutions to such critical appraisal'* (O'Neill 1995: 144. Original italics).

In the face of these issues a far better dialogue is needed between different practitioners than has been evident from past and current practices. At one level we need a process in which we understand that what are held to be self-evident truths about how we know reality are contestable claims, while also recognizing that social processes have real effects and consequences despite this recognition. In this sense reflexivity as sensitizing, orientating, checking and opening up fields of relations to social investigation is one thing. If it pronounces upon the constitution of social reality, that is quite another. Caution should be exercised when it comes to proclamations about what are the basic features of social reality as if those were unproblematically separate from the variable procedures that may be adopted in coming to know that reality.

Forms of justification that underlie context and which may carry transferable lessons may be too readily placed to one side in favour of a contingency beyond which nothing legitimate can be spoken of. Yet acts of representation are routine in social life from the mundane and everyday, to the very dynamics of capitalism that constitute commodities as desirable and add to forms of consumption that are indifferent to the characters, contexts and consequences that make up their production. It is not that they take place, but the conditions and consequences through which they are constructed, received and acted upon that is at issue.

There is no shortage of those who are willing to undertake this endeavour on the basis of their power, ignorance and prejudice. While differentiated terrains, such as the economic and cultural, are taken as targets of modernist thinking, so too should be the presumption of collapse. Designations in relation to academic tribes easily become counterproductive to a critical-pragmatic practice that seeks to examine the causes and consequences of modern practices and policies and add its voice to better understanding, improvements in social and economic conditions and overall, a greater respect and tolerance among people.

In the face of these interrogations in Part 1 of the book, the need to reconstruct now rears its head. In the background is recognition that there are simple foundations upon which to base claims to truth, justice, fairness and freedom and so these things must be continually achieved rather than assumed. The 'philosopher-king' as the bearer of absolute knowledge should be uncrowned (Bourdieu 1990: 33), but we are not then led into a reflexive free for all. Deconstruction in the name of reflexivity is not the end, but reconstruction. Politically engaged and committed as he was, Jacques Derrida was aware that deconstruction did not readily translate into a programme for action (Bernstein 1992: Chapter 7).

Therefore, just how far should we go, bearing in mind those responsibilities that are about not only celebrating strengths, but also knowing limitations? Works about the relatedness of science to society, whether claiming to unproblematically reproduce the philosopher-king, or collapse social science into a position whereby there is no interpretative challenge to a reader by assuming there can be no vantage point of insight or practice demarcation, both reproduce sterility by default. Social science has more to offer than the latter holds and a lot to offer without recourse to legislative argument. As a check against self-referential indulgence and scholastic slumber, while engaging with the social world, we need a dynamic that recognizes not only differences, but also limitations, and does so in the spirit of contributing to human betterment.

PART 2

CONSEQUENCES

REFLEXIVE PRACTICE

4

In a North American town people began to notice small marks appearing on the windscreens of their cars. Other people then saw the same marks on their windscreens, with the result that the whole population became preoccupied with this new phenomenon. What was the reason? Quite simply, instead of looking *through* their windscreens, people had started to look *at* them. The pit-marks had always been present and resulted from small stones being thrown up by car tyres. From that time onwards windscreens were checked for marks, as well as being the means through which the road ahead was observed.

Could this story be used to illustrate the approaches to understanding reflexivity in Part 1? It is attractive, but problematic for many. A distinction between the knower (driver) and the known (road) exists, with the driver employing a medium (windscreen) to observe the landscape ahead. As we saw in Part 1, these ideas have all been subjected to sustained critique. It is the windscreen(s) and not the road ahead upon which the methodological and theoretical gaze now tends to fix itself.

The consequences of the content of ideas on reflexivity vary according to their interpretation against a background of pre-reflexive assumptions. These require continual scrutiny in order to develop ideas from new experiences and understand the relations between the production, transmission and reception of knowledge derived from research. It is perfectly possible to dismiss such considerations by regarding them as trivial. Equally, however, 'fixity' in assumptions is required on the part of the researcher in order to examine the social world in the first instance, without which one would collapse into infinite regress. The question is not whether this occurs, but how and with what implications for the practice of research and our understandings of the world?

We have seen all sorts of moves to avoid ambivalence from production through to dissemination, reception and application. These issues exist across all dimensions of research from the humanities, through social sciences to physical sciences, but have variable consequences. In general, we have had falsification and paradigm shifts; hermeneutic idealist proposals; definitional operationalism and whole collapses of sense and reference as manifest in systems theory. In the work of Niklas Luhmann (1982), this latter move is achieved in the primacy of the relations between system and environment in order that the former can break itself off from the external world in a self-referential vortex enabling it to be operative. The consequence is: 'What the refracting view sees, in the moment of its collapse into the inner, is the void of the subject world, the blank surface on the back of the skull that has become *indistinguishable* from the purely external' (Brunkhorst 1996: 98. Original italics).

Another path is open to us in understanding the relations between content and consequence. It investigates the relations between culture, practices and institutions in the production of research and enables us to understand variations in the content, context, consequence and the expectations placed upon knowledge. In the first stages of this investigation, I consider the consequences of these critiques in terms of how we can understand variations in degrees of effect upon practices, as well as a productive differentiation between forms of reflexivity that neither fall into infinite regress, nor collapse. For this reason I will focus upon epistemic permeability: that is, the extent to which knowledge is the province of particular groups enabling them to control a separation between production and other elements in the knowledge process.

What are the influencing factors on degrees of epistemic permeability? These relate to the capability to keep separate the justification *for* research and the application *of* research. The conditions for this include: the political economy of research funding; the institutional context of knowledge production; the attributed value afforded to the work by public and/or elite audiences; the operating norms within a research community for what counts as good work; the organization and power of a professional group who, having a sufficient consensus or power among them to prevent what is seen as contamination by outside forces, operate closure around the means of production and finally, the existence of intermediary organizations that work to apply the results of research and so act to break and/or pick up the implications of the production-transmission-reception-application process.

In relation to the work of intermediary organizations I am thinking, in particular, of the proliferation of knowledge transfer activities populated by personnel of varying backgrounds, as well as spin out companies in and around universities, numerous consultancies and the increasing drive for economic development driven by investments and patents in science. I will return to these issues in Part 3 where the focus is upon the context of knowledge production. Beth Perry and I will then develop insights based on the extensive work we have undertaken on knowledge, universities, science and economic development and innovation and knowledge exchange. First, with epistemic permeability and its consequences for research practice in mind, this chapter is based upon a distinction between endogenous and referential reflexivity.

Dimensions in Reflexive Practice

Endogenous reflexivity refers to the ways in which the actions and understandings of researchers contribute to the modes in which research practices are constituted.

There are specific expectations, often latent and unarticulated, that are made of the practices and forms of knowledge that are deployed in particular disciplines. In addition, methods of work may be embodied in instruments of production or practice that form non-reflexive elements in the research process: for example, computer-based modes of qualitative and quantitative analysis and coding; researchers subcontracting the collection and analysis of data to third parties and implicit expectations concerning working methods as manifest in normal practices.

Diversity characterizes scientific production settings (Knorr-Cetina 1999). There is often no evident, articulated consensus among research communities. Equally, however, witness what is mobilized when it comes to defences of procedures, or during times for promotion and recruitment and how, all of a sudden, diversity becomes uniform. The same tendency is evident in times of crisis when universities threaten to close whole departments in the name of rationalizing the mode of production according to criteria justified by external 'demand analysis'. It is also possible for particular research groups to exist in university and other settings that set themselves aside from others and in so doing, mobilize particular expectations of their staff. To this extent, culture, context and content combine to enable the existence of such settings. Beyond these cultures of inquiry, endogenous reflexive practice refers to how we think and act in our social and cultural milieux. That, in turn, produces a knowledge that informs, and is informed by, actions oriented to those practices and localities.

What is accounted for in this domain of practice is that the knowledge deployed in social inquiry is similar in form, if not content, to that deployed in other forms of culture. The difference is that practices of inquiry anchor particular meanings through a process of translation in order to analyse them in the first place and so turn subject into object, while those meanings are more widely diffused and contested in the social world. We can therefore say that: 'Inquiry is practice of a deeply cultural sort, which can become reflexive only by investigating these relationships through inquiry itself' (Hall 1999: 255).

Referential reflexive practice assists in understanding degrees of epistemic permeability. It refers to the consequences that arise from a meeting between the reflexivity exhibited by actors within the social world and that exhibited by a researcher as part of a social scientific community. It takes place where the production of accounts meet contexts of reception that seek to render events, conditions and experiences intelligible via a meeting of points of view. The power to ignore or act upon these is variable among and between different groups and that also informs the extent to which production and reception are differentiated, conjoined in various ways or collapsed into the same domain of activity.

Here we find forms of knowledge that are, potentially or actually, generated as a result of having the routines in social life disrupted by sudden changes in social conditions, or by meeting circumstances that are not amenable to reproduction within the normal conditions of everyday life. It thus implies not only a set of conditions that give rise to further questions, but also the potential to learn and act through an engagement with alternative viewpoints. The ability to ignore, as well as have access to such potential, comprises this realm of understanding – along with puzzlement, confusion, uncertainty and resistance. Rhetorical persuasion, and not just the production of systematic accounts of social life, also informs the decisions of those who are the recipients of social scientific knowledge.

The movement from endogenous to referential reflexivity may be character- ized as one from reflexivity *within* actions to reflexivity *upon* actions, enabling connections to be made between individuals and the social conditions of which they are a part. In other words, to bring attention to not only the conditions of action at the level of intersubjectively shared lifeworlds, but also the effects on action manifest as constraints and enablements upon others and so not necessary amenable to immediate understanding within the particularity of our lives. Highlighting the world in this manner has the potential to demonstrate how the objectivity of the social world is not only a presupposition *in*, but also an ongoing achievement *of*, everyday interactions.

Consequences and Contingencies

The history charted in Part 1 may be characterized as a fluctuation between refer- ential and endogenous concerns. One tendency may be detected in this unfolding history: towards an inward-looking practice that prioritizes observation and pro- duction, over the process of observation and its relationship to reception. Alternatively, they are collapsed, as suggested earlier, with the result that any sense of learning through engagement evaporates. The consequence is a failure to ade- quately understand the role and place of research in the study of social life.

The study of endogenous reflexivity within lifeworlds starts with how people understand meaning. This is not a subjective state of affairs, but an intersubjective one that represents a process of acculturation manifested through publicly avail- able forms of communication, including language. In order to adequately grasp the meanings used in everyday life, Alfred Schutz introduced his postulate of adequacy for the practice of social science. In the terms employed here, this may be expressed via the idea that a mirroring of endogenous reflexivity within the lifeworld provides for endogenous reflexivity in the practice of social research.

As discussed in Part 1, limited concepts of endogenous reflexivity are sympto- matic of an absence of a referential dimension to practice. Instead of examining this issue, it is sidelined in favour of meticulous descriptions of everyday accounts of language use. Two consequences follow. First, the lifeworld itself appears devoid of meaning, and second, the analyst appears to be able to free themselves from their own language games without due concern for mediation between frames of meaning and their contribution to its constitution (May and Powell 2008). We need better ways to understand how social research contributes to social life, other than to describe the order and conventions of the social world which is represented as homogeneous, with the subject expunged as a result of a focus upon linguistic conventions. Contingency reads as necessity because of seeking to avoid the problems of a 'reflexivity of reflexivity' (Ashmore 1989). Epiphenomenal trouble within the lifeworld arises in terms of misunderstandings that require interactional realignments; alignments that are explicable in terms of the rules of conversation and/or categorization.

Such approaches lead to a sharpening of the technicalities of method within the endogenous domain of research practice, but should not be overextended as if that alone granted the grounds for understanding the relations between research and social life. Here we can detect empiricist leanings that are manifest in different research techniques. It is well known that the validity of question-naire design can be predicated upon congruence between the respondent's inter-pretation and the researcher's intentions in the framing of their questions. Various methods are then employed in order to cross-check for validity through, for instance, asking the same question using different phraseology when employ-ing Likert techniques. The point is not to suggest that questionnaires are neces-sarily problematic, nor is linguistic analysis, it is simply that particular approaches bracket issues that result in partial understandings via method-based solutions in a triumph of endogenous technicism over referential understanding.

The assumption that accurate recording of the lifeworld is both a necessary and sufficient condition to attain reflexivity within the social sciences, or represent that within the lifeworld, is a characteristic of different research traditions which exhibit the same overall tendencies. It permits a distance from considerations of forms of reflexivity and so a better understanding of the place and possibilities of research in the world. These may be seen with respect to comparative research. Researchers may be grouped into the categories of 'purist', 'ignorants' or 'totalists' (Øyen 1990). However, none of these are 'comparativists' who exhibit an attention to reflexivity along both of the dimensions discussed here via their sensitivity to issues of and implications for, the study of social life. There is no assumption here of context-dependence, but a context-sensitivity that has the potential for context-revision.

It is not only empiricism, but also 'theoreticism' that replicates the 'illusion of absolute knowledge' (Bourdieu 1992a) in the endogenous dimension. This relation-ship should be open to examination through the process of 'problematization':

> Problematization doesn't mean the representation of a pre-existent object, nor the creation through discourse of an object that doesn't exist. It's the set of discursive or non-discursive practices that makes something enter into the play of the true and false, and constitutes it as an object for thought (whether under the form of moral reflection, scientific knowledge, political analysis, etc.). (Foucault 1989a: 456–7)

Therefore, it is a continual process of seeking to understand what the sciences see and the manner in which they construct it, while considering their place within and contribution to, social relations more generally. In the process, it is recognized that 'practical' interventions in the organization of social life are central to their endeavour, as well as being vital to their futures.

We can see the tendency towards theoreticism in 'totalising' critiques. Into this group one can place elements of the 'Frankfurt School' tradition and postmodernism. The tendency of the latter to gloss over the lifeworld and so the potential for 'lay' reflexivity has been attributed by Jürgen Habermas (1992a) to the influence of Nietzsche. Methodologically speaking, attention to the internal ordering of social scientific accounts leads to a glossing over of the dimension of referential reflexivity. Equally, allusions to particular ideas of the autonomous subject in terms of the reception of social scientific knowledge place a burden upon that which cannot possibly live up to its apparent promise. Disparate paths may then terminate in the aesthetic dimension of life as retreat rather than being complementary in a journey of discovery, as first epistemology and then ontology cannot live up to the expectations placed upon them by philosophers, social theorists and methodologists.

In our journey we also found that interpretations of the content of works inevitably have consequences for research activity itself. The popularity of contemporary ways of thinking can mean a bracketing of whole perspectives within a tradition of thought that enables us to pursue a relational understanding (Letherby et al. forthcoming; J. Scott 1998). Take Richard Rorty's (1979, 1982) use of James and Dewey to the exclusion of the 'other' pragmatism of Charles Peirce. Peirce, while critical of Cartesian thought, did not surrender truth to instrumentalism and empiricism (Apel 1995; Mounce 1997). The links between Mannheim's sociology of knowledge and the work of Peirce actually provide for a different way of looking at knowledge in the above process in relation to referential reflexivity. Peirce's maxim is stated as follows:

> For the maxim of Pragmatism is that a conception can have no logical effect or import differing from that of a second conception except so far as, taken in connection with other conceptions and intentions, it might conceivably modify our practical conduct differently from that second conception. (Peirce quoted in Mounce 1997: 33)

Two criteria are now side-by-side. First, the constitution of the social object itself and/or the problem to which the social researcher turns their attention is intersubjectively validated within the scientific community (endogenous dimension). Second, however, the resulting knowledge can act as a communicative contribution to a community. Here, different traditions do learn from each other. Marxism can learn from pragmatism that it cannot make predictions from history and pragmatism can learn it has to abandon the link between theory and praxis as if it were simply the same process as scientific experimentation (Apel 1995). At this point we turn to the potential for the creation of dialogic communities in which the possibility exists for moving beyond relativism and objectivism. Now, firmly within the realm of a practical task, divergent thinkers such as Rorty, Gadamer, Habermas, Arendt and Foucault, come together (Bernstein 1983).

Consider Jacques Derrida's aim to expose subject-centred reason as the 'disingenuous dream' (Boyne 1990) of Western thinking. Allusions to 'voices' in the research process are said to open up the research text to 'multiple readings'. Methodological translations of his work take paradoxical forms whereby critiques of the authority of the author actually lead to accounts that reproduce ego-identity! At one level this has opened up a whole new publishing industry for textual reflections on the futility of past attempts to grasp something called 'social reality', thereby enabling careers to continue through written confessions of past, misguided practices.

The effect of these moves is to render representation so incoherent that engagement for the purpose of illumination is difficult, if not impossible. These accounts appear 'strangely self-contained, sealing themselves off from comment and criticism' (Law 1994: 190). The act of repudiating the authority of the author ends up reproducing the very targets of Derrida's critique: textual closure and the centrality of the researcher in the production of the research account. A particular game is being played here leaving readers bewildered in the wake of self-serving textual reflections conducted within the limits of the endogenous realm.

Authority is not abandoned in Derrida's writings. What Derrida did is not to place it beyond question:

> the value of truth (and all those values associated with it) is never contested nor destroyed in my writings, but only reinscribed in more powerful, larger, more stratified contexts...And within those contexts...it should be possible to invoke rules of competence, criteria of discussion and of consensus, good faith, lucidity, rigour, criticism, and pedagogy. (quoted in Norris 1993: 300)

His work posed transcendental questions in order to avoid the traps of empiricism, while seeing this as a never-ending quest in order that it does not succumb to the reproduction of the idea of Truth as final. What authors have done is to take this approach and turn it into an inward fate for social research through an over-extension of philosophy as the under-labourer. Derrida was clear in his aims whose limits for the practice of social research require active translation in their implications, not regurgitation without such responsibility: 'I take extremely seriously the issues of philosophical responsibility...I have been led back over the past thirty years...to the necessity of defining the transcendental condition of possibility as also being a condition of impossibility' (Derrida 1996: 81–2).

Bruno Latour's discussion of meta-reflexivity and infra-reflexivity picks up on the issues raised by the translation of clarifying philosophical positions into apparently methodologically resolved outcomes. For him meta-reflexivity is characterized by a concern with the knower, not the known. An abandonment of the work of representation then occurs in which the naive view becomes that which conceives of the text as a referent: 'Reflexivity is supposed to counteract this effect by rendering the text unfit for normal consumption (which often means unreadable)' (Latour 1988: 168). The result is that: 'Reflexivists fully endorse the scientistic agenda when they believe there is no other way out of empiricism than language, words and self-reference' (Latour 1988: 173).

Latour suggests that social scientists should speak of the world not the word in order that the proper object of reflexivity is the work of representation. Without this in the forefront of considerations, the balance between deconstruction and reconstruction tips in favour of the former with the result that social research loses its relevance for understanding and explanation. Alvin Gouldner (1975) was clearly aware of this tendency when he wrote how disciplines that begin with disenchantment concerning the world only end up disenchanting themselves. A conference on reflexivity can easily be imagined as one in which the audience emerges with a profound sense of the futility of their enterprise. The speakers, on the other hand, are delighted that the proceedings will appear in an international journal, only adding to the sense that their enterprise is alive and well and leading to yet more invitations to do the same at other conferences.

We end up with an absence of context-sensitivity to inform research engagement. Within academia a principle applies such that certain works may be absolutized by dehistoricizing them. In turn, this provides for their apparent ability to solve problems that are not sensitive to historical change or the conditions under and through which they were first produced (Bourdieu 2000). What I am suggesting here is that a process of forgetting is at work that frequently characterizes 'innovation'. At one level this allows a practice that remains indifferent to the original reasons and conditions of its possibility and how these relate to contemporary issues. A lapse into indifference and ultimately arrogance may serve to produce an insularity sustained by those who will not challenge what is apparently beyond question. All disciplines and all members of those disciplines may be subject to such a process and while these are variable in effects, we need cultures that are not only robust, but also sufficiently open-minded to have preconceptions challenged and practices open to change as a result.

Opening up the practice of research to scrutiny has a number of consequences. At the experiential level of the researcher, a tension will be felt between the centrality of their experiences, measured against the aggregate of social values and practices they seek to understand. In this way they can appear as inconsequential as their individuality is absorbed in totality. As we saw in the work of Max Weber, this existed as a tension between an ethic of commitment and one of responsibility. In the absence of a supportive research environment, this tension so easily becomes unproductive. Expressions of individual inadequacy may result, or exaggerated claims to expertise occur, or there is allusion to the futility of research while enjoying the conditions it affords. Individuals or groups of individuals opt for particular schools of thought, thinkers or methods as such allegiances provide for a relief from this basic tension or, alternatively, yet another deconstructive critique of social research, which does little for our understanding of its role in social life, then occurs.

At the same time for those who regard any critical distance as a luxury in the face of apparent necessity, we can reserve the term 'doxosophers'. To refuse to grant self-evidence to an existing states of affairs is often seen to be symptomatic of a naivety or bias because of its 'refusal to grant the profoundly political submission implied in the unconscious acceptance of *commonplaces*' (Bourdieu 1998b: 8. Original italics). The doxosopher's view combines with that of those who do not submit academic positionality and its implications for the production, transmission and reception of knowledge to critical examination. Contingency is necessity by default, as there is no understanding of the conditions for existing states of affairs and the means of production are held to reflect an unproblematic environmental urgency, or react to an individualized demand by those who feel their work is of the utmost importance in an over-blown extension from narrowly bounded spaces of production to reception.

Concern focuses upon the conservation or subversion of the structure of capital within the field, as opposed to a consideration of the potential for its reconstitution and the consequences of that for knowledge production in different environments and disciplines. We all have a stake and a place within such relations and cannot but contribute to reproduction at some level. However, to what degree and with what consequence? Those who benefit from current arrangements will tend to defend orthodoxy when it speaks in their name. History, including their own biographical trajectories and positions in the field, may be displaced in a process of the naturalization of the present. Yet if the resultant strategies and tactics fail to take account of the reconstitution of fields of knowledge production according to new forms of control and changing institutional conditions of production, misrecognition will be the consequence whether it originates from an orientation to presentist empiricism or abstracted theoreticism.

A number of these consequences are in no way unrelated to academic practices in the pursuit of recognition via forms of dissemination based on narrow areas of specialization. As citation indices are increasingly seen as indicators of prestige, so too will practices alter to take account of the new game. It is not suggested that the content of these acts of dissemination or reporting may not be valuable in themselves, but it is important to avoid conflating clarification *for* practice with resolution *in* practice across the research process. All too easily there is a slide from the sensitizing and revising to the regulative via limited understandings of domains of practice. In this respect, too many cultures of inquiry are poor learning environments where mutual understanding is put aside in favour of celebrations of products, rather than the quality of the process that enabled their production in the first place.

Clarification and Engagement

Intelligibility and the conditions under which it takes place are not the same as the analysis of the conditions that give rise to an event or process that is being analysed. The difference between the endogenous and referential dimensions requires effort aimed at understanding. To reduce one to the other is a conflation giving rise to such things as methodological individualism and structuralism. 'Solutions' have been sought between the analytic and experiential for a long time, right through to the current post-metaphysical stage. Methodological legislation is permitted through such conflation and so are corresponding claims to expertise in the shadows of particular understandings of the practice of the physical sciences. This legacy continues through strategies of distancing and talking to other experts and conflating clarification with resolution thereby over-extending domains of influence by default.

In finding connections between domains of practice, the place of knowledge-ability and capability as components of agency are explicated in terms of specific understandings and social environments, as are the construction and consequences of the relationship between social scientific knowledge and social life. In social life more generally, to focus upon the relations that exist between social determinants, reflexivity and practice enables the possibility of acquiring a greater freedom from the influence of such determinants. We then have the potential to become free 'from the illusion of freedom, or, more exactly, from the misplaced belief in illusory freedoms. Freedom is not something given: it is something you conquer – collectively' (Bourdieu 1990: 15).

The process of constituting objects of social scientific discourse results in a demarcation between 'theoretical' and 'practical' knowledge. The effect of this is to create a 'distance' from the topic of social inquiry through invoking a set of pre-reflexive assumptions that, in relation to understanding the logic of practice, condemn the analyst 'either to wring incoherences out of it or to thrust a forced coherence upon it' (Bourdieu 1992a: 86). To consider endogenous reflexivity alone would not allow us to see the implications of this separation and how it is that the social sciences are constitutive of social relations. What would then be replicated is a one-way hermeneutic whereby social research is simply separated from social life. In this sense, the study of referential reflexivity can be seen as an understanding of the consequences of a 'double hermeneutic' (Giddens 1984). That idea, however, requires considerable modification for the purposes of this discussion.

The issue here is how the relationship between social scientific knowledge and action is dealt with. Within the philosophy of social science, for example, reflexive predictions have been held as a problem. Here we find the assumption that it is feasible to have a strict separation between subject and object. Therefore, if a prediction is made concerning the social realm, we would have to hold back from any form of dissemination otherwise it would be self-fulfilling and thus not amenable to a verifiable hypothesis according to a particular conception of scientific work. The 'dissemination problem' is then addressed through a focus upon formulation such that only some predictions may then be said to be reflexive, depending upon how they are constructed and of what they comprise (Romanos 1994). Intriguing as such arguments are, they rest on certain characterizations of science and assumptions of epistemic impermeability. Here we are led to questions concerning whether a separation is either possible or desirable between expert and lay cultures.

Civil society is constituted by the expectation that expert knowledge feeds into rational deliberation with a resulting progression, politically speaking, towards better states of affairs. In this way an educated public is said to exist alongside other interests with the result that different voices are mobilized according to some conception of the common good. However, expertise and democracy are not harmonious (S. Turner 2003). Communities of professional practice require long periods of initiation into their own mysteries and, to that extent, the best we might expect is that the public accord legitimacy to such specialization, based upon recognition of the importance of the resultant knowledge.

What is actually agreed upon is a separation between the content (endogenous) and consequences (referential) of knowledge: the former being the province of professional disciplines, while the latter is subject to different criteria. Here, assumptions that power and knowledge are always intertwined or easily separable may be examined and worked through and conditions made possible for examining implications away from the influence of elites. In this way it is possible to maintain the legitimacy of research in order to be operable.

The relations between social science and civic discourse constitute a fundamental aspect of the referential dimension (Brown R.H., 1992). It is within an understanding of this dimension, in terms of the relations between research practices and social life and the knowledges that are produced, that the potential to see under what conditions and utilizing what resources, reflexivity may be enhanced. By reflecting upon social circumstances, it is not held that we can simply escape from our socio-cultural milieux, but it is suggested we can more satisfactorily reflect on the relations between freedom and necessity. In knowing the social world in this manner, transformation is possible alongside a greater understanding and tolerance of the differences, as well as commonalities, in our lived experiences.

These questions link reception and production. Yet they seem difficult to address for they question that which is so often assumed at the level of production: for example, the hierarchies in research communities and how they work to structure fields of interest and the research process itself. These are the 'de-bunking' aspects of reflexivity to which I alluded at the beginning of this chapter. Those wielding power in the research hierarchy will be genuinely mystified by the attention called to its exercise. To this extent we may say that: 'Misrecognition…enables objectivity to become subjectivized by agents of power' (Cicourel 1993: 102).

An examination of the interactions between social research and other communities assists in making the pre-reflexive assumptions of the research community more clear. This should not mean, however, that we lose sight of the ways in which the results of research are interpreted, used and with what consequences. To do so is to translate the need to study the rhetoric of research texts themselves into the endogenous dimension which can end up being self-referential. That tends to happen in methodological reflections that focus upon how language and reality are inextricably linked within a homogenous particularity of world views. Horizons of meaning are more likely to be challenged when the implications of relationism stretches them further from reach. However, this in no way relieves research of its role in translating between the general and particular.

A framework for research enquiry can now take on board the possibility of the existence of intransitive objects that furnish the conditions for agreement in the shared meanings of different theories (Bhaskar 1989) and that of communicative reason (Habermas 1984, 1987, 1992b). I take these two positions as being concerned with 'ontology of already existing things' and 'ontology of ethically significant, developmental activities' (Shotter 1993: 100). Despite the different theories of truth – coherence and consensus respectively – being regarded as reconcilable (Outhwaite 1991), that is a matter of practical, lived experience and which requires those concerned to 'engage with differences as a *problem of understanding and explanation*, and ultimately, as a problem common to our lives' (Holmwood 1996: 134. Original italics). We need, therefore, to attend not only to the endogenous, but also to the referential dimensions of reflexivity if we are to unleash the potential in their meeting to inform practical actions within the lifeworld.

Those who castigate others for questioning the self-evident meet with those for whom the limits of critical questioning arise when it comes to an examination of the positions from which their pronouncements are made. When a critical disposition and position are separated what evaporates are the relational understandings that are highlighted in taking this meeting seriously. Knowledge can be divorced from context and packaged for resale on the basis of excellence to one's peers, or it can be sold on the basis of its content-relevance to those for whom its findings are nothing more than confirmations of their world views. There is no moving beyond the objectivity–relativism debate, it is just repackaged in new guises.

In discussions upon reflexive modernization in this interaction we can see a tendency to focus upon 'expert', as opposed to 'lay' cultures (Beck et al. 1994; Giddens 1990). The idea of reflexive modernization is located in a trust in 'expert' systems, whereas those such as Ulrich Beck base their analysis in a 'distrust' of those same systems (Lash in Beck et al. 1994). While such an emphasis seems to align itself with issues that inform referential reflexive practice, a subject–object dichotomy is repeated that should be a topic of investigation, not an assumption. It is achieved through providing social scientific practices with a place from which generalized reflections on social life can be made. Yet, this is separate from 'lay', endogenous reflexivity (Giddens 1990: 40–1). Two issues that require analytic attention for the purpose of understanding the role of research in social life are then closed to scrutiny.

First, there is the hermeneutic dimension of the modern self which has ramifications for an understanding of endogenous reflexivity. Rather than an iron cage or protective domain for the self, we can see difference as a source of knowledge, not an impediment (Calhoun 1995). Second, in invoking a subject–object dichotomy in terms of an overly drawn demarcation between expert and lay knowledge, the hermeneutic dimension to scientific practice is relatively neglected. What is excluded is a consideration of how it is that the role of 'expert' is itself constructed in an encounter with the object of its attention.

Such a distance is understood through an examination of varying degrees of epistemic permeability. Rather than close this off through a theoreticist or empiricist flattening of the dimensions of reflexive practice, this needs illuminating through the following question: how do translations between lay and professional frames of meaning occur and how are they negotiated and acted upon and with what consequences? The idea of a 'trust' in expert system, or simple epistemic privileging, is thus replaced by a more complex understanding of the relations between the social scientific and 'lifeworld' communities, particularly given the difficult, if not impossible task, of bracketing the social scientist from the conditions of their own everyday lives.

What we find in this relationship is ambivalence. It is a space in which trust 'is at least heavily qualified by the experience of dependency, possible alienation, and lack of agency, though there are of course many areas of experience where relationships between expert and lay publics are well integrated and non-alienated' (Wynne 1996: 52). How these situations of trust and scepticism arise, for what reasons and with what consequences, are the topics of our understandings. The consequence of this move is bound to question a simple fact–value dichotomy. With this separation in place, social science may act as a legislator between the true and the false, as opposed to an effective contributor to a participatory dialogue over means and ends based upon the production of systematic intensive and extensive findings.

The dimension of referential reflexivity acknowledges the distinction between legislators and interpreters. It questions the idea that social researchers enjoy the authority to arbitrate in disputes through appeal to past ideas of 'objective' knowledge to which they have a privileged and unmediated access. Instead, the role of social research is seen in terms of being a facilitator of communication between traditions. However, it does not follow that 'anything goes' (see Feyerabend 1978). Rather, attention must be devoted to the rigours of translation in acts of mediation between 'communities of meaning' (Bauman 1989: 197). Attention is then called to a 'critical hermeneutic' (J. Thompson 1981) dimension to referential reflexivity in terms of the relations which exist between power, language, interpretation and practice. In this way, the potential for referential reflexivity within the lifeworld is open to investigation via a 'strong hermeneutics' (N. Smith 1997) and not closed off by fiat.

In terms of the analytic and experiential, research will resonate with the latter and engage as a translator between particular experiences and matters of social, political, economic and environmental concern. In these acts of translation, there is recognition embodied in interpretation and so it can become a 'nuisance'. Between the general and the particular is translation. This is not side-stepped by fancy reflexive arguments, or sophisticated mathematical or textual procedures, but practical interventions in which there are no guaranteed outcomes. It is a division of labour that inheres in our understanding of and condition of being in the world. We may produce an excellent explanation, but it does not follow it is relevant to a particular context. That does not make it irrelevant, contrary to particular pragmatist orientations simply that it does not, in that context at that time, provide a basis for actions among particular persons or groups.

Equally, we may find an 'elective affinity' (Weber) between ideas and material circumstances such that they are taken up for reasons other than a clear understanding of their content and consequence for subsequent actions. For these reasons it does not help to conflate the values that inform the constitutive realm of social research practice with the contextual values that adhere in the referential domain. Following a piece of research that has illuminated a facet of social dynamics, there is no automatic resolution to the question 'How do we proceed?' Here we enter the terrain of practical engagement where contestation may, or may not, reign. Knowing this enables us to know the value of what we do, avoid disappointment about what we cannot achieve and see the strengths of limitations of the value of research in society.

Where we have been tied up in knots about the relations between the general and particular, it has been over the imperatives of representing experience as context-dependent, against those of explanation as context-independent. To move beyond this requires context-sensitivity. It is the science of the probable, not the certain. How you constitute a sense of expertise in the public realm in order to legitimize the role of research on the basis of this recognition, is about issues that lie beyond scientific discourse and practice. It is informed by it, but it is not a matter for it. As writings about social science are said to move beyond stale dichotomies, justifications for practice in everyday life also repeat them. 'The facts speak for themselves' will always be deployed in the service of those for whom context-sensitivity is an impediment to righteous pronouncement about reality. Selectivity will remain with us in the domain of reception for those who conflate how we justify our forms of analysis with its assumed implications for what should then be done. Let this conflation be challenged by a modest research practice that has so very much to offer social life.

Different groups, in different ways, sever the links between these processes and they, in turn, are afforded the possibility of building these into their reflexive practices through institutional conditions. Frames of reference can then freeze, for example, at the relation between production and reception in the production of articles in journals. These acts of dissemination suffice in situations where the practices and integrities of research are said to be undermined if excellence gives way to relevance. Other forms of research, on the other hand, are held to be excellent only when they are relevant and sufficient boxes are ticked in order to demonstrate end-user satisfaction.

In resultant spaces, the logic of supply and demands is allowed to continue unchecked in thinking about knowledge, for, while such practices continue, so too do the assumptions of neo-liberal conceptions of individuals. Thus they either consume knowledge according to the maximization of individual preference or, in a move to join economics with behaviourism, manipulate their environments according to changes that include knowledge about those conditions. Another way of thinking about this issue is to see it as existing in agonism. As we will see, institutions intervene in reflexive work by enabling its absence through varying degrees of epistemic permeability.

I use the term 'agonism' here deliberately. We can see this agonism in the frustrations that people have in understanding the accounts of the world produced by researchers because they are not within their experiences, challenge their preconceptions, or that they regard it as either illegitimate or out of the realm of comprehension: for example, participant observation studies of deviant and criminal behaviour because they are acts of interpretation, are also seen as implicated in the acts they describe through bringing recognition to a more general audience. These accounts bring to the public realm what is regarded as unacceptable forms of behaviour. It then leads to debates about how understanding is not acquiescence, nor is to explain action to condone it. Similarly, at the level of an ethical code for the conduct of research, it raises particular questions for the researcher in terms of the over-identification with forms of behaviour that they find unacceptable (see Fielding 1982), or the conflicts that may arise in undertaking evaluation due to the effects of power (McKie 2002).

Varying degrees of epistemic permeability inform the efforts needed for such boundary work. It may not be recognized in situations where, for instance, the publication of critical texts exists alongside a practice that is out of line with the content of such writings. Perhaps praxis never did make perfect? This is hardly unheard of in academic life and raises issues about character, culture, content and context. Such issues took Alvin Gouldner, despite his undoubted insights, into a romantic-individualist realm, no doubt in large part due to the frustration of seeking a more general reflexivity in social scientific practice.

Such domains may be collapsed in order to inform those who appear to embody contrary forms of knowledge from their pay masters. Talk then focuses on practices that are not sustainable in the 'real world' with its self-evident necessities that demand certain actions. There is no shortage of attempts to ignore these distinctions in relation to market-driven initiatives (Amit 2000; E. Martin 1999). What this points to is the need to keep these spheres as part of reflexive attention, not to collapse them in practice. We often then see individuals reacting to this state of affairs by speaking of their individual autonomy and producing texts on the death of the subject.

Resonance appears to capture the inevitable ambivalences that arise in research when findings stretch away from the person. Of course, this will vary in terms of the content of particular forms of research and its audiences. Against what may be the intense particularity of experience, there is also the experience and understanding of others, as well as the analysis of conditions that arise from research. Proximity and stretching then varies according to the place particular forms of research have on a scale between the intensive and extensive and with resulting issues over the translation of meanings.

It is not only the endogenous constitution of the object in research we are dealing with here. We are also concerned with conditions of being within social research practice, some of whose manifestations may be placed under the umbrella of 'disappointment' (Craib 1994) that witnesses a move from the hope and promise of science to its apparent demise. Where science was to manipulate objects in the desire for control, we now have a science that apparently cannot live up to any promise. Of course it could never live up to the expectations placed upon it because it was held to be the only human activity 'to resolve questions without raising any' and in so doing 'it would be released from the need for questioning as well as from any burden of responsibility. A divine innocence it would possess, a marvellous form of extraterritoriality' (Castoriadis 1991: 263).

Recognition of ambivalence when dealing with these domains of practice and engagement is part of maturity (Ferrara 1998). It is the ability to discern differences and not place unrealistic burdens upon that which cannot live up to unrealistic hopes. Research practice will be populated by those who are disappointed if a simple relationship is assumed to exist between research, reception and transformation. It becomes an over-extension of desire into terrains that cannot fulfil it. These issues are culturally closed when individual recognition for the social researcher follows from the production of what is regarded as an excellent piece of work by their peers. Yet this closure conflates elements of the research process and leads to inevitable frustration if those forms of justification then spill over into the realms of interpretation by others. Reactions to this state of affairs are expressed in terms of the failed possibilities of research, or the ignorance of society or particular groups.

Summary

Bringing different elements of reflexive practice together contributes to clarification, rather than obfuscation. Autobiographies, for instance, can be open to examination as an important aspect of research and not as a means for engaging in indulgent introspection. It is therefore possible to provide an insightful account of identity and the self using autobiographical material not as means for a confessional, but as a starting point for the development of a general account of self-identity being conducted in the service of positive social change (Griffiths 1995). The same impulse is evident in understandings of the self as a process of exclusion linked to class – without over-burdening it with too many expectations born of past frustrations with the failed promises of class analysis (Skeggs 2004).

Philosophical and socio-theoretical insights into research are sensitizing devices. Such accounts should not be abandoned wholesale, but continual caution should be exercised in their overextension into different domains of activity that rely upon each other for their legitimacy and efficacy. We seek boundaries around phenomena in order to act, but in so doing need to recognize that they do not exhibit simple separations or collapse into each other. Boundary work in the referential dimension of reflexivity can be difficult and requires effort on the part of all of those party to the interaction. At an endogenous level, striving for objectivity in social research requires a consciousness and form of practice, but it should not lead to reflexivity being deployed as an accusation of deficiency in which a person is told they are not 'reflexive enough' or 'where is your reflexive account', as if that were a guarantor of good work. These demands work as deficit models of practice by collapsing domains without any sense of mutual learning about what is meant and what can realistically be achieved in different contexts and according to what contents? Research is valuable for what it tells us about the world and that comes through what we can show for our efforts, not just our methodological or even philosophical arguments (Fay 2009).

Allowing ourselves to be overcome by theoreticism or adherence to particular methods when addressing such issues enables a continuation in the endogenous dimension of practice. At some level, however, we assume a relevance to our work and that there will be an audience for it. Our orientations are informed by contingency and a responsibility for what we say to others. With that responsibility comes a choice for what we are saying, how we are saying it and why we are doing so. To illuminate those choices is no different from what we take others (our audience) to need from the product of our efforts. We are then left with a central question:

> How is the space of possible and actual action determined not just by physical and social barriers and opportunities, but also by the ways in which we conceptualize and realize who we are and what we may be, in this here and now? (Hacking 2004: 287. Original italics)

In seeking to understand the dynamics, contents and contexts of our lives, we seek clarification *for* practice and through adherence to belief systems or by virtue of taking our environments for granted, action exhibits resolutions *in* practice. Reflexivity can be the unbearable grit in the oil of these relations. While calls to reflexivity may be seen as part of the recognition that we live in an ambivalent age, I have argued that this has the potential to translate into sterility and paralysis. We may recognize ambivalence, but that does not relieve practitioners of the need to consider whether that is a characteristic of the world itself and hence reflected in their practices, or the result of a disciplinary uncertainty that comes from an inward-looking, non-engaged, set of practices, which implicitly and explicitly overextend the discipline or draws its boundaries too narrowly. If the latter predominates, the balance tilts in favour of concentrating upon the mode of production and places a burden upon social research which it cannot fulfil. If the former, it confuses domains and relieves practitioners and audiences of the effort needed in reaching understanding and the possible consequence of knowledge for subsequent practices.

Research practice and reflections upon the research process fluctuate between these two domains. One is manifested in the 'kind of self-fascinated observation of the observer's writings and feelings' (Bourdieu in Bourdieu and Wacquant 1992: 72), while the other reproduces an epistemic superiority enabled by a scholastic point of view. In this history we have witnessed denials of professional and lay knowledge and celebrations of practical consciousness and epistemic superiority.

Equally, as will be argued in Part 3, variation in the attributed values of different knowledges can enable endogenous practices to remain relatively unaffected by any sense of engagement with those who are not within its boundaries.

The balance for renewal and engagement comes in a greater understanding of the relations between dimensions of reflexive practice. At the same time this necessitates scepticism with respect to ultimate foundations in order that knowledge is sensitive to change. We have no need to lapse into the futility of such an enterprise for that is what gives it a vitality, while world views will be deployed regardless of such writings as an instrument of power. It is important to be mindful that there are no shortages of those who speak in the name of a false universalism from the particularity of their positions, as well as those who speak in the name of a false relativism that celebrates a situatedness via its denial of relationalism and how we are linked up with each other and our environments.

A retreat into pure critique or scientism without engagement can be avoided in the service of 'epistemic gain' (Taylor 1992). In the process a movement towards greater adequacy without allusions to fixed ideas of what is true and false is possible. Rigour is not abandoned in the process. It is the working through of these implications, without a resort to the complacencies of either unity or fragmentation that is one of the most important issues facing the reconstruction of research practice. In this process there is no use in saying that some practices are interest-bound and thus no different from any other. More heat than light is generated by this and underlying it is nothing more than the desire to do science better than the scientists. The dimensions to help us understand practice then slip over into being a dichotomy rather than a continuum. As I have suggested, a deficit model of the subject then arises in which ignorance from lay people meets the knowledge of experts. It leads to feelings of frustration when dealing with the reception of knowledge that allow an implicit 'here is my solution, now show me the problem' mentality to prevail.

These expressions are the reserve of not only those for whom societal problems have technological solutions, but also those for whom ignorant publics should give way to superior understandings via a hypodermic model of knowledge transfer. Learning opportunities, in terms of different knowledges and their roles in society, are totally lost in such processes. More mundanely, what are also lost are understandings for the relations between knowledge and practice in life and what we can *and* cannot realistically expect of different endeavours in terms of their limits and potentials for our lives together.

5

POSITIONING AND BELONGING

In this chapter I wish to examine reflexivity in terms of the relations which exist between positioning and belonging. The overall purpose, as with the book as a whole, is to inform social scientific engagement with social life in order to explore the potential for illumination and social transformation. As throughout the book, I will seek to separate clarification for engagement, with assumed resolution in practice.

I am concerned here with an orientation that is informed by the division of reflexivity into the dimensions provided in Chapter 4. What I will be arguing here is that the oscillations that occur between those two senses of reflexivity also inhere within social life as a result of dynamic interactions between positioning and belonging. In addition, the ability and capability to conduct research and the extent to which it resonates with social life is informed by this relationship, hence its vitality in social life. Beth Perry and I will develop this in Part 3 when examining the institutional contexts and cultures of knowledge production within the university, a setting which directly informs positioning and belonging in research production and hence the content and potential consequence of the knowledge that is produced.

Belonging and Positioning

The consequence of social scientific analysis for action within the referential domain may be oriented by the question: 'How do we proceed?' A revelatory hypodermic does not exist such that the knowledge produced by research and subsequent practices is assumed to be aligned. There is no linear relationship. As discussed in Chapter 4, outcomes are matters of practical engagement between parties and may be influenced by factors that are not related to the research purpose, process and product. The catalysts for this lie not only in the encountering of conditions that appear intransigent to change, but also in positions and dispositions and ways of life, whereby journeys from the self to the other and back to the self, lead to reflections upon the taken-for-granted constitution of social life. The dimensions of the interaction order and the influence of wider forces are therefore of importance to this inquiry.

Following discussions in earlier chapters, it is acknowledged that this process may become a reactionary force that forms itself in opposition to the 'other'. Forms of nationalism and fundamentalism are two forces that seek to fix meanings through the repression of identities that are believed to threaten the bases of their existence (Bauman 1997; Calhoun 1995). While exclusion and violence may work to *stabilize* identities – as in the case of slavery – it is within dialogic conditions that the *formation* of identities is enabled (Joas 1998: 15): 'When we consult ourselves about who we are, that entails something more than the negative reflection on "who we are *not*". It is also a matter of autobiography: of things we know about ourselves, or the persons we believe ourselves to be' (A. Cohen 1994: 120. Original italics). How and under what conditions this takes place, with what effects in terms of the antagonisms and the spaces of opposition and dialogue that are created are open to examination.

An examination of the type proposed here asks what lies between disposition, action and social context? Social phenomena produce regular effects that exhibit clear patterns within social life and lead to particular consequences. These patterns are causal in the sense of being tendencies, rather than determining of all actions. A disposition that is informed by belonging to a social class, for instance, influences cultural affinities and forms of identity, but affects life chances by virtue of being positioned in particular ways, yet it is not determining of all persons who are part of a particular group or strata. Properties are those of the world in terms of the consequences they have for the actions of people and cannot be confused with models through which researchers seek to capture them.

Categorization is related to what is categorized. Categorization systems can display an ambiguity or openness; they can work to exclude and they can provide a mode of framing that allows for pre-reflexive assumptions to be operative that enables action and intervention. They are political and cultural productions (Bowker and Star 2002). To this extent a reflexive practice can be framed as standing guard against those who conflate the model of reality with the reality of the model and so allow clarification in the endogenous realm of scientific practice to unproblematically spill over into the referential realm. When objectivism is confused with objectivity we can be sure this is happening. The latter includes recognition of limits and a willingness to learn, while the former knows no bounds and does not submit itself to an interrogation of its presuppositions and the positions from which it arises. When researchers seek to position themselves as experts in the sense of having ready-made solutions to problems not yet identified, or when dialogue aimed at understanding contexts of action is absent, or when those who criticize the very practices that have institutionally enabled their utterances to be heard in the first place claim a privilege of insight without that recognition, we can be assured that the ambivalence that accompanies engagement in the referential realm is being eradicated at the alter of partial understandings.

I suggested in Chapter 4 that disappointment in the potential of knowledge to be 'applied' to resolve issues is a frequent reaction to this state of affairs. Equally, there are those who reside in the cosy slumbers of an elective affinity between their ideas and prevailing ideological justifications that allow their falsehoods to be perpetuated. Research practice, however, cannot live up to being a domain in which one rages against the world. Disappointment might be argued to have its place in life (Craib 1994), but recognition of ambivalence is also a mark of maturity (Ferrara 1998).

In these ways, the world has a tendency to remind us that it is richer than we can know at any one time. We discover this in our practices when we reach limits and are confounded by circumstances beyond our control. To shut down such considerations is to perform epistemic closure enabled by an impermeability, thereby representing a conflation that produces a distance from the world which, while necessary for analysis, so easily spills over into a denial of the reality of the world via indifference, arrogance or displays of 'irresponsible utopianism and irrealist radicalism' (Bourdieu 2007: 9). It assumes that 'being' may be reduced to 'knowing' in a universe where hermetically sealed practices are readily conflated through illegitimate overextension. The same mistake is repeated in reflective philosophies whose belief is 'that the thinking subject can absorb into its thinking or appropriate without remainder the object of its thought, that our being can be brought down to our knowledge' (Merleau-Ponty 1989: 62).

Recognition of these factors may witness retreat to specialized divisions of labour to increase a sense of well-being through belonging. That, in turn, relies upon being institutionally positioned in the first place to enable such a distance to be maintained. Nevertheless, the world does not simply conform to a silo mentality. Equally, in the face of radical diversity due to the absence of *any* structural effects in social life, what is there left for the social scientist to do but to describe fleeting cultural configurations that have disappeared before their descriptions are disseminated to a wider audience? Caught in a vortex of symbolism without referents, the time has arrived for the social scientist to seek alternative employment and for the potential of a positive reflexive practice to finally disappear without trace.

Aside from the world exhibiting certain tendencies and having consequences for individuals, groups and populations, particularly in times of crisis and upheaval where forces are unleashed (and we can be assured that it is the powerless who will be its victims), it is routinely taken by socio-economic forces to be a predictable place subject to manipulations in their name. Even if the world does not conform to such dominant expectations, governments appear to be predisposed to exercise their powers to mould reality to meet its needs as its tentacles have spread to saturate our lives.

It would be irresponsible in the face of such consequences to leave the terrain to those who are less reserved in their willingness to speak in the name of 'reality' based on nothing more than prejudice and unexamined presuppositions. To do so according to the idea that there will be a transparent relationship between individuals and the social processes in which they participate through the deployment of social scientific knowledge represents an idealist dream. It is extraordinary just how many academics remain frustrated by the refusal of others to listen to their apparently self-evident solutions. A retreat then takes place to the familiarity of the endogenous realm in which the joys of peer review, competition for research council grants and publication in an increasingly elite concept of 'appropriate outlets' as guarded by the bastions of quality assurance, editors and appropriated by publishing companies, reign supreme.

In terms of the dynamics of the relations between knowledge and action, researchers seek to bring to recognition forms of explanation that run on a continuum from the familiar to abstract and acceptable to contentious. Social transformation does not follow from the acceptance of unfamiliar and contentious findings, for several factors stand between reading, recognition, illumination and transformation. First, as noted, there is the power to ignore or dismiss on the part of those whose interests are not advanced by research findings. Second, 'scientific discourse misses the fact that the ability to deny is an amazing human phenomenon, largely unexplained and often inexplicable, a product of the sheer complexity of our emotional, linguistic, moral and intellectual lives' (S. Cohen 2001: 50). Third, power can work through a process of misrecognition whereby privilege is ascribed rather than achieved (Bourdieu 1992b). In reverse this works for the non-powerful: that is, systems of classification position people in particular ways and a dialectic exists between the classified and classification systems (Hacking 2004): 'Discerning how positioning, movement and exclusion are generated through these systems of inscription, exchange and value is central to understanding how differences (and inequalities) are produced, lived and read' (Skeggs 2004: 4).

Finally, if we deploy reflexivity as the capacity for engagement in this process, we should not overstretch this dynamic, nor reduce it to the exceptionality of character separate from culture via a romantic ideal. For a more nuanced understanding and to inform the belonging-positioning orientation, we need to subdivide reflexivity. It is one thing to recognize, it is another to be positioned in terms of being capable of taking insights forward in action. Therefore, we can think of forms of reflexivity in positioning-belonging in the following ways: communicative; autonomous; meta- and fractured. The first refers to those internal conversations that require external confirmation before resulting in action. The second refers to those who engage in such conversations which lead to actions without external validation. The third captures both a critical ability concerning internal conversations and the effectiveness of subsequent actions, while the last can lead to an intensification of uncertainty, rather than a clarity that informs subsequent actions (Archer 2007: 93). To these dimensions we should add the ability to possess sufficient self-esteem and coherence and understanding to engage in critical reflection, as well as how one is positioned in terms of the potential to take these forward into action.

Research findings lie against this background and so are contestable, while actions bring about different consequences that require new understandings. Understanding limits, as a condition of learning and regarding modesty as a positive attribute of research, makes sense because there are conditions beyond the control of agents, even if they were to agree upon the implications for actions of research and put those into practice. Recognition, in other words, should not be confused with assumed effects: for example, in relation to subsequent redistribution of resources (Fraser and Honneth 2003; McNay 2008) and as such, revelation does not automatically lead to transformation.

All of this adds up to producing research accounts that render not only recognition of actions, events, processes and conditions more likely, but how they might (and might not) contribute to potential transformation: 'Social regularities present themselves as probable chains of events that can only be combated, if this is deemed necessary, on condition of their being recognized' (Bourdieu 2008: 195). In these moments, we see the fusion of the 'who', 'what', 'where, 'how' and 'why'. That fusion has the greatest potential to occur in the oscillations that exist between belonging and positioning. In the following sections, I wish to elaborate upon this argument.

Persons and Positions

We are all situated within the socio-cultural milieux of which we are a part. We exhibit varying abilities to submit those to analysis, as well as to exercise a semi-transcendence in our practices that turns our actions and the conditions in which they take place into matters of contemplation. In the idea of habitus in Pierre Bourdieu's work, we find a link made between history and being in terms of 'socialized subjectivity'. As embodied in human beings, it is manifested in ways of talking, walking and making sense of the environment. Here we find a disposition that guides, but does not compel, situated reasons for practices. Parallels are evident here with Karl Mannheim's idea of *Weltanschauung* (world view). In his work we find recognition of being situated in a way that gives rise to certain values, while at the same time being a *mediated sphere* that provides the grounds for different forms of knowledge in the relations between existence and validity (Mannheim 1960).

In this sphere an investigation of the relationship between thought, social conditions and action takes place. In the process of discovery, the basis for understanding their interrelationships is made more manifest in terms of a situated objectivity (M. Williams 2005), not in order to escape from social conditions, but to create the space for reflections upon them in order that understandings and even possibilities for alternative forms of social existence then emerge. An emphasis upon analysis of relations within the social world in terms of how they bear upon knowledge and action informs accounts for justification of the ways in which the social world can be known. In such a project, Mannheim (1970) had a clear aim: 'to develop a theory, appropriate to the contemporary situation, concerning the significance of the *non-theoretical conditioning factors* in knowledge … Only in this way can we hope to overcome the vague, ill-considered, and sterile form of relativism with regard to scientific knowledge' (Mannheim 1970: 109. Italics added).

An admission of the issues associated with speaking of an external reality beyond particular standpoints does not surrender to relativism. Through the deployment of 'relationalism' we can see how all knowledge is at least partially true: 'It may be genuine or sincere, cynical or manipulative, but it is an authentic expression of the interests, experiences, concerns and circumstances of those in a particular social location' (J. Scott 1998: 111). A meeting between perspectival and relational understandings informs practical actions orientated towards the developmental implications of research. The link between knowledge produced by social scientific work and practice occurs in terms of rendering intelligible the constitution of our actions and those conditions that appear to be impediments to our understandings and aspirations.

I have suggested that endogenous reflexivity refers to an awareness of the knowledge that is born in and through the actions of members of a given community in terms of their contribution to social reality. The sphere includes an understanding not only of 'what' someone appears to be, but also of 'who' they are and 'how' others view them. It is at this point that research connects with everyday life. Particular approaches to reflexivity, as discussed in Part 1, can fail to address these issues and also ask what texts are influential upon actions and for what reasons and under what circumstances?

Suggesting in Chapter 4 that it is by our efforts as researchers that we will be judged and taking a broad definition of text as the 'production of a discourse as a work' (Ricoeur 1986: 219), we can ask to what extent interpretations then clarify conditions of actions. Any possible resolution, in the domain of reception, is a matter for the referential realm. The potential for individuals to achieve distanciation in relations between endogenous and referential reflexivity within a mediated sphere therefore requires investigation to better understand this process and its potential consequences. An endogenous project is implied here in terms of locating the means through which understanding is normally carried out, in relation to a referential component whereby attention is drawn to an explanation of the conditions in which actions occur via a meeting of perspectives. These components relate to the ability to monitor one's own actions, how one is positioned by others, the conditions in which actions take place and its consequences and potentials.

Introducing the idea of belonging enables an understanding of how the social world is experienced. The study of positioning enables the investigator to see where an individual is located from a relational viewpoint. Methodologically speaking, the focus then falls upon 'mediating concepts' between lay and social scientific knowledge:

> The mediating system we need is that of the *positions* (places, functions, rules, tasks, duties, rights, etc.) occupied (filled, assumed, enacted, etc.) by individuals, and of the *practices* (activities, etc.) in which, by virtue of their occupancy of these positions (and vice versa), they engage. (Bhaskar 1989: 40–1. Original italics)

Although it is the study of the relations between positioned-practices that is suggested here, the implications for this at the level of the individual will vary according to the differing dimension of reflexivity introduced earlier. Some relations are internal: 'such that the related being is what it essentially is by virtue of the relation' (Collier 1994: 150).

At this point we move away into the terrain of identity. Following Alessandro Ferrara, the following components are important for the fulfilment of individual identity: coherence, vitality, depth and maturity. Coherence refers to a narrative dimension in which it is possible for an individual to sum up the changes that have taken place during a lifetime. Sense of unity and cohesiveness are key here. Vitality refers to a sense of fulfilment in terms of progression towards who one wishes to be and is seen as being. Depth refers to the ability to have a sense of the constitutive elements that make up an identity, while maturity concerns the ability to come to terms with the facts of the world in relation to internality without compromise to coherence and vitality (Ferrara 1998: 80–107). To cut oneself from social dynamics in these relations is to starve oneself of these possibilities. To take account of these factors and their relations to research texts, 'belonging' is introduced in practice-positioned relations. Several points of clarification are required at this stage in the argument.

The fact that people are differentially positioned relates to their capacity to mobilize resources in order to position themselves. Positioning relates to situations of co-presence in the interaction order as so beautifully illustrated by the work of Erving Goffman (1984). A time–space dimension also exists that stretches from the familiarity of daily routines and is manifest in terms of its effects on the life-world and life chances through more abstract systems as discussed in relation to the insights of Simmel. However, remembering the continuing value of Michel Foucault's insights, how does this relate to a network of power relations? He would suggest that a call to reflexivity that focuses upon positioning-belonging according to an idea of the self introduced above is itself an exercise of power. While I agree that first having to submit to the norms of recognition we are being worked upon, it does not follow that we cannot then produce a critical distance in order to reflect upon our being at the 'borders of recognizability' (Butler 2002).

Introducing the above idea of the self in relation to belonging-positioning is deliberately designed to address a key question in this investigation: 'How can the growth of capabilities be disconnected from the intensification of power relations?' (Foucault 1984: 48). An understanding of illocutionary force in relation to position is required for this purpose. In the absence of such an analysis:

> efforts to find, in the specifically linguistic logic of different forms of argumentation, rhetoric and style, the source of their symbolic efficacy are destined to fail as long as they do not establish the relationship between the properties of discourses, the properties of the person who pronounces them and the properties of the institution which authorizes him to pronounce them. (Bourdieu 1992b: 111)

The capacity of the individual to position themselves along the dimension discussed above will relate to how they are accommodated within cultural views with respect to the dimension of belonging. Here we find a continuum from active embrace and implicit accommodation through to estrangement, hostility and violence. If positioned as dependent, a 'cry of pain is hearable as a plea of help'. On the other hand, if a person is positioned as dominant, 'a similar cry can be heard as a protest or even as a reprimand' (Harré and van Langenhove 1991: 396). To this extent positions delimit speech acts and also provide for pre-interpretations of what people say or do (Harré and Slocum 2003). At an individual level, this relates to the attributes that a person possesses within given constellations of social relations or, in Pierre Bourdieu's terminology, 'fields'.

Fields are those things that 'present themselves synchronically as structured spaces of positions (or posts) whose properties depend on their position within these spaces' (Bourdieu 1993: 72). A relation exists between habitus and field in terms of a 'fit' between the individual and social position. Habitus works to constitute the field as meaningful: 'a world endowed with sense and value, in which it is worth investing one's energy' (Bourdieu in Bourdieu and Wacquant 1992: 127). It follows that there is a two-way relation between the habitus and field: 'Social reality exists, so to speak, twice, in things and in minds, in fields and in habitus, outside and inside of agents' (Bourdieu in Bourdieu and Wacquant 1992: 127).

The capacity to act is linked to being accepted according to cultural definitions and those, in turn, relate to the attributes that are valued within given fields; all of which informs expressions *and* feelings of belonging. To the capacity to belong, therefore, must be added the power to position oneself. A person might, for example, be able to exercise sufficient power via their mobilization of resources without relying upon cultural expectations within a given social setting. Symbolic acceptance may not then follow and so material power is circumscribed in particular ways. To this extent, symbolic capital refers to sedimentations of

power within a field of relations, accumulated by past struggles, that grants recognition of a position and also a capacity to intervene in circumstances when that
is threatened (Bourdieu 2000).

There is no need to allude to consensus to understand this process, merely to
note that at given times and places an acceptance of particular definitions enables
our self-orientations in order to provide for a sense of belonging. Yet this must
also take account of how individuals are positioned in terms of existing power
relations and what their reactions and actions are in those contexts. In terms of
positioning, an alignment of the individual with the normal expectations extant
within a field of social relations provides for a doxic acceptance or 'ontological
complicity' (Bourdieu in Bourdieu and Wacquant 1992: 128). A misalignment,
on the other hand, leads to a 'Don Quixote effect' where 'practices generated by
the habitus appear ill-adapted because they are attuned to an earlier state of the
objective conditions' (Bourdieu 1986: 109).

Although Bourdieu is clear that the habitus is only activated and amenable to
study within fields, there is less elaboration in his work of the movement from
pre-reflexive doxic acceptance to endogenous reflexivity at the level of the
agent and from there to referential reflexivity. Without this in place a sense is
given that ontological complicity is overdetermining, despite his observation
that: 'Politics begins, strictly speaking, with the denunciation of this tacit contract of adherence to the established order which defines the original doxa'
(Bourdieu 1992a: 127).

To analyse this movement a consideration of the willingness that people
exhibit to be positioned in particular ways and how this relates to those elements of identity noted above, in terms of the dimensions of reflexivity, is
required. What we need is an elaboration of 'how the habitus is transformed
from pre-discursive doxa into reflexive, discursive consciousness' (Burkitt
1997: 194). As argued, we should avoid hermetically sealing off research from
social life by concentrating our energies on scientific practice and the 'oxymoron of *epistemic doxa*' (Bourdieu 1998a: 129. Original italics), by which is
meant those presuppositions that thinkers leave unthought in their practices.
On this topic – endogenous reflexivity within the social scientific community –
Pierre Bourdieu was at his best, most consistent and most provocative. As with
Michel Foucault, he embodied the attempt which is also being investigated in
these pages: 'to hold together autonomy of research and commitment to political
action' (Bourdieu 2008: 385).

Thinking, Acting and Text

As discussed earlier in the book, both the hermeneutic implications of Schutz's
(1979) postulate of subjective adequacy and the depth-hermeneutics of the
early Habermas (1989) are seen in Foucault's work to provide the regime of

truth with the role of final arbitrator. Yet problems arise in a wholesale rejection if seeking to address his question about power and capabilities. Here we need to further understand the relations between texts and actions and what implications they have for coming to know ourselves differently in the service of transformation. The point was made earlier that to avoid the idea of freedom and truth as simply being laid at the service of self-making, Foucault undertook a body of work that was placed in the service of a truth for self-making (Taylor 1986).

Hermeneutics has contributed a great deal to an understanding of the relationship between thinking, acting and text without resort to subject-centred reason. Take the study of 'technologies of the self'. Refusing a history of ideas and a social history as an artificial separation between the study of how people think without acting on the one hand and act without thinking on the other, he wrote: 'Everybody both acts and thinks. The way people act or react is linked to a way of thinking, and of course *thinking is related to a tradition*' (Foucault 1988: 14. Italics added). Conflicts between pressures to conform and act differently in various traditions illuminate how people might possess a different relationship to themselves through an alteration in their relationship to others. Here is the process through which self-consciousness is born and from these confrontations 'must issue a new relation of forces, of which the provisional profile will be a reform' (Foucault 1982a: 34).

Within the domain of everyday life both the ability and capability to conform and think and act differently arises. A study of this domain enables us to answer why: 'To the same situation, people react in different ways' (Foucault 1988:14)? Herein lies the possibility for producing referential spaces in which power does not play as 'evil' and through which we can explore the 'limits to appropriation of discourse' (Foucault 1991b). Foucault's (1982b) idea of agonism between freedom and power, such that the exercise of power presupposes a free subject, makes sense only 'if someone has several courses of action open but chooses the one congruent with the wishes of another. The capacity to choose in any meaningful sense requires the existence of a human will that is not merely an effect of discourse' (Flax 1991: 231).

To discover how and under what conditions people think and act differently requires an understanding of how people think of themselves, through others, as having particular attributes, values and characteristics, in relation to an explanation of the conditions that seek to constitute them as subjects and objects. To reiterate: in the argument presented here, it is how a person experiences their own identity and through interaction with others that endogenous reflexivity is born. From that point, through practical efforts of engagement, during times of abrupt changes in social conditions, or acts of refusal or exclusion, or being predisposed to comprehend the normal as well as pathological, referential reflexivity is born.

The beginnings of the means for this analysis are the modes through which language provides for powers of self-reference and expression in relation to social positioning. Between belonging, practice and positioning lies the key to referential reflexivity in terms of opening up the spaces for understanding and from there, potential transformation. A world of possibilities may be disclosed in a critique of the self-evident in relation to self-definition. In discussions of 'capitulated selves' or 'multifaceted selves', the question should be asked: how is it that the analyst has a vantage point for such reflections? The effect of distance is analytically advantageous; it can also produce knowledge that is hermetically sealed off from understandings within lifeworlds.

Social research, as conceived of here, is the systematization of an understanding of the relations between self and environment in the interactions between endogenous and referential reflexivity, without simple resort to ideas of exteriority–interiority. From this point of view, celebrations of contingency not only are an over-corrective to the idea of self as 'entity', but also effectively seal off reflexivity and render accounts of the potential for social transformation problematic, if not futile. These arguments represent the throwing out of 'the baby (subjectivity) with the bathwater (metaphysics)' (Madison 1995: 77). As commentators on the 'Death of the Subject' thesis have noted, there is a rich vein of knowledge to be found in past writings (Benhabib 1992: 218). An engagement with these writings may be avoided by believing that any reference to intersubjectivity necessarily reproduces subject-centred reason. Equally, to read off linguistic analysis as sufficient without an understanding of the structures of experience, or role of emotion in social life does not grant sufficient recognition to its experiential dimensions and how identities mutually interpenetrate and constitute themselves (Craib 1998).

What we see here is an antiseptic, endogenous outlook spilling over into what then becomes a referentially barren terrain. Illumination, as well as potential transformation, is bracketed. The consequence is that research becomes a self-serving activity at the level of endogenous reflexivity. Not only can social scientists then forget how they are positioned themselves, but also when it comes to perpetuating such ideas on the self:

> Those who flaunt the most radical denials and repudiations of selected facets of modern identity generally go on living by variants of what they deny. Thus … defenders of the most antiseptic procedural ethic are unavowedly inspired by visions of the good, and neo-Nietzscheans make semi-surreptitious appeal to a universal freedom from domination. (Taylor 1992: 504)

Without an understanding of belonging, theorizations of the self produce those antiseptic accounts that do not resonate with everyday experiences and render the results of social scientific investigations sterile. Resonate – not simply reflect. It concerns having a 'point of view' which is needed when meeting the results of research as being 'a point of view on points of view' (Bourdieu 2004). It is about the singularity of one's experience which is constituted in the knowledge that this is not an isolated position as such, but knowledge generated in the dialectical relations that exist between sameness and selfhood (Ricoeur 1994).

At this point a gap often appears. Here is where positioning and belonging play their part. The study of fields enables an examination of the relations into which individuals enter and are then positioned in particular ways and with what consequences. As Foucault notes of 'statements', we should not so much analyse the relations between a speaker and what they say, but 'what position can and must be occupied by any individual if he is to be the subject of it' (Foucault 1989a: 96). The problem then arises in constituting identity solely in terms of positioning. Such ideas need to be supplemented by the experience of that positioning, as belonging or not belonging and with what effects? Attention is then called to a need to understand the subjective and intersubjective realms of human relations. It is this, as a starting but not finishing point, that allows social scientific knowledge to resonate with everyday understandings and so generate new interpretations with the potential for social transformation.

The ability to choose is related to the capacity to bring about the results of that choice. A study of this heightens an understanding of the relations between knowledge, social action and positioning. The study of positioning enables one to see how the agent either has, or does not have, the capacity to act in terms of the knowledge possessed – of self, of others and of the conditions under and through which they act, or are prevented from acting, in particular ways. Thus, the movement from practical to discursive knowledge is bound up with the relations between belonging and positioning. An analysis of both components of agency then follows: a capability to act and the ability to understand action in relation to social identity.

A paradox exists in resorting to the idea of an ego for illuminating this second dimension to agency for it leads to the conclusion that 'the self that seeks is the self that is sought' (Harré 1998: 12). The problems associated with a resort to the analytic philosophy of language to overcome this issue have been noted. Paul Ricoeur's (1994) approach to these issues enables us to see the tensions between sameness and selfhood that, as argued, constitute the basis for research to resonate with the experiences of everyday life, as set against the constraints and opportunities available for people to realize their potentials, limits and experience exclusion and even violence.

Acts of self-consciousness and self-monitoring, in expressions of belonging and in reflections upon actions, need not resort to the idea of the self as unproblematic entity. Those dimensions to self-identity outlined earlier may be seen as the ability 'to give discursive accounts of and commentaries upon what we perceive, how we act and what we remember' (Harré 1998: 12). Yet less this collapse into yet another linguistic move to eradicate ambivalence at the level of the individual, the emotional intersubjectivity that Merleau-Ponty alluded to plays its role. In other words: 'First we feel, and then later we learn to speak about our feelings' (Craib 1998: 174).

An understanding of this process in relation to positioning provides for a study of how limits and exclusions are practised (Foucault 1989b: 73). What is revealed are the experiences, in terms of the consequences, of being positioned in particular ways. The question posed of ourselves at this level is: 'Who am I?' (Ricoeur 1994: 118). Here the singularity of our experience is of prime concern and is ordered by reference to our bodies. How commitments to self-definition relate to positioning in given contexts is an empirical matter. The important point for the purposes of the argument being constructed here is that the asking of 'who' questions does not necessitate resort to a unity of self, nor does the fragility of this sense of self necessitate a collapse into celebrations of contingency and multiplicity.

This sense of selfhood – Ricoeur calls it 'ipseity' – derives from where one is located and the events in which one is a part. It is the articulation of a sense of self in time. Rom Harré expresses it in the following manner:

> My field of awareness, though centred in a singularity, is a complex structure of relations to my environment, past present and future ... To be one and the same person my point of view must be continuous relative to an all encompassing material framework, including the world of other embodied beings. (Harré 1998: 91)

It concerns the position of the speaker in relation to other things in the social universe, as well as being a performative utterance in the sense of being someone who is trustworthy. Thus, not only does it enable an understanding of the location of the embodied speaker, but also it is the means through which responsibility is taken for being positioned. An ethical dimension to selfhood thereby prevents the simple absorption of self-identity into social identity in the study of positioning. It allows for a sense of continuity in the self over time that can lead to the disjuncture that Pierre Bourdieu (1986) calls the 'Don Quixote' effect.

To steer a middle course between 'epistemic exaltation' of the self that is evident in Cartesian formulations and its 'humiliation' in the hands of Nietzsche, Ricoeur's idea of the self employs the term 'attestation' to denote the kind of certainty that is appropriate at this level: 'Whereas doxic belief is implied in the grammar "I believe-that", attestation belongs to the grammar of "I believe-in"' (Ricoeur 1994: 21). Clearly, this can lead to a resort to the kind of guarantees reminiscent of the Cartesian problematic. It is the contingency of the questioning itself, however, that prevents such resort by providing vulnerability via a 'permanent threat of suspicion'.

Before collapsing into ideas of self-annihilation, we find the relationship between attestation and testimony expressed as *credence*. As we are concerned with reliable attestation so we move into the realm of trust:

> attestation is fundamentally attestation *of* self ... attestation can be defined as the *assurance of being oneself acting and suffering*. This assurance

remains the ultimate recourse against all suspicion; even if it is always in some sense received from another, it still remains *self*-attestation. It is self-attestation that, at every level – linguistic, praxic, narrative, and prescriptive – will preserve the question 'who?' from being replaced by the question 'what?' or 'why?'. (Ricoeur 1994: 22–3. Original italics)

In this sense the keeping of a promise challenges time, via a denial of change, despite an alteration in social conditions: 'even if my desire were to change, even if I were to change my opinion or inclination, "I will hold firm"' (Ricoeur 1994: 124). Here we find the oscillations between personal and social identity via self-attestation that leads to the first moment of endogenous reflexivity. Nevertheless, to commence the link to the possibility of referential reflexivity within everyday life, requires a sense of self that refers to the question of 'what' in terms of possessing a set of attributes, 'how' those attributes are viewed by others and 'why' this relates to positioning.

There is a sense of self that refers to 'an ever-shifting set of attributes that characterizes a person at any one time' (Harré 1998: 5). It is not the same as the 'self' as *point* of view, but is an expression of 'person with attributes' in the form: 'proper name + object name' to 'characterize oneself as the owner of an object, an attribute' (Harré 1998: 28). Here we find a sense of self-esteem and self-definition being fundamentally connected to an enacted environment for the realization or frustration of the additions of points of view and attributes. Therefore, consideration must now be given over to the impressions others have of these shifting sets of attributes, as well as the referential context in relation to how and why positioning plays a role.

A misalignment or alignment between point of view, attributes, actions and context, may exist. One may wish to belong, but attributes and/or points of view are in disjuncture to symbolic acceptance. Having a point of view of 'who' one is, relates to what one 'does', how it is performed and how others value one's contribution and opinions. This is the sum of impressions that others have of us in terms of our changing patterns of dispositions and attributes. These local and variable presentations of the self are 'drawn from a culturally available repertoire' (Harré 1998: 87). Although there may be an ontological complicity at work, as Pierre Bourdieu suggests, we often find oscillations and ambivalences between a point of view, a set of attributes and how the enacted social environment accords, or does not accord, with a sense of belonging in being accepted or rejected. Endogenous reflexivity comprises these oscillations between personal and self-identity that are derived in interactions with others.

Erving Goffman (1984) appears to capture this sense of self in his observations on everyday interactions. He terms 'role distance' the process whereby the norms of a role are given within a social setting, but the manner of its performance is variable:

> The manner in which the role is performed will allow for some 'expression' of personal identity, of matters that can be attributed to something that is more embracing and enduring than the current role performance and even the role itself, something, in short, that is characteristic not of the role, but of the person. (Goffman 1974: 573)

Yet this relation is variable and as a result: 'One can never expect complete freedom between individual and role and never complete constraint' (Goffman 1974: 269). However, to explain this, what is the space for selfhood? We need to characterize this as a series of tensions produced between the questions stated earlier: 'Who am I?', 'What attributes do I possess?' and 'How do others see me?'

While a sense of self as 'essence', as both Jacques Derrida and Michel Foucault argued, is constituted by the exclusion of a negative, they invoke their work as a guard against complacency. One was to emphasize the inevitability of undecidability to guard against finality, while the other would not see their work as being informed by consensus, but stood against non-consensus. What is being argued here is that an idea of the self stands neither as static nor infinitely variable. Ultimately, to invoke ideas of ourselves means a journey through others. Our singularity is made up through the invocation of others via a gallery of character interactions, typifications and expectations. In terms of their space–time content, they run from familiarity through acquaintance due to proximity to descriptions via inference. Acts of self-identification require discursive resources that are drawn from one's environment: *'The assessment of the maxim of one's intention, as these embody moral principles, requires understanding the narrative history of the self who is the actor; this understanding discloses both self-knowledge and knowledge of oneself as viewed by others'* (Benhabib 1992: 129. Original italics).

There is dialectic at work in identity (not in the Hegelian sense of the term) between sameness and selfhood. The keeping of a promise, as someone who is trustworthy, may produce a disjuncture between selfhood and social identity. The idea of the self presented here tackles the issues surrounding 'calendar' and 'internal' time via an 'ability to integrate an account of the self within the context of a larger temporal framework' (Rasmussen 1996: 17). Self-monitoring activity is then amenable to understanding via narrative accounts.

The self is socially located and may become dislocated as well. To move us from the self to issues associated with both dimensions of reflexivity requires a journey into positioning. While the absence of an understanding of intersubjectivity distorts the daily experience of social life, the idea of intersubjectivity should not collapse into continual intersubjectivity (Joas 1998), as is clear from the distinctions drawn above. Character, culture and conditions come together, but do not simply collapse into each other. That much is evident from the individual moral judgements and acts of political courage that are littered throughout history – what Ricoeur refers to as 'holding firm'. Struggles for recognition are about the creation of spaces for having a voice and are concerned with 'the politics of moral geography and, as in all delicate environments, when the weather changes for some, sooner or later it changes for all who inhabit the territory' (Lemert 1997: 129). The task is to map that territory and its consequences. Equally, there is more to identity politics than 'being', there is the question of what is 'done'?

In terms of the relations between where one is positioned and the possibilities that are held open for the future, we return to an earlier question in this chapter: 'How do we proceed?' Now we are dealing with the relations between ontology of what exists and an ethic of development. In the introduction to this chapter, types of reflexivity were noted that related not only to a person's ability and insight, but also to their being able to bring into being their aspirations, perhaps through an alignment of their dispositions with positions. Here we encounter the issues of how positions within fields are presented not only synchronically, but also diachronically in terms of their tendency to reproduce particular individual and group 'trajectories'.

These tendencies relate to the distribution of types of capital that are mobilized in the struggles that take place within particular fields. There are those whose actions contribute to conservation (orthodoxy) and those who engage in strategies of heresy. Not only is the power to confer meaning upon objects, attributes and characteristics (symbolic capital), but also there are the skills and knowledges that people possess within a particular field (cultural) and their differential access to wealth and material resources (economic capital). A study of strategies and tactics within fields then enables an explanation of not only where, how and why people are positioned in particular ways, but also what forms of capital constitute the field itself and with what consequences?

To explain this process it is necessary to move beyond the realms of subjectivity and intersubjectivity and make links between personal identity, self-identity, agency and power. Mapping the territory in terms of the relations of power that constitute a field enables one to see the spaces within which referential reflexivity may be born. How are these spaces to be delimited such that critical distanciation in the form of referential reflexivity may be achieved? It is within the examination not only of who and what, but also of how and why? Positioning tends to deal with the latter in order to inject a relationalism that does not collapse into celebrations of situated subjectivity or relativism and as such, tends to be extensive, rather than intensive, in the domain of reception.

In analysing relations of power Michel Foucault wrote of the need to examine specific rationalities, as opposed to invoking an over-arching idea of rationalization. He took this to be a more empirical approach that was attuned to contemporary society: 'Rather than analyzing power relations from the point of view of its internal rationality, it consists of analyzing power relations through the antagonism of strategies' (Foucault 1982b: 210–11). When doxic appearance is ruptured in these antagonisms, the question of whether any resulting resistance is transformative is raised. It then becomes necessary to move into the terrain of explanation in terms of the conditions under which actions are performed, as well as the limitations that are placed upon forms of power. How this relates to structured antagonisms is a focus of empirical interest. The question is how might a form of analysis proceed that seeks to examine the forms and limits of power relations in order to unleash the potential for transformation in the referential realm of research activity? In the next section, I outline an approach to this issue drawing upon the above arguments.

Logics of Routine and Transgression

Roberto Unger makes a distinction between the logics of routinization and transgression. He characterizes these as 'trance' and 'struggle' respectively (Unger 1987: 205). To employ this distinction enables a sense in which there is a 'fit' with objective conditions (Bourdieu), or agonism between freedom and power (Foucault), or a dialectical tension between sameness and selfhood (Ricoeur). Bearing in mind the points made in relation to oscillations and ambivalences within the self, including among social scientists in terms of the apparent promises of their disciplines, we often act according to two different logics:

> We behave as if we were the passive objects of the formative institutional and imaginative contexts of our societies and the victims or beneficiaries of the tendencies and constraints that shape these frameworks of social life ... however, we sometimes think and act as if our pious devotion to the practical or argumentative routines imposed by these structures has been just a ploy, to be continued until the propitious occasion for more open defiance. (Unger 1987: 202)

In turning outwards towards the environmental conditions that are studied, an understanding of the unstable relations which exist between the logics of routinization and transgression is required. In exploring transgressions within the lifeworld, so too must research communities be open to innovation by turning those tools of investigation back onto themselves. After all: 'The logic of context breaking persists as an inconvenient residue in even the most routinized social situations' (Unger 1987: 203). Attention to this aspect enables us to face the weaknesses which result from the one-sidedness of so many calls to greater reflexivity:

> The Cartesian claim to a 'view from nowhere' is to be avoided not just by invocation of the excluded other, nor even by the location of subjects within the realm of concrete experience and social relations, but by the recognition of tension that opens up the possibility of critique and change. (Calhoun 1995: 187)

Here we find a project taking place without allusion to simple certainties or celebrations of fragmentation.

People vary in their willingness to be positioned in specific ways, as well as how they are positioned. An analysis of acts of refusal and resistance must be related to the above points in terms of the capability to be effective in such aspirations; all of which permits a study of limits of appropriation to expose false necessities. Logics of routinization are frequently invoked in the service of tidy descriptions of social relations in both modernist *and* postmodernist accounts. Transgressions become the uncomfortable residues that must be subsumed under generalized accounts. To collapse routinization and transgression, as well as degrees of willingness into objective locations, is to commit the fallacy of the capitulated self. Presuppositions of homogeneity within cultural traditions, invoking ideas of multifaceted selves with no point of view, or the totalizing capacity of power, are three routes towards this end.

A lapse into a celebration of everyday practices to the exclusion of the ways in which such practices are themselves constrained, as well as enabled, by the conditions in which they are enacted is not a way forward. What is being suggested is that the study of positioning and belonging in relation to practice enables an understanding not only of endogenous reflexivity, but also of the spaces for referential reflexivity which, it must be emphasized, requires effort aimed at understanding. By producing social scientific accounts employing the ideas on the self outlined above, alongside explanations of the conditions that give rise to positioning, the potential for transformations in social practices are opened up.

The task is to assist research in illuminating those areas of struggle that inhere in everyday circumstances via a fusion of what has been termed the critical and pragmatic stances (Bénatouïl 1999). In terms of the ethos of social science a critical, but engaged, practice may then be arrived at in the fusion of endogenous and referential reflexivity and from there, a greater resonation with the struggles that go on within everyday life and with that, the potential for social transformation.

A two-stage critique is implied. First, there is an immanent critique from the point of view of the internal relations between identity, experience and actuality. Second, there is a movement towards transcendence by opening up the possibility for change via building upon the ambivalences and oscillations within the former through revealing how particular conditions inform actions and aspirations. Studying the relations between positioning and belonging enables us to examine how it is possible to move beyond the current constraints on potentiality imposed by existing configurations of power relations. It enables us to see ourselves and modes of relating to one another in different ways. Therefore, explanatory power is obtained from the relationship between an understanding of social actions, including the points of view and attributes of those involved and how they are seen by others, in relation to the explanation of conditions under which those actions take place. To repeat, however, this is a practical task and not a taken-for-granted element of the outcomes of research.

These two elements comprise sense and reference without collapsing into scientism. The relationship between the empirical, actual and real is brought forth in terms of the possibilities for transformation given through an explanation of the relations between actions, aspirations, dispositions and the conditions through which they are enacted. A process of re-cognition does not imply that self-consciousness of the relations between actions and social conditions is a given, it is a task that seeks to illuminate how our conceptions of the world are themselves social and historical products and so amenable to transformation. In acts of interpretation issues are then disclosed in such a way that they are recognized. We may then enter into a process of social becoming in which actualities and potentialities are linked across time (Sztompka 1991).

By linking through time and across space, research will stretch away from the individual. Many methodological writings have been devoted to this issue and closing the gap between extensive and intensive accounts of social life. Those include the idea that accounts should be not only intelligible, but also agreed upon by the individuals who have been part of the investigations, as if that alone guaranteed validity. Equally, in terms of the former, I have noted there is the assumption that this is resolved through a commitment to technicism derived within the endogenous realm of the scientific community.

The critical and hermeneutic can be brought together. The abstractions often associated with the former become rooted in the idea of tradition that is associated with the latter, while also correcting for a tendency to resort to tradition to locate meaning. The transitive and intransitive are brought together in terms of the potential for transformation. What operates at this level, employing the above ideas on the self in relation to explanations of conditions of action, lies between reflections upon tradition and the anticipation of freedom. It plays upon the strengths of both ideology critique and hermeneutics (Ricoeur 1981). Social becoming sees acts of retrospection informing present action and thus viewing the potential for difference as a projection into the future. Retrospection acts as a check upon simple allusions to transcendence, while at the same time revealing misunderstanding and the potential for greater understanding in the future as a check upon the status quo.

The issue is reformulated in terms of the 'inner life of hermeneutics' as a dialectic: 'between the experience of belonging and alienating distanciation' (Ricoeur 1981: 90). In the process the deception that lies in 'the alleged antinomy between an ontology of prior understanding and an eschatology of freedom is revealed' (Ricoeur 1981: 100). We can certainly agree with Michel Foucault when he wrote:

in saying that we are much more recent than we believe is not a way of placing all the burden of our history on our shoulders. Rather, it puts within

the range of work which we can do to and for ourselves the greatest possible part of what is presented to us as inaccessible. (Foucault 1982a: 35)

Summary

We cannot overburden reflexivity as an idea that does not require a commitment to engagement with all the practical difficulties that means. Such commitment is not only for researchers, but also for those who are party to the
research, but the resources needed for such a purpose will vary. Nor should
reflexivity be deployed as yet another sword against which to slash at our inadequacies. There is much pleasure to be gained and needs to be met through an
absence of reflexivity and positive feelings of belonging from a suspension of its
exercise. However, when this is constituted through the exclusion of the 'other',
we easily see how struggles for recognition spill over into a demand enacted
through exclusion and attribution, with unpleasant and sometimes disastrous
consequences.

There are more mundane and exclusionary mechanisms in operation. They are
not so spectacular in gaining the public eye: for example, the relations between
the informal and formal in organizational life, sports clubs and social gatherings.
To bring attention to the process that constitutes such exclusions is to risk further
ostracization or meet with denial. The limits to referential reflexivity will then
inhere in a studied indifference towards the plight of the excluded by those
whose positions have been afforded by processes that are now seen to be in question. One can see this very clearly in the clashes between social and environmental sustainability that exist between rich and poor countries.

Selected repudiations of that which constitutes the ability to act seem, from
the outsider's point of view, nothing more than the exercise of bad faith by
those who have enjoyed the advantages of particular positions. We can go
further and say that it is the positioning enabled by those very conditions,
informed by a fit between self and environment, that has permitted distance in
the first instance. Distanciation is achieved by a set of pre-reflexive conditions
which, for many people in different positions, are the objects of necessity in
managing their day-to-day existences.

The symbolic forms that place value upon the points of view and attributes of
persons within the intersubjective world work in an objective sense. I mean by this
that they not only refer to particular objects, but also place certain evaluative
meanings upon those objects, characteristics and attributes from which individuals
draw in order to make sense of their environments. As noted, the 'Who?', 'What?'
and 'How?' can lie within a congruity of meaning or, as Bourdieu puts it, ontological complicity. The Don Quixote effect is apparent not only in movements
between fields, but also in actions which challenge the meanings that constitute
fields of relations.

Individuals experience existential concern in the dialectic between sameness and selfhood either through their attempts to change those conditions which may persist despite such actions, or by having change imposed in such a way that states of flux and uncertainty result. The process of organizational change is one example whereby previous attributes that were valued may no longer be held in the same esteem. Relations of power are then altered by 'technicians of transformation' (May 1999, 2006) with the result that individuals may no longer feel valued, but evaluated. To study relations of power requires that the resources that are mobilized within a field are explained in relation to an understanding of belonging, as well as positioning.

In illuminating such issues I have suggested that the findings of social science will inevitably vary in how they resonate with the experiences of everyday life. They will not simply reflect, but could become a vantage point from which to consider a retrospective–prospective link in terms of their implications for action. Without some connection, calls to reflexivity and the potential for transformation are devoid of substance. However, there is no necessary relationship between this illumination and transformation. In considering spaces of dialogue and potential in which research findings and their potential implications are considered, there is a fundamental feature of the social world that we encounter in our actions and forms of analysis: the interplay between the processual and structural. Here the referential dimension of reflexivity may be seen to inform the endogenous dimension through a movement from practical to discursive reasoning. This encompasses a movement from reflexivity within actions towards reflexivity upon actions in terms of an understanding, via an encounter whose implications cannot be written in advance.

Where discussions of validity and reliability occur within academic communities, so too should discussions of reception according to this background, for that guards against endogenous reflexivity speaking in the name of the referential dimension. This is the inevitable tension that arises in the sense in which 'belongingness' is not the same as 'positioning', for that would be to assume symbiosis between a feel of place and the capacity to act. This is not to suggest that this does not happen, but it is to suggest that their relations are open to empirical inquiry. In contemporary times, it seems, this understanding is being filled by measures of research 'outcome', 'output' and 'impact'.

I have argued that the practice of social research should be the systemization of links between personal and self-identity and the enacted environment. Endogenous reflexivity is born in the first movement from personal to social identity as a journey of oneself through others. The second movement, however, to the enacted environment, while rooted within the systemization of this relationship, is not reflective of it. Referential reflexivity is not just a reflection of everyday life, but begins with that experience. The end point is a more extensive one and comprises a work of understanding in how actions and dispositions are constrained or enabled by environments and how those environments are also produced and reproduced by actions.

PART 3

CONTEXT

WRITTEN WITH BETH PERRY

6

THE POLITICAL ECONOMY OF KNOWLEDGE:
RELEVANCE, EXCELLENCE AND REFLEXIVITY

The discussions in Part 2 of the book introduced degrees of epistemic permeability in disciplines, referential and endogenous reflexivity and positioning–belonging. Researchers in academic settings exhibit differences in their senses of belonging, as well as how they are positioned in their institutions and position themselves in respect to the knowledge they produce, disseminate and represent. Oscillations occur between engagement in the spirit of the public intellectual or the lone researcher or group and the idea of the scholar as detached observer. Underlying and informing these dynamics are varying degrees of epistemic permeability which, in turn, are informed by how different forms of knowledge are valued in society.

The aim of this chapter is to discuss these shifts in knowledge production and how they manifest themselves in different contexts and with what implications for how knowledge is seen in society. Having looked at these changes at the level of political economy, in Chapter 7 we supplement this discussion on positioning in relation to the university as an institution of knowledge production. We then move on in Chapter 8 to look at belonging through the lenses of the dynamics of cultures of production. We seek, therefore, to provide an understanding of the pressures on modes of knowledge production in the so-called 'knowledge society' and how those are mediated through different political, economic and institutional contexts. In so doing we seek those spaces of potential in which the distinction of the social research that is produced in universities may be distinguished in the face of those forces that seek to undermine its independent insights.

At the level of theory-development and policy expectations, profound shifts can be identified in how knowledge is conceptualized and treated and the assumptions made for its potential transformative effects on modes of production. Transformations are presumed to occur on the basis of having an effect upon epistemic permeability that then open up forms of knowledge to external pressures, leading to revised modes of knowledge production. At the level of practice, political-economic, cultural and institutional contexts combine to mediate external pressures that vary from the preservation of the status quo to having profound consequences for how and why knowledge is produced. These factors, along with positioning and differing levels of attributed value being accorded to forms of knowledge, all inform the context in which the position and disposition of academics is forged.

The relationship between the discourse, the person and the institution which authorizes them is of interest in this respect. Rhetorical allusion becomes powerful when aligned with institutional position. In this way:

> the ubiquity of rhetoric, indeed, is unlimited. Only through it is science a sociological factor of life, for all the representations of science that are directed beyond the mere narrow circle of specialists (and, perhaps one should say, insofar as they are not limited in their impact to a very small circle of initiates) owe their effectiveness to the rhetorical element they contain. (Gadamer 1977: 24)

The Pursuit of Knowledge for Competition

Knowledge has always played an important role in relation to the constitution of social, cultural and political identity and been attributed with varying powers and value. From the early relationships between universities and different ecclesiastical or monastical orders to the roles played by students in the European socio-political revolts of the 1960s, the relationship between intellectual institutions and the development, enhancement and critique of society has been close. Any history of ideas shows periods of greater or lesser circulation of influence between the direction of research and broader societal developments. As such, popular accounts of knowledge as produced within 'ivory towers' not only are anachronistic but also have arguably never been entirely accurate. Take, for instance, the close relationship between industry and the growth of universities in the United States in the early twentieth century, or the unprecedented amounts of public expenditure directed towards strategic science priorities in the periods preceding and after the Second World War (Guston 2000; Newfield 2003). What we see emerging, however, is not the idea that relationships with industry are new, but a particular type of relationship with different sets of expectations (E. Thompson 1970).

Given the discussion in Part 1 of the book, a need exists to become more sensitive to the continuities that inform current knowledge-based trajectories as much as historical ruptures. In respect to physical scientific activities, for instance, we need to guard against those who present them as unitary activities, as if values and choices have not always been present in their activities (Canguilhem 2007; Pickstone 2000). Yet despite the contestability of popular discourses on the glories of a past autonomous age, there remains a traditional image of the individualized lone scholar pursuing largely independent research trajectories as a product of the exceptional and isolated mind.

Universities have never been simply protected or insulated from broader social, economic or political forces but despite this, attributing 'usefulness' to disciplines is highly problematic (Graham 2005). Relative to other institutions, social tolerance and acceptability of the uniqueness and privilege of their place in society has been valued in popular consciousness, albeit often latent and unarticulated. In the European context the Second World War provided a specific catalyst to public acceptance of the autonomy of the university as a result of the misappropriation and colonization of science by malevolent political forces. What we find, therefore, is a degree of acceptance around a view of *relative* academic autonomy and the unique position of knowledge as pertaining to a tolerated yet elite set of cultural practices, right up until the late twentieth century.

A different set of assumptions emerged from the late 1980s and early 1990s onwards, even taking the above point about continuity and change into consideration. The speed and integration of previously disparate political-economic trajectories now began to produce particularly vivid and articulated accounts of the social and economic role of knowledge. The Cold War came to an end, heralding the possibility for new political and economic alliances to be forged. The European Community was moving ahead with the Single European Market, including the removal of barriers to movement of trade, goods and services. Conservatism in the UK led to an entrenched neo-liberalism taking hold that subsequently came to influence and penetrate middle-ground European social democratic ideologies (Marquand 2004). Globalization was accompanied by the formation of regional trading blocs, such as the Southern Common Market ('Mercosur') or the North American Free Trade Agreement and economic relations began to first replace and then constitute new political ones.

Like any premised break-point, the date is inevitably slightly arbitrary, for the roots of these shifts can be traced back throughout and before the twentieth century – yet it is around this time that global trends began to constitute new political and economic discourses around knowledge. Then along came the armies of the representatives of globalization, including academics, who were to limit the political in the name of an apparently unproblematic idea of the 'economy' (Cameron and Palan 2004). Once again, only this time for different reasons, choice and value evaporated in the naturalization of global competition.

For developed countries the combination of neo-liberalism and globalization led to concerns about competition from developing economies. The discourse of the 'knowledge economy' began to be consolidated, drawing on work from the 1970s and subsequent analyses of the implications for competitiveness of a post-Fordist, post-industrial economy. As global capital has little affiliation in its frenetic search for profit, so manufacturing began to move to developing countries, leading to questions over new forms of production and consumption. Deregulation and a lessening of control of markets within nation-state boundaries led to a separation of industrial capital and the circulation of private, money-capital with a resulting deterritorialization (D. Harvey 2006; Lash and Urry 1987).

Writers on the subject of the 'knowledge economy' have tended to locate the origins of its name in the influential work of Daniel Bell (Allen 2000; Bryson 2000; Scarborough 2001). *The Coming of Post-Industrial Society* (Bell 1973) charts the perceived shift from manufacturing to a less tangible world of services and information. According to this argument, we see a move along a path towards a post-industrial economy in which the singular driving feature is knowledge and in particular, codified abstract knowledge (Allen 2000). Accounts of the knowledge economy tend to congregate around a single point: the most important source of competitive advantage is now knowledge. Putting it simply, the 'new' economy is based on creating, doing things to or with knowledge (Bryson et al. 2000; Castells 1996).

A set of key assumptions underpin the 'new' – or at the very least, strengthened – knowledge paradigm. Knowledge is viewed as a panacea to specific economic problems, with a strong instrumental and strategic role. We cannot simply see science as a practice being produced in the service of interest-free illumination, or even emancipation, but bound up with the very reproduction of the economy. Knowledge more generally now becomes a tool which can be appropriately wielded to produce competitive advantage. To achieve this aim, it is to be harnessed, codified, managed and stored. The commodification of knowledge and its translation into direct economic advantage becomes paramount, as does the ability to measure, define and demonstrate success in knowledge hierarchies through metrics and league tables of innovative output in the struggle for economic-symbolic advantage. Universities and their members are not immune from this process. What we then witness is the continued search for the unattainable in the name of the intangible. To question this process is to constitute oneself as one who does not understand the self-evidence of 'necessity'.

Accompanying this neo-liberal economic discourse is another, less popularized, debate concerning the 'knowledge society'. Here similar assumptions are made about the potential solutions or fixes offered by knowledge to societal problems. While seemingly offering a more civic or social view of the role of knowledge, popular conceptualizations of the knowledge society still trace an economic output logic in terms of more education = better skills = economic competitiveness. This is reflected in policy statements regarding the learning society, lifelong learning or widening participation in higher education. A second element to this debate, however, is less instrumentally driven, in terms of the changing role of knowledge, evidence and expertise in policy-making itself (S. Turner 2003). This has led to greater integration of 'experts' into governance systems across a range of policy fields – though whether this is the result of an increasing recognition of the importance of accurate evidence-based policy, or the result of processes of de-politicization and technocratization of decision-making is varied.

Academic work is critical of these developments and also complicit in their reproduction as it affords its own competitive advantage for those of its producers. Critique and analysis stems from within different schools of thought: from political science and state theory (Jessop 2000) to sociology (Hirst and Thompson 1999), social studies of science and technology (Fuller 2000), economists who work as the conscience of their profession (Galbraith 1992; Sen 1997) and economic geography (Gibson-Graham 1996; Leyshon et al. 2003). Such accounts tend to take issue with assumptions over the idea of preference as the motivation for human interest; flows of knowledge and its alleged gaseous or ubiquitous nature; the 'stickiness' or 'embeddedness' of knowledge within particular contexts or places; the relationship between competing policy objectives for cohesion as well as competitiveness; or the relationship between knowledge as a public good and its attributed market value.

The extent to which such critiques inform policy discourses is limited. Policy rhetoric has remained largely insensitive to the nuances of this intellectual debate regarding the viability of underpinning assumptions and instead reproduces deeply problematic assumptions. This often leads to those who have been the problem becoming heralded as the solution in a bizarre twist of reason! Greater openness appears to operate *within* dominant paradigms, particularly within certain fields of knowledge management and innovation. Here, however, there is a tendency for complicity in the starting assumptions regarding alleged paradigmatic changes, with work tending to focus more actively in the construction of generic tools for 'managing success' within the new hegemonic order. There is no shortage of those in the method army who produce ever greater and more sophisticated means of measuring 'effectiveness'.

Despite critiques, the general tone of academic writing on knowledge economies and societies is to support the overall thesis that there are transformations in the ways in which knowledge is being conceptualized and treated and the assumptions and presumptions made over its justification and application. We then witness a set of changes that place knowledge both theoretically and rhetorically at the centre of contemporary economic and social development. More broadly, this draws attention to the emerging strategic and political issues that face academics – and their institutions – in knowledge-based economies and societies, in terms of the stakes involved (increased funding from market/ public agencies); the risks entailed (characterization as 'not engaged' or 'difficult' academics) in working around this agenda and differential institutional positions that provide varying degrees of shelter, complicity or resistance to these changes.

In Pursuit of Excellence in the Age of Relevance

The relationship between knowledge, economy and society is under scrutiny whether in terms of wealth creation, the rhetoric of social inclusion, or public understanding or expertise. Knowledge has become the subject of policy aspirations across a range of fields, no longer confined (or protected) within the black-box of science or research policy. The result can be seen as a challenge to the differentiation of boundaries between the academy and the world of business, as captured in the idea of 'soft capitalism' (Thrift 2005). The implication is to profoundly affect the purpose, function and form of knowledge-producing institutions and more importantly for this analysis, modes of production themselves, particularly in relation to criteria for justification, contexts of application, forms of reflexivity, the content and context of knowledge and degrees of epistemic permeability.

The treatment of knowledge as a tool in the management or resolution of economic and social issues implies that the criteria of 'relevance' and 'usefulness' assumes increased importance in defining *what* knowledge should be produced and *how* it should subsequently be judged. Rather than seeing the role of the state to predominately protect curiosity-driven research as a cultural obligation, the current era has led to a greater emphasis on strategic research priorities, meeting the needs of industry and the application of knowledge for economic gain (Gibbons 2001; Ruivo 1994). As already highlighted, to posit that 'relevance' is in any way a new criteria is to rewrite the history of sponsorship of and influence over the evolution of knowledge-producing institutions. Nonetheless, it is the pervasive nature of 'relevance' as an allocation and evaluation tool that characterizes the changing research climate (Barnett 2000: 41).

That particular trend was highlighted in the mid-1990s (Gibbons et al. 1994). Relevance has heightened as a key goal, along with social accountability, as new criteria of efficiency and use have joined that of scientific excellence. Increasing links between universities and industry, in the context of research budget pressures, are said to have led to an emphasis on research for economic purposes and less institutional separation of the production, distribution and deployment of knowledge.

A focus on relevance appears to sit at odds with excellence-driven basic research. Research funding, whether through research council systems or otherwise, has largely been allocated on the basis of funding the best research regardless of research topic, with quality control assessed through processes of peer review. 'Excellence', within an international community of scholars, has formed the criteria for justifying whether research should be funded in any given area, as well as an evaluation mechanism for assessing its 'impact' and relative academic merit.

Within the excellence paradigm, other criteria for the justification or application of knowledge are not deemed to be significant. A by-product of research may be economic or social relevance but certainly not the funding rationale itself. As the coverage of the 'Ig Nobel' prizes highlights, research into the relationship between human presence and ostrich arousal, or the dynamics of avian defecation in penguins, is a celebration of the triumph of the curious over the instrumental. The point is simply that knowledge for knowledge's sake – once the bastion of the academy and still a source of cultural intrigue – is seen to be under threat by an encroaching relevance.

With this trend the objectivity of knowledge is also seen to be at risk. While much critique has already been levelled at the biases that are innate in peer-review systems, based on personal networks and entrenched cultural prejudices, or the extent to which objectivism in knowledge is itself a realistic ambition, a widespread acceptance of peer review as the best available means of guaranteeing scientific excellence and therefore objectivity, prevails. An 'objectification' of excellence-driven processes goes hand-in-hand with the popular perception that the opposite also holds true.

What we see here is a connection between *relevant* with *relative* knowledge which is of less value and more contestable than knowledge produced through traditional modes. This perception stems from the range of criteria that might be taken to constitute relevance, whether the strategic military interests of states; the economic interests of commerce; the political interests of parties or the social interests of community groups. The view that relevance implies the involvement of different interests in the research process and therefore a 'contamination' of research integrity is commonly held. A concern for relevance, along with recognition of its inherent contestability, involves a greater degree of preparedness to enter into the domain of referential reflexivity. That these pressures drive, fund, shape and validate work requires reflection not only between and within academic communities, but also by the individual researcher and assumptions concerning the 'outside world'.

As we have discussed, within traditional modes of knowledge production, justification is characterized as taking place within bounded communities with values being attributed to different knowledges and activities on the basis of assumed internal norms and practices. Application has been absent, accidental or delegated, but importantly, often not a direct part of the justification process itself. Relevance collapses these distinctions as application (requiring the effort of referential reflexivity) bleeds into justification (which at the level of a research community concerns endogenous reflexivity). As we have noted, however, those moving into the terrain of relevance, without due concern for the content and context in which knowledge is produced, end up in a state of capitulation to the assumption that knowledge is a one-way street to be judged according to its contexts of application. The context-revising nature of knowledge and the efforts needed to make it work in those contexts are then bracketed and with that the potential for learning.

Changeable dynamics between justification and application are regarded as characteristic of transformations within a broader framework of societal change in which increasing complexity, uncertainty and dialogue between science and society is leading to the 'contextualization' of a more socially accountable science, intrinsically linked to enhanced reflexivity on the part of the researcher. The social distribution of expertise and the fragmentation of established linkages between expertise and institutional structures play a role in determining the nature of this reflexivity, in light of the absence of a single point of scientific authority (Nowotny et al. 2001).

Relevance and reflexivity point to the need to re-examine the relationship between the content and context of knowledge production. On the one hand, there are scholars of the philosophy of science for whom, despite preoccupations with issues of methodological rigour or the defining lines between the arts, social and physical sciences, broader issues of institutional, spatial or socio-political context have not been considered as relevant factors. Here it is perfectly possible to produce insightful discussions concerning epistemic cultures, but say relatively little about the institutional conditions, in relation to the university, which shape the development of and attribution of value to different knowledges (Knorr-Cetina 1999).

On the other hand, within the science, technology and society (STS) community, we can see how context can become everything, leading to a relativization of knowledge claims, without any real concern for the content of the work itself (Barnes et al. 1996). As a result, understanding how knowledge is taken up, and translated in different contexts according to its content, evaporates. In both of these cases, the content and context of knowledge has been divorced. Preoccupations have focused either on micro-level analyses of processes of knowledge production or else on ideas of content without consideration of *what* knowledge is produced and *how* its reception is shaped and informed by particular conditions.

As relevance criteria grow in importance, the disjuncture between content and context becomes ever more problematic. Context increasingly informs not only what work is funded, but also how it is performed and the conditions in which value judgements about its ultimate worth are made. Questions which define the boundaries of work are not only what research, but also how, with whom and where? Problems are set and solved in the context of application, widely understood as being outside the university, not only in industry, but also within broader social and political arenas. Indeed, context operates at multiple levels. Although often interpreted through an interpersonal dynamic or at the micro-level, as indicated through laboratory-based studies, contemporary politico-economic pressures necessitate a broader understanding of context in, for example, institutional and spatial terms.

The single most important site of knowledge production has traditionally been the university. This is not to ignore other sites that have emerged (or disappeared) over time, but to recognize the status that the academy has enjoyed as the foremost acknowledged source of legitimate, objective, excellence-driven knowledge. The structures, norms and processes of such institutions provide a fundamental context in which external pressures and expectations are met, managed or mitigated. The implications for universities of the changing international political economy of knowledge have been variously understood, from those who chart the recasting of university roles and functions and subsequent internal reorientations, to those that predict its diminished role vis-à-vis other knowledge-producing institutions (see, for example, Eggins 2003; Odin and Manicas 2004). In this view, the net effect is to undermine the academy's role in creating and defining value: 'in the future, universities will comprise only a part of the knowledge producing sector and they are no longer in a strong enough position to determine what still counts as excellent' (Gibbons et al. 1994: 72).

Contexts of knowledge production are also spatial. Indeed, it is at the local or regional level that the dynamics of different knowledge capitalisms, from policy conceptualization to conditions of production, are most apparent. Regions and cities are devoting increasing resources to participating in the knowledge economy, redirecting funding from policy objectives relating to housing, regeneration or traditional business support. The aspiration is that excellence and relevance can come together in context, in other words, the 'embedding' of academic institutions and scientific expertise in particular places and spaces. Spatial context therefore provides a crucible in which issues of politico-economic, institutional and disciplinary contexts react and collide (May and Perry 2006).

As context shapes content, so the reverse can be said to be true. The increased economic and social relevance attached to knowledge leads a plethora of actors, whether within national states, regional or local environments or university governance structures, to consider the relative strengths and weaknesses of the pre-existing knowledge base. Across Europe we see efforts to reshape regional and local identities through harnessing the 'brand' power of science and technology. Knowledge capitals, silicon alleys, BioValleys, digital cities or, more broadly, capitals of culture have sprung up, as pre-existing strengths within the knowledge base become the foundation for broader socio-economic strategies for competitive success. A similar rebranding can be seen at the institutional level with, for instance, the specialization of academic institutions in niche areas or around clusters and centres of excellence. Where institutions wish to build up specific areas of expertise but have little pre-existing research 'content' with which to work, the dynamics of the international political economy are such that context then exerts greater influence, with a resulting response to dictated or assumed 'market' demands. The point, in either case, is that taking the dynamics of the international political economy seriously, leads to a mutual definition or reshaping of the content of and context for knowledge production.

The extent of these changes has been said to signal a fundamental transition in modes of knowledge production brought about by the emerging contours of the knowledge-based society (Gibbons et al. 1994). These authors offer an extended discussion of how changes in the international political economy of knowledge have interacted to produce an emergent mode of knowledge production along-side the traditional mode. They argue that the familiar cognitive and social norms which must be followed in the production, legitimation and diffusion of knowledge – aka 'Mode 1' – have been undermined by radically different ways of conceptualizing knowledge, its organization, reward systems and quality control mechanisms.

A new 'Mode 2' knowledge production process is characterized by the following: knowledge produced in the context of application; transdisciplinarity; non-hierarchical structures; heterogeneity and transience of organizational forms outside traditional university structures; multiple actors in the research process; social accountability; reflexivity and wider criteria for quality control than those implied by excellence and peer review. By bringing these trends together within a single thesis they offer a persuasive account of how, not singly, but collectively, a paradigm shift in modes of knowledge production is occur-ring. It is the fact of synthesis and articulation in the context of discourses on knowledge-based economies, rather than the identification of individual change factors per se, that gives the Mode 1/Mode 2 its particular resonance to contem-porary debates.

Returning to earlier discussions, the pressure for relevance and heightened forms of reflexivity relate to varying degrees of epistemic permeability. Surrounding and informing this is the extraordinary idea that knowledge is amenable to a supply-demand model. A demand-led, problem-solving or strategic approach to defining research agendas entails drawing on whatever relevant knowledge or expertise exists to address the assumed issues at hand, apparently regardless of discipline, faculty, learning and consequence. All of this is assumed under the banner of necessity and application. Policy discourses have therefore increasingly emphasized the need for cross-disciplinary working in order to produce more effective 'useful' knowledge.

Some of these effects may be seen as beneficial in overcoming the silo mental-ity that exists within professional communities in the public, private and volun-tary sectors. This may be through multidisciplinarity, interdisciplinarity or even transdisciplinarity; the latter referring to the transcending of normal epistemic boundaries via work on common problems and the creation of new forms of working outside of traditional disciplinary frameworks. This might, as some have argued, include working with those outside the academic community, such as citizens, public policy-makers or other community or business stakeholders (Boix Mansilla et al. 1999; Klein 1996; Klein et al. 2001). While there remain definitional conflicts, what is at stake is the extent to which the boundaries between disciplines remain porous or permeable within new collaborations.

Framing degrees of epistemic permeability across disciplines remains a key focus for the issues discussed in this book. Here we must return to the importance of context. If epistemic permeability is an essential prerequisite for the changes in modes of knowledge production posited in the contemporary era, according to the assumed logics of a capitalist international political economy, the political-economic, spatial and institutional contexts of knowledge production need to be better understood. Indeed, what is missing from many accounts of the apparent unrelenting march to a knowledge-based future is an understanding of how power flows, hierarchies, institutional positions, political and research cultures or place-based realities interact to mediate pressures for change.

Practices in the Pursuit of Excellence and Relevance

There is little doubt that governments across Europe are staking the future economic competitiveness and social fabric of their nations and places on knowledge. Its translation takes particular forms and is associated with such things as 'science', 'technology', 'innovation', 'creativity' (including 'creative industries') and 'skills'. At a European level, the Commission has set a number of initiatives in place to ensure that innovation, research, education and training are core to the European Union's internal policies. These include the creation of a European Higher Education Area (EHEA) and the agreement to create a European Research Area (ERA) to lay the foundation for a common science policy across the European Union through coordinating national research policies in order to combat fragmentation and duplication. Within such policies, universities are seen as unique in their contributions to the core functions of the knowledge society in producing new knowledge, in knowledge transfer and dissemination and in new industrial processes or services (European Commission 2003).

Both the EHEA and the ERA initiatives aim at coordination and harmonization rather than the creation of a federal European system of higher education and research. However, the debate over the appropriate levels of coordination of diverse national traditions and cultures has remained a vibrant one, particularly in the context of the development of the European Research Council (ERC). This objective is linked in with previously instrumentally driven targets, yet takes the European Union into the province of basic research, previously an exclusively national domain (European Commission 2005). Concern may then focus upon issues associated with international competitiveness and the methodological rigour of benchmarking for the purpose of producing a 'customized' European system according to a nuanced understanding of inputs and outputs (Bonaccorsi and Daraio 2007).

At the national level the policy emphasis on the knowledge economy has been apparent, particularly since the late 1990s. Across Europe emblematic examples of national efforts to embed knowledge within economic and social policy can be seen. Within the UK this is best exemplified in the 2004 ten-year framework for science and innovation and enhanced by a science and innovation strategy (see Perry 2007). In the French context key policy initiatives have included the Pact for Research (2006) under which institutional structures have been created; mechanisms initiated and a series of employment-related measures outlined in relation to research and higher education (see Crespy et al. 2007). Two planks of policy best represent Germany's approach to building a knowledge-based economy: the High Technology Strategy and the Excellence initiative. While the former emphasizes employment and economic growth through knowledge, the latter focuses specifically on enhancing basic research and development.

Across Europe the need to harness science, technology and knowledge as a precondition for economic and social survival in a globalized world is seen as paramount. Competition is seen to be knocking at the door, not only from the United States and Japan, but also from emerging economies such as Brazil, Russia, India and China. These trends are echoed in the restructuring of numerous government departments to reinforce the central relationship between economic development and science-based innovation (Dresner 2001; Perry and May 2007).

Those preoccupied with policy analysis are apt to say that 'all changes' when the policy moves, as they have a stake in maintaining an expertise associated with the presumption that history evaporates when policy pronouncements are made. Yet in times of crisis or upheaval, we can see a reinforcement of messages and so there appears to be few (written) discourses that indicate any form of deviation from or questioning of the underlying assumptions and presumptions about knowledge economies and societies. To that extent the exportation of Western ideologies and doctrines to other parts of the world is also appearing, with little sensitivity to context or concern for transferability. Examples include the embrace of the Mode 2 thesis in South Africa (Jansen 2002; Kraak 2000) or the similar success experienced by the idea of the 'Triple Helix' in parts of Eastern Africa. In each case, we can see the propensity for models of reality to slip into the reality of models that are regurgitated by individuals and groups without due consideration of their content, limits or contextual factors.

Two points of convergence are apparent. First, in the European context a central plank of economic policy is increasingly to focus on the 'supply-side' of knowledge: that is, the university. Universities are characterized as not only catalysts for, but also barriers to, knowledge-based change. Manifestations in the UK include government restructuring to bring innovation and universities together as well as the 'Research Excellence Framework' (Department for Education and Skills 2006). In France and Germany universities are being encouraged to become more entrepreneurial through changes to legal frameworks designed to increase autonomy. In both latter contexts, the fundamental issue has been characterized in terms of necessary reform of slow and bureaucratic research structures in the name of competitiveness and efficiency. The aim is to replicate a UK competitive model of higher education and research, through reducing direct state influence, performance-related evaluation, increasing indirect mechanisms of incentivization and introducing greater instability and flexibility into the system through, for instance, a reduction in recurrent funding.

Second, we have also seen a widespread, albeit often unintentional, regionalization (or even urbanization) of policy for science, research and higher education taking place within Europe and internationally (Perry and May 2007). The range of actors involved in the formulation and implementation of knowledge-based policies has broadened across the spectrum from basic research to skills (European Commission 2001). What is important about the involvement of multiple levels in research policy is the scope for different challenges to traditional modes of knowledge production. As physical scientific activity, for example, is taken to be more relevant to smaller spatial units, so issues of relevance, context, interdisciplinarity (through the emphasis on problem-solving) and multi-partnership working become more prominent, requiring greater reflexivity and context-sensitivity on the part of the researcher.

Despite these convergences, there are a series of differences that remain evident. Scholars of political science have already identified clear evidence of divergence behind the apparently unanimous embrace of modern capitalism, giving rise, for instance, to differentiations between Atlantic and Rhineland capitalism and an emphasis on models of European social democracy. Equally, however, we see recognition that the restoration of any democratic sovereignty over the private economy needs an internationally shared agenda as its precondition (Crouch and Streeck 1997). The same is applied to the manifestations of 'knowledge capitalisms'. Looking across the realms of state, industry, civic society and science we see differences emerging in how knowledge discourses touch down in different places. Behind these differences lies the presumption that knowledge should be harnessed as a core economic driver.

Taking the two examples above, approaches towards university reform are strongly influenced by cultural attitudes towards research. The autonomy of the professor and their right to determine their own affairs is constitutionally enshrined in Germany as a result of the consequences of misappropriation of science and research in the Second World War. While our interviews with German civil servants in the Ministry of Science and Innovation revealed a frustration with levels of professorial autonomy, there is no appetite to undermine the fundamental freedom of research. In France the widespread striking of scientists in reaction to proposed reforms to the research system in 2004 led to a reversal in French policy, but the same trends are, once again, apparent in the reforming intentions of politicians.

The campaign 'Sauvons la recherche' appealed to a long history of French intellectualism against the machinations of the budget-cutting state and attempts to engage public support for research in a way that seems highly improbable in the English context. French and German academics are civil servants and continue to enjoy 'jobs for life', compared with a widespread acceptance of more neo-liberal principles into the higher education sector in the UK context. This translates into variable capabilities to steer university research *in practice* regardless of stated preferences. At the same time we find politicians frequently alluding to a need to reform universities in the name of adapting them to the challenges of the twenty-first century.

In terms of regionalization and how these trends are conceived and interpreted, we see not only the importance of how respective roles are allocated to and expected from state, industry and the academy, but also how they affect the form and content of central–regional relations. The direction of influence and drive for regional science and innovation policies differs. Developments in the UK have been largely bottom-up, with reluctance on the part of national agencies to accommodate a growing regional appetite for science and technology. In France top-down pressures dominate, with variable yet increasing regional acknowledgement of STI (science, technology and innovation) and higher education as legitimate policy domains. Issues of political expediency are predominant in Germany, with decisions over the governance of science, research and higher education bound up in the wider debates over reform of the Federal state.

The extent to which sub-national actors have any constitutional or officially delegated powers in these domains varies. That, in turn, affects the freedoms, flexibilities and expectations of and for research. Even prior to the regionalization of science policy, coordination, steering and interest aggregation is difficult in countries where regions have responsibility for research (Senker 1999). Indeed, scientific communities in Germany have traditionally exploited the difficulties in reaching political agreement between the Federal and Länder governments to obtain an unusually high degree of autonomy (Dresner 2001: 110).

Rhetorically there is evidence that a more instrumental approach to knowledge is being advanced. Through written documents at European, national and regional levels, the aspiration is clearly that relevance is not merely an equal to excellence, but a defining feature of how 'excellence' has come to be understood. At European level, the distinction between pure and applied work has been replaced by an understanding of 'frontier science': that is, basic research linked to application through a driving concern to reinforce excellence in scientific and technological competition (European Commission 2005). It is this understanding that has underpinned support for a new European Research Council as a primarily excellence-driven initiative.

Despite this there are differences in how the relationship between excellence and relevance is represented in different national contexts. Hence policy texts in Germany emphasize industrial competitiveness and growth as the driving concern, with excellence in basic research as a key mechanism to achieve this. This contrasts with the tone of French policies that tend to focus on the need to commercialize and exploit physical scientific research for competitive advantage to maximize investments made – for other reasons – in science and research. Differences can also be seen in the relationships between excellence, relevance and place: for example, in the extent to which science and research objectives are seen as exceptions from or contributors to goals for balanced development or redistribution.

We can draw a contrast between a neo-liberal acceptance of the spatial consequences of excellence-driven investments in science and technology (UK) and a social democratic approach to managing out conflicts that arise between potentially conflicting policy objectives. While supra-national frameworks are pushing for greater centres of excellence, networked across Europe, hence ensuring that selectivity is key, it is less culturally acceptable in other contexts to concentrate resources in particular regions as a result of historical and political circumstances.

Despite evidence of heterogeneity in how knowledge-based discourses touch down in different contexts, an overriding concern with justifying investments in science and research according to largely economic criteria can be seen in policy statements, along with assumptions about how such investments should subsequently be assessed.

Dimensions of Excellence–Relevance

The above leads to differing dimensions in the excellence–relevance relationship. In practice cultural attitudes embedded in discourses on science and research can reinforce unreflexive stances towards 'excellence' as a goal in and for itself. Particular forms of knowledge can have their cultural authority reinforced by an expansion of their boundaries into other domains of activity (Gieryn 1999). Through our work on regions and science policy at different scales of governance and across policy realms, five non-exclusive dimensions to the excellence–relevance debate can be identified.

First, we find a *disembedded excellence*. This may be seen as traditionally non-spatial and amenable to global logics in which processes of knowledge production are divorced from the context in which they are produced. Distributive issues are secondary to quality as judged by peer review. Academics in particular institutions have a stake in the reproduction of this form of knowledge production as it celebrates content and the mobility of expertise and ideas without concern for context. Relationality then evaporates and the idea of an absolute space in which excellence takes place, reigns supreme. Knowing about practice is then separated from knowing in practice.

Second, and associated with the above, there is *competitive relevance*. Here we find a de-contextualized interpretation of relevance that places emphasis upon application to specific economic or social issues and strategic priorities as a pre-condition for global success. The focus on biotechnology, nano-technology and genomics is symptomatic: research may be 'applied' but does not have a direct advantage to any particular community or group. This is the politics that revolves around – but will not commit to – populating a missing middle between content, context and consequence. It focuses upon an exemplary politics of the model for all to emulate that seeks to avoid questions of place according to the logic of a naturalized and globalized idea of competition. Once again, context evaporates in favour of an exemplary politics that privileges the transferable model in a market of ideas.

Third, a *relevant excellence* discourse highlights the indirect benefits of science and technology to particular places and spaces. This does not relate to changes in processes of knowledge production, rather it seeks to exploit, extract and attract knowledge products and institutions for territorial benefit. Here universities who position themselves as, or are seen as, significant economic actors in their own right in their localities can capture and exploit the product of research process through the construction of spin-offs or patents. The local or regional then becomes a space of funding, with the consequence that it becomes a place that benefits via an indirect consequence of research activity.

The partner to this discourse is our fourth type: *excellent relevance*. Here we see a concern with what is produced in terms of the generation of co-produced research priorities and agendas through a linking of content with context. The distinction between relevant excellence and excellent relevance is subtle but important: it is not the criteria of excellence that is at stake, rather the extent of interpenetration into processes of knowledge production itself and how the benefits will then be realized. Issues associated with the integrity of process, divorced from product are taken seriously in this scenario, yet it is also the consequences of knowledge for significant actors or organizations etc., that inform the impetus for the research itself. Knowledge is not just context-sensitive, it is potentially revising. For all parties concerned, therefore, we find a challenge to the normal ways of producing and receiving research in a situation of 'active intermediation'; a subject to which we will return in our suggestions for a way forward.

Finally, there is *contextual relevance*. Here we find research investments being driven by narrow political or economic objectives, without any concern for the quality or content of the work. This articulation of the relationship between science and regional economic development can be found only at the periphery of policy opinion. It is not a clearly expressed or implicitly held preference, rather it exists as a negative fear that the growth of a regional dimension to science policy will lead to 'second-rate' science. Equally, it can lead to the capability to capture and mobilize resources at different spatial scales for the purposes of reproducing excellence in terms of the idea of 'untainted' interference from outside forces.

It is the fear of contextual relevance that has provoked a backlash from the scientific establishment. Disembedded excellence and competitive relevance have come to dictate the contours of the emerging neo-liberal knowledge economy as they converge around an aspatial politics whereby we see a conjunction between commodification and models of reality. The dominant view is that neither space nor place are valued in the search for global success and any understanding of the contexts within which excellence or relevance can be built is limited and partial.

In the face of these pressures, shelter is provided by those institutions who can position themselves as being relevant in the pursuit of excellence. While clear intra-institutional differences exist between disciplines and where they are positioned within faculties, particularly when it comes to appropriate levels of resources allocation, inter-institutional differences also play their part. Here, it seems, concern with the recognition of contingency can be read as destiny and constructed as a threat to the pursuit of excellence. All have a stake in this pursuit if the institution provides a shelter from what are regarded as contaminants deriving from outside forces. Equally, the power of attributed value can work to provide this shelter for those disciplines and institutions whose relevance is taken to be derived from their excellence.

Excellence is a game in its own right, with an emphasis on positioning in international league tables, emblematic science investments and the pursuit of prestige. The global is invoked as necessity by those within institutions who operate more like sport teams, seeking position as a demonstration of capability. The result is a competitive situation in which an increasing concentration of research excellence in particular localities leads to a 'survival of the fittest' mentality, without due regard to the actual concentration of expertise, or even the benefits that such areas may derive from such an existence. The logic of the global finally meets the pursuit of excellence.

Perhaps most tellingly excellence is increasingly mobilized as a defence or justification for particular decisions or processes in order to invoke the appearance of objectivism, despite those decisions being based on criteria invoked from within other domains of activity. Particular examples can be seen in relation to the location of scientific facilities (Perry 2006); the limits to which policy-makers can reasonably steer research trajectories, or in relation to attributed value placed on universities in terms of their strategic orientation and their variable institutional power to resist, co-opt or co-produce these expectations. In so doing excellence operates as a full stop. It can seemingly be mobilized at any point in order to halt the perceived encroachment of relevance within traditional modes of knowledge production.

Places and Practices in Knowledge Development

Nowhere is this more apparent than in developments at the sub-national scale around science and economic development. Such a focus provides a powerful lens through which knowledge dynamics can be illuminated and magnified. In the UK, a paradigmatic shift has taken place in which funds for regional economic development have been redirected away from regeneration or traditional business support towards basic and applied research and innovation activities in the public and private sectors. In Germany, where research is more of a matter for regional government, increasing policy measures nonetheless seek to embed knowledge and innovation as building blocks of sub-national growth. Contrary to those that posit the demise of the university, an emphasis on the supply-side has also been reinforced, with funds specifically available for universities to encourage greater links with businesses. Such developments give the appearance of an increasing coincidence between particular scalar and spatial contexts and research trajectories.

As science and research become legitimate policy targets for those whose primary emphasis is on a narrowly based economic development of places, the potential for new modes of knowledge production as a response to – or even precondition for – growth and competitiveness increases. This is reflected in the range of measures within regional and city contexts to build science regions or innovation ecosystems.

From our research on universities and their roles in local knowledge-based initiatives, three alternative ways of seeing knowledge-based development (KBD) can be identified at the sub-national level: process-driven, product-driven and acquisition-driven, each with different implications for the role of universities as sites of knowledge production and for the disciplines within them. First, KBD may concern new processes of knowledge production. This view draws on the Mode 1/Mode 2 thesis, as well as the distinction between codified and tacit (or embedded) knowledge (Polanyi 1962, 1966) or the distinction between 'knowing how' and 'knowing that' which Gilbert Ryle (1990), with Schopenhaeur as his inspiration, made in *The Concept of Mind* (1949).

Core to the process-driven view of KBD are fundamental questions relating to how knowledge is produced, for what reasons, by whom, for whom and how it is subsequently judged? In relation to research, this involves multiple stakeholders in the definition of priorities, research questions and the conduct of the research itself. Action research or policy-oriented work becomes more commonplace which is taken to be populated by active and constant communication between stakeholders throughout the research process. Such concepts apply equally to pedagogy in terms of new working patterns and modes of engagement between academics, students and/or local partners, such as new curricula to meet the skills needs of industry, placements or continuing professional development. For the university the significance of a process-driven view of KBD is threefold:

it involves new ways of working that are seen to have the potential to break the pursuit of excellence within the ivory tower; it requires engagement with academic staff at different levels of the university hierarchy outside of senior management; finally and relatedly, it is characterized by multiple, fluid, informal and formal external interactions, almost impossible to map, let alone manage and so represents a challenge to the narrow managerialism so characteristic of universities. In other words, it has the potential to represent a wholesale change in the fundamental 'business' of the university.

Second, KBD may concern the exploitation of particular knowledge products, with processes of knowledge production hermetically sealed from 'outside' interference. More consistent with a 'Mode 1' of knowledge production, the research process is detached from the subsequent harnessing of knowledge for socio-economic benefit. Here the emphasis is on a linear model of innovation and knowledge transfer or on the mechanisms through which knowledge is managed and communicated, such as networks or information-communication technologies (ICTs). Here knowledge-based development relates more to the changing nature of the industrial fabric, for instance, in terms of knowledge-based industries and the linkages between universities and businesses as a precursor for commercialization and spin-offs, rather than to the redefinition of academics' research agendas and ways of working.

What we see here is a more 'managed' or 'institutionalized' view of KBD as evidenced through the growth of technology transfer offices, business departments and academic-linked science parks or business incubators. Across different contexts, individual academics are implicated in terms of intellectual property to greater or lesser degrees (Charles 2006), but relationships can be mediated or brokered through specific liaison offices at the institutional level. The extent to which this is encouraged depends on the relative importance at a strategic level that is accorded to income generation and spin-out activities.

A third view of KBD draws on literatures relating to urban growth coalitions and the new urban entrepreneurialism (A. Harding 1997; Oatley 1998; Salet et al. 2003). Increasingly, cities have become more concerned with marketing, branding and global success and position. The concept of the 'ideopolis' – or 'city of ideas' – has found particular resonance with policy and practitioner communities as a means to capture the essential ingredients of a post-industrial city. The 'ideopolis' was initially seen to have three key elements: a set of key physical and economic features, a particular social and demographic mix, and a specific cultural climate and set of commonly held values (Canon et al. 2003).

The 'ideopolis' vision puts the 'urban' into knowledge-based development, with a key leading role for local authorities as well as broader cross-sectoral city partners. Yet this is essentially an acquisition-driven view, about the ingredients that need to be acquired within cities as the basis for competitive success, rather than how knowledge itself can be harnessed for wider socio-economic benefit.

These ingredients include, for instance: high-tech manufacturing; knowledge services; a university, or universities with strong networks to commercial partners; an airport and/or major communication nodes; architectural heritage and/or iconic physical development; a flourishing service sector; large numbers of high skill professional and front line service positions; a vibrant city culture and diverse population; an ethos of tolerance and significant local political direction and policy autonomy (Canon et al. 2003: 16). Here we have a different conceptualization of what KBD might mean. Knowledge itself as a process or product has a role, but this is within a broader vision in which the acquisition of talent, research expertise, the development of assets and external symbols of success or marketing and image are equally, if not more, important – as tools in global positioning as much as urban regeneration.

Universities are seen as tools, instruments, assets and status symbols to be acquired, harnessed and their benefits extracted. In an acquisition-driven view, universities are one among many participants, operating on an institutional basis within strategic alliances and little formal engagement with individual academics being recognized in the process. In the context of the knowledge-economy, universities may be part of urban growth coalitions that have been attributed with delivering urban renaissance. Yet they may alternatively be absent – as it is their existence that is deemed important as assets, rather than the knowledge they produce. 'Knowledge' as research is of secondary concern. At the forefront of these activities is an understanding of the 'knowledge city' as being clever, smart, skilful, creative, networked, connected and competitive.

It is this latter view that tends to dominate sub-national knowledge-based developments. Acquisition is seen as a goal in its own right, without due consideration of the factors that then lead to positive knowledge-based outcomes (Simmie 2002). Instead, across the case studies we have examined, interventions in research policy are best understood as *physical, symbolic* or *additive* – with *transformation* assumed to occur automatically as a result and according to narrow economic outcomes. In none of these cases is 'knowledge' expected to have a positive transformative effect in relation to understanding, equality or even the environment as a whole. Instead, it is conceived of as an asset (physical), an emblem (symbolic) or a magnet (additive). The power of attributed value leads to a symbolic politics, with positions in national and international league tables commonly quoted as evidence that regional interventions are 'working'.

Once again this relates to how the relationship between excellence, relevance and place is regarded. A concern with distribution, equality or social cohesiveness is undermined by the pursuit of scientific prizes as symbols of regional identity and growth which limits the extent to which context and content come together in practice. In this it is the search for the exemplar of good practice, such as Silicon Valley, that can be transplanted from one context to the next that dominates, rather than concern for the difficult and yet also necessary conditions for success: that is, the creation of context-sensitive strategies, partnerships and actions. It is not of course the case that experiments in new ways of working do not exist in terms of initiatives aimed at bridging the gap between excellence and relevance or universities and industry. They remain, however, just that: experiments at the edge of the mainstream, or exceptions that prove the rule.

Alternative articulations for knowledge production, transmission and application do exist at the sub-national scale, more so than at other levels of governance, and are often widespread. Through debates around specific initiatives, such as the location of scientific facilities or the development of regional science councils, economic development managers and local politicians express the desire, coupled by frustration, for research to be funded, conducted and assessed differently. Aspirations for reformulated modes of knowledge production, tied to the needs of regions, industries or communities and subsequently carried out through more interactive, heterogeneous ways of working, are commonplace. To this extent, there are voices that have the potential to populate the 'agora' (Nowotny et al. 2001) and that can be taken as evidence of society speaking back to research. The key issue in evaluating whether this is the case is to understand how and where those views are expressed.

The 'agora' is intrinsically about a *public* space where the values for and of knowledge can be deliberated upon in terms of their consequences for subsequent actions and ways of life. We would then see a way of society and science entering into a dialogue in the 'belief that an open, self-confident and self-critical society is a prerequisite for the successful management of scientific and social change' (Irwin and Michael 2003: 158). These public spaces do not currently exist and instead publics are introduced to scientific activity along the lines of the hypodermic view, in which ignorance is assumed and a meeting of knowledges as having potential for different ways of seeing, dismissed.

Views that challenge accepted wisdom are often seen as unacceptable in open fora or policy debates. The gap between views expressed to us by policy-makers and academics in interviews and subsequent action was striking: an almost unanimity in private opinion against an uncritical excellence-driven paradigm translated into silent complicity in support of the status quo. All too often this appeared to relate to position and authority: real concerns about how economic value may be extracted from research or the strategic orientation of academics seemingly vanish when policy-makers are faced with university managers whose positions, like those in the private sector, are often attributed with a particular set of characteristics. The emerging consensus view on the relationship between science, economy and scale is therefore not the result of a conflict of values: the absence of debate is deafening in its silence. Questioning these narrow understandings is almost taboo, as preconceptions of spin-off opportunities, narrow constructions of economic outcomes and elite universities as guardians of excellence, all meet around that which is never questioned.

It is the role of the university and its position within the knowledge economy that is critical here. As already highlighted, policy statements both written and verbal increasingly emphasize the centrality of the university as a central actor in knowledge-based development. Universities have varied roles to fulfil: to educate and train students; to produce excellent research according to peer-reviewed criteria; to innovate in order to enhance productivity through collaborative relations with external partners; to produce relevant research according to the needs of client organizations; to make socio-economic contributions to their localities and businesses in general and to enhance civic value in the public realm (Clark 1998). Taken together the diversity of roles ascribed to universities has given rise to the notion of the 'third mission': that is, the acknowledgement that universities have functions beyond research and teaching that relate to their wider economic, social and civic roles (Harloe and Perry 2004). The rise of 'third leg' funding accompanies this shift, as public spending on research and development alone falls well short of international or national targets.

Sub-national actors are vocal proponents of the third mission and increasingly look to universities, within broader science and innovation policies, as tools of development and engines of growth (Castells and Hall 1994). Regions have increasing expectations from universities, as STI (science, technology and innovation) is hoped to deliver reversals in economic fortune and the rebirth of new territorial identities. From the point of view of universities, a complex mix of altruism and instrumentalism incentivize this engagement, in terms of acknowledging the legitimacy of demands upon them as institutions that receive, either directly or indirectly, public funding, coupled with the need to search for additional finance in the context of budgetary constraints.

Inherent in these diverse roles are sets of expectations that embody different values. Their overall balance is mediated via different frameworks for action at multiple levels of scale with incentivization through alternative funding streams. It is here that the international political economy described earlier comes into play. Mixed messages are apparent in the drives for international excellence and collaborations for regional benefit. It is held that research needs to be conducted at an international level in order to meet criteria of world-class excellence. Yet it also needs to be embedded in local and regional contexts if the kinds of benefits expected from knowledge for the economy are to be realized within its locality.

The dominance of the disembedded excellence or competitive relevance discourses gives rise to assumptions about connections between research, teaching and third mission activities which dictate 'appropriate' measures of success for the university. Ideas of knowledge transfer, for example, tend to rest upon outputs that are measurable according to patents and/or the setting up of new companies. Matters of organizational accountability are set according to targets; performance is judged by the ability to attract resources; economic impact is mediated through the production of spin-out companies, patents and the attraction of inward investment, while research and teaching scores are taken as demonstrable indicators of excellence. Clear tensions can be seen in the aims and aspirations for universities: the civic role of the university, for instance, sits in tension with the idea of knowledge as a commodity.

A confusion of expectations and incentive structures leads to demands from policy-makers, politicians and university managers for programmes in the short term to demonstrate relevance, as well as more sustained and long-term programmes of work in the pursuit of excellence. 'Quick hits' are seen to drive demands for knowledge to service the economy, as if nothing has been learnt from this short-termism, the result being what has been referred to as 'academic capitalism' (Slaughter and Leslie 1997). Equally, the search for excellence produces hierarchies according to abstract league tables; their flaws are widely noted, but this does not stop the frenetic drive among universities to attain a place in the rankings and for academics that then place a premium on their critical capacity to repeat them, as if they stood as an unproblematic representation of activities.

Institutions tend to compete, rather than collaborate, aiming for the elusive label of being 'world-class' or 'regional'; except where collaboration is itself a stepping stone to global visibility or the enhancement of relevance. New managers may then enter institutions in the promise of delivering them to new heights in a struggle that is never questioned. For these reasons we find universities that are 'in', but not 'of' their localities (May and Perry 2006) and academics themselves exhibit ambivalent attitudes towards the spaces in which their institutions are housed. Those elements of 'third mission' activities that support this world-class role, such as collaborations with industry or the receipt of regional monies, are embraced as a stepping stone to global position; the result is that the less visible, yet arguably more socially relevant, activities that are not seen as excellent, are relegated to the domain of the less prestigious universities.

Diversification in role accompanies stratification in university systems with the 'third mission' becoming the last choice for those universities outside the upper echelons of the global hierarchy. The issue is that sub-national expectations are not equal upon all universities. Elite universities, in the top world rankings, are highly valued for their assumed benefits, or by virtue of being 'world class' receive funding to pursue knowledge exchange as if that were an unproblematic relationship – yet it is other institutions that must deliver on agendas relating to the third mission. What we witness is a certain power of knowledges to protect themselves within particular institutions – noting of course, as we have said, that there are intra-institutional conflicts and movement of monies between disciplines.

Despite professed expectations of universities, our work also reveals a high degree of public support for the autonomy of the university in general. Legitimation still counts, despite the games being played in the guise of necessity. The extent and nature of this autonomy is debated between university managers and policy-makers. However, a paradox emerges: on the one hand, the deficits of an 'inflexible', 'bureaucratic', 'elitist' university system, as expressed through interviews, are widely noted, with a desire for greater steering of universities towards particular agendas; on the other hand, this has been accompanied by shifts to greater autonomy for universities, with incentivization through funding streams remaining the only tool to influence behaviour. Even in more neo-liberal systems, regional demands on universities are largely restricted to being physical agents, attractors and economic actors, with little consideration of their civic role.

This raises real issues over the relationship between science, expertise and democracy and the overall relationship between governance and knowledge (Stehr 2004). We see value attributed to science and assumed by universities, without any accompanying debate on the values of or for science. It is this situation that many (largely research-intensive) universities have exploited through occupying positions of strategic authority on Science Councils, regional economic boards or local development agencies. Those in senior positions hold the enviable position of increasingly being able to claim credentials as businesses and economic actors, while alluding to the public services they perform and their societal duties. In so doing, they can first act as 'guardians of excellence' and so retain their value-defining role. Indeed, it is through allusions to the roles of academics within policy-making processes that the criteria of excellence (and not second-rate science) is said to be met.

At the same time universities can claim to be sources of relevance through their very existence. In the process, 'new' sources of funding for relevance-driven research at the sub-national level are often co-opted in support of existing research agendas and strategic university priorities regarding the achievement of world-class excellence. For this reason senior managers often speak of the attraction of companies to their campuses, or the value of their real estate, rather than directly about the activities that occur in the buildings themselves and what is distinctive about the knowledge they produce, with whom and how and with what consequences for different groups?

None of this is to suggest there are not direct and indirect benefits that flow from the presence of disembedded, world-class excellent, research-intensive universities to local economic development. Nor is it to suggest that unintended consequences will not remain a thorn in the side of those who seek to mould the world in their view. Yet inherent within product-driven or acquisition-driven knowledge-based developments is the assumption that 'having' a world-class research-intensive university is enough for economic development. The power of attribution is also one of misrecognition and filling in this gap in understanding means going against strong, entrenched interests, around which not only university managers circulate, but also the academics within them.

Summary

In Chapter 4 we defined variations in epistemic permeability around the extent to which the control of knowledge becomes the province of particular groups which then enables them to constitute a separation between production and other elements in the knowledge process. We then suggested that the important conditions for this to take place included the political economy of research funding; the institutional context of production; the attributed value afforded to the work by different audiences and the culture informing the production process itself.

In this chapter we have described changes in relation to the knowledge economy and their effects in relation to institutional and national contexts. Degrees of epistemic permeability are influenced by these environmental factors. Differential and conflicting expectations of universities and acquisition-based strategies, coupled with an absence of real debate over the value of different knowledges, leads to a disconnection in understanding the relationship between the cultures, structures and contexts of knowledge production and the realization of knowledge-based visions and with that, more reflexive understandings.

What we have are emblematic and popularized examples of 'stakeholder' or 'entrepreneurial' universities (Clark 1998; Marginson and Considine 2000), or short-cut ideas that are held up by those seeking to popularize acontextual understandings in the pursuit of recognition for their models of reality. In the meantime there remains a widespread mismatch between a co-produced approach to research and the traditional structures of university work that divide academic research into disciplinary silos. This is not only reflected in organization, but also reproduced within policy and funding frameworks with negative and positive results, depending on where one is positioned in disciplinary terms and institutional hierarchies.

Certain universities are able to offer 'shelter' to academics from external pressures, dependent on their position in global, national and regional hierarchies. Just as universities are differentially positioned, so are forms of knowledge. The 'privilege' of shelter from the demands for epistemic permeability is not offered equally across disciplines, with value attributed to different knowledges on the basis of their assumed contributions to economic development. Within policy statements and reflected in funding decisions, there is a widespread tendency to conflate the search for the world-class, excellent, disembedded university with particular forms of knowledge. Value is often attributed to a narrow understanding of science and technology without a concern with how that value is to be realized, or the value of different knowledges. Within the field of culture we see the 'creative industries' being held up as emblematic for ways forward in the search for competitive advantage, or culture being important as an attractor for the recruitment of 'world-class' academics.

Contemporary discourses treat knowledge as a single homogenous entity. We can see the tendency for a merging of distinct histories of knowledge into a single powerful 'knowledge-dynamic', without any differentiation between how the sciences, social sciences and humanities may have figured or disappeared at critical junctures in time. Claims are made about the relevance of knowledge to modern day economic or social problems, in the absence of context-sensitivity. What this means is differential degrees of contextualization of disciplines in the international knowledge economy, resulting in the need for different levels of engagement and reflexivity dependent on where and how researchers are positioned. We can see how distinct epistemic cultures influence how people know and what they know (Knorr-Cetina 1999). It follows that external pressures will not affect all disciplines or institutions equally.

The factors that will influence varying degrees of referential and endogenous reflexivity include not only internal norms, codes and conducts of areas of research with differing embeddedness in context, but also the position occupied by the discipline and individual in relation to the institutions in which they are housed. Questions arise over the relative permeability of disciplinary boundaries to external pressures, the extent to which epistemic osmosis takes place between disciplines and the institutional conditions for endogenous and referential reflexivity according to the new pressures on knowledge production.

In this spirit of inquiry we have outlined the different appropriation of discourses in respect to the knowledge economy as they manifest in practice across different national and regional contexts. An overview of policy statements reveals sufficient evidence that knowledge-based developments are being taken seriously and are driving national strategy across a range of areas. Global shifts are mediated through national structures producing distinct knowledge capitalisms with varying consequences. One of the deficits of the Mode 2 thesis is precisely the failure to fully account for the range of contextual factors – including place-based historical legacies, political and cultural dynamics – which influence *how* the dynamics of the knowledge-based economy are translated in action in different places.

At a rhetorical level a more instrumental approach to knowledge production, justification and application appears apparent. Yet in practice it is the attachment to an undetermined, illusive 'excellence' that often drives developments. Relevance has increased in importance, but also mixes with a fear that relevance, relativism and second-rate science are inevitable. There is a clear limit to which it is culturally and publicly acceptable to express alternative views in relation to the questions of how we should judge, fund and value different forms of knowledge.

Belonging to an academic community of scholars then implies a value judgement on the quality of work produced, informed by how individuals are positioned within professional and institutional contexts. As we have seen in Parts 1 and 2 of the book, the need for referential reflexivity becomes once again bracketed, with endogenous concerns obtaining the hierarchical high ground and rendering the attainment of any productive agonism between the two dimensions difficult.

These conditions continue despite greater awareness of the relevance of spatial context. Science and research policy are increasingly governed at multiple spatial levels, from the global, to European to the sub-regional. In theory, this provides a wider potential for context-based 'Mode 2' forms of knowledge production; indeed this is the aspiration for interventions aimed at reinventing territorial futures or transforming the economic and social fortunes of places. Yet, in practice, the search for the global excellent-driven 'fix' continues according to logics that are not properly interrogated, with interventions emphasizing acquisitions or physical repositioning more than new modes of knowledge production.

The absence of legitimized public forums for debating the relative merits of science, knowledge, technology and innovation in relation to other public policy objectives is critical here. There is no 'agora' – even where relevant forums exist, the deference accorded to and presence and strength of strategic university managers and private sector executives often precludes meaningful and frank exchanges of views through their allusions to economic necessity. Universities are central within policy frameworks, yet have values ascribed to them that would be expected in relation to the corporate sector, which subsequently devalues their role in society. They are then able to present themselves in multiple guises, speaking on behalf of different communities (academic, civic, economic etc.), within diverse, often conflicting forums. In the process the distinctiveness of the university is undermined and the basis for making a coherent and defensible argument for its value eroded.

Variability according to institutional position and disciplinary area is strongly evident. The ability of universities to protect themselves and 'their' academics is dependent on position in international knowledge hierarchies. It is the world-class, research-intensive, science-based university to which maximum value is attributed, despite an acknowledgement, again largely in private, that it is other institutions and forms of knowledge that are more engaged in meaningful collaborations in practice. A silent complicity between all those involved permeates so-called strategic partnerships, where issues may be acknowledged behind doors yet allowed to continue unchallenged in public. Expectations of the knowledge-based economy will not be realized, until honest debate about roles, responsibilities, capacities, capabilities, positions and dispositions takes place.

It is not the intention here to erode contextual differences between places through outlining the above as a common set of dynamics. As has been clearly noted, distinct knowledge capitalisms are developing with sets of responses at the sub-national level exhibiting variation. Exceptions exist where attempts to create new partnerships and ways of working between academics and societal actors are evident and the international political economy of knowledge is rapidly changing. Nonetheless, a cross-national and cross-regional comparison does support the contentions above. More importantly, our evidence indicates that a general reading of the contemporary economy as being dominated by 'Mode 2' is inaccurate, with practices revealing greater complexity than can be understood from a single converging knowledge history.

The content and context changes and manifestations outlined here inform the arguments proffered in this book and the day-to-day realities that face social researchers in their practices. Often faced with being the application arm of scientific funded research, they are also positioned within their own institutions in different ways according to the knowledge politics outlined here. External validation and value attribution to particular forms of knowledge frame the daily realities of knowledge production. These include where funding comes from and how much; how research is expected to be carried out; assumptions made over what constitutes 'legitimate' interference; the expected timing and outcomes of work and, more broadly, the relationship between the researcher and wider society. Rhetorical positioning, coupled with differential degrees of institutional shelter provided by universities, are critical in understanding the ways in which different disciplines are placed within the international political economy of knowledge, which in turn informs the dispositions, positions and sense of belonging of academics – and with that the extent to which degrees of endogenous and referential reflexivity might emerge. It is to these differences and how they are manifest in the institutional setting of the university to which we now turn.

UNIVERSITIES AS RESEARCH SITES

7

In this chapter we elaborate on the university as an institutional context in mediating, absorbing or transcending external shifts in values attributed to knowledge. Expectations of knowledge abound within a redefined political economy of knowledge, yet the extent to which changes are manifest in practice is informed by the mediation of external pressures through diverse institutional contexts. This relates both to the structural organization of the university, as well as the values that are internalized for its corporate rebranding in an era of knowledge politics.

The shifts outlined in Chapter 6, as we suggested, have particular consequences for universities that lead to both inter- and intra-institutional variability in the conditions for the production of research. Inter-institutional differentiation occurs through the extent to which universities are remoulding themselves according to values attributed to the market and the extent to which this is mediated by a range of contextual factors. These factors, historical and geographical, have implications for the strategies that universities adopt, as well as the *generic* employment contexts for academics. Intra-institutional differences also exist, as universities, with different research traditions, mediate external values attached to particular forms of knowledge in different ways. Here the implications are more *specific* in relation to the position of forms of knowledge within different academic contexts.

The consequences for the practice of research are varied. Universities offer constraining and enabling conditions for the development of a practice that brings endogenous and referential reflexivity together. Institutions provide more than a mirroring of social forces, but a structure for managing interests and a modification of rules, norms and expectations of political behaviour (March and Olsen 1989). The constraining elements may be more evident, with enabling environments persisting despite, not because of, dominant institutional structures and norms. Such variable contexts inform the degrees of effort needed on the part of those who wish to engage in the name of the idea of the 'public good' of knowledge.

Public Goods, Universal Provision and Autonomy

We have said that there is no single history of the university. The 'university' is not a homogenous concept, but a hybridization that rests on the coalescence of alternative trajectories. In the English context, the University of Oxford has roots dating back to the eleventh and twelfth centuries originally serving ecclesiastical interests, while Manchester universities were founded in the nineteenth century through Victorian wealth, aimed at least in part to encourage the development of scientific knowledge that supported industrialization. Institutions founded in different ages have been dominated by different social interests and hence been encouraged to produce partial knowledge in support of a particular order through, for instance, the provision of a managerial humanism for reproducing the economic system (Newfield 2003). To that extent while institutions exhibit differences, they have been underpinned by the same conceptions of their roles and functions, and it is around ideas of their success in so doing that hierarchies emerged.

While caution has been exercised in adopting a romanticized view of reflexivity, so it is the case concerning those institutions that enable and constrain its potential. It is an airbrushed view that sees the university as a public institution serving the public good, given the industrial foundations of many such bodies and their exclusivity to narrow, educated elites for much of their history. Nevertheless, in their broadest terms, universities have come to 'serve' society, regardless of their roots, with a broad understanding of their civic role in relation to the production and dissemination of knowledge. Throughout the years, this idea of the university has undergone various iterations – from Plato's Cave and the Greek Academy, to the medieval idea of a university, to that of Newman and finally, Jasper's idea of higher education (Barnett 1990). While it is the case that the transmission of value of these institutions in terms of what they stood for is not new and has been documented in earlier studies (Green 1969), we have suggested a relatively stable period until the latter parts of the twentieth century.

The primary functions of these institutions have been the pursuit of knowledge and the provision of a liberal education to the elite, as part of a more general aim to create a more knowledgeable and enlightened population. It is not a coincidence, therefore, that science has traditionally been treated as a subset of cultural policy in European countries, with Germany being a case in point. Several key principles have been seen as sacrosanct in the definition of the university. Newman, writing in 1854, from a particular theological point of view and Humboldt, writing in 1810 on the foundation of the University of Berlin, may have disagreed about the relationship between teaching and research, but were united in an understanding of what should be provided for and how: universal knowledge, across disciplines and subject areas, under conditions of (relative) autonomy.

The pursuit of knowledge implies no *necessary* hierarchy between science, social science and the humanities – of course, subjects have changed over time as new branches of knowledge have developed or, more precisely, been refined, transformed or rebranded. Whether through the provision of theology or criminology, all branches of knowledge have traditionally had the right to equal status and place within the academy. Such concepts find their resonance in the ideas of the 'full range university' or 'universal provision'.

The provision of education to elites has been variously characterized as both a precondition for and consequence of the university's cultural, social and civic roles. It has been held, on the one hand, that only through self-governance and autonomy from state interests can broader societal values be produced, reproduced and potentially revised. On the other hand, autonomy has also been characterized as part of a 'pact with the state' in return for furnishing its cognitive requirements (Delanty 2001). Whether assumed or accorded, autonomy and self-governance have been the basic operating conditions which guarantee the quality of the knowledge produced within the university by virtue of eliminating the potential for external contamination.

Boundaries between the outside world and the university, represented physically through the image of the courtyard or inner sanctum, in which scholars are provided spaces within but apart from their immediate localities, have been replicated within these organizations. Traditional university structures have divided disciplinary areas into silos for the purposes of management and organization, but more importantly, according to methodological and epistemological orientations that define 'communities' and who is included and excluded. Such practices have led to characterizations of 'academic tribes' (Becher 1989) bound by disciplinary affiliations. Universities have been divided into faculties, schools, research institutes and ever smaller subgroupings that represent not only mechanisms for management, administration, control, discipline and reward, but also cultural differences in modes of production. Nested academic identities result, in which affiliation to immediate research groupings is followed by affinity with broad disciplinary communities across institutions, rather than within a single university setting.

What this has meant for the practice of research up until the contemporary knowledge era is the provision of contexts which, by their effects, inform varying degrees of epistemic permeability and endogenous and referential dimensions of reflexivity. While the physical sciences have a long history of development in diverse institutional settings outside the academy, such as in private research laboratories, government research settings or industry, under recent conditions the university's traditional monopoly on social research has been challenged by consultancies, think tanks and other knowledge 'gurus' peddling their social wisdom. In addition, large multinational corporations may offer funding for more experimental forms of research whose outputs may not be evident, but whose dividends may provide for competitive advantage thereby justifying the risk associated with investment. Endogenous reflexivity within the academy, therefore, is variable in terms of its insularity from what are professionally defined as outside 'contaminants'.

We do not wish to imply the existence of static disciplinary boundaries, nor an absence of relevance or relational understanding. Rather, relational understandings do not necessarily translate into referential reflexivity, for this varies with institutional context, cultural norms and the political economy of research funding. In urban studies, for example, we see both a strong degree of epistemic permeability in terms of the reformulation of disciplinary boundaries over time in relation to definitions of the 'urban' and the changing nature and complexity of urban phenomena (May and Perry 2005). Its development is shaped by globalization and cosmopolitanism, as well as the diversity of its own practices (Le Gales 2005; Marcuse and van Kempen 2000). Social settings have been seen as laboratories in which relevance – either through the generation of knowledge about urban dynamics or knowledge for urban policy – has played a key role. Chicago not only was a 'laboratory' for early urban scholars, but also provided a 'heuristic space' through which to understand larger dynamics in industrial capitalist societies' (Sassen 2005). Yet relevance here is a by-product of or context for research, an inherent starting condition for the justification of research or an accidental effect of application, but not necessarily integral to its production; until, that is, the public speak back and require it as a condition of entry to such places.

Given the above, we need to make a distinction between forms of epistemic permeability: between the boundaries of disciplines (multi-, inter- and transdisciplinarity); between disciplines and their institutions and their relations with the outside world. These are not connected and it is in part their conflation that is responsible for the degree of attributed value to particular forms of knowledge. Changes have taken place within boundaries, provided and structured by the university, in which awareness of and reference to external changes, in terms of subject focus, has not repositioned or affected the disposition of academics. Reflexivity, in the social sciences, can be linked to contextualization but in a 'consciously detached manner' (Gibbons et al. 1994: 105). It becomes not a matter of social science interacting with society, but very particular versions of such practice being in, but certainly not of, those societies. To this extent, Max Weber's answer to being an academic who was a civil servant without being a state functionary was an allusion to value freedom. Yet, the condition of being able to criticize institutions is itself dependent on capacities that are afforded by those institutions. A pact is then entered into between the university and the state with self-censorship being the price to pay for the freedom to speak from a position of authority (A. Scott 1995).

The relationship between social research and the outside world, as mediated through the university as the dominant context of production, contrasts with the implicit contract we can see between the physical sciences and different institutional settings. Here, knowledge-producing conditions have been subject to variability both institutionally and in relation to the expectations of the state. Particular scientific activities have been expected to deliver industrial outputs, define strategic economic direction and underpin technological possibilities and developments. Consideration of the broader socio-economic value of the social sciences do not feature in state-level rhetorics in the justification of science and research spending throughout the early twentieth century and post-war period. It is notable that early discussions over the creation of a European university, initially linked to the French idea for a training and a research institute for nuclear energy, came to focus on the humanities and explicitly rejected the attachment of economic value to university education (Corbett 2009). What this points to is a differential starting point for disciplines, across contexts, in relation to the degrees of permeability to change from outside and within.

To the extent that universities have continued to remain committed to the concept of a full-range university in both research and teaching, differences in the institutional context for and expectations of disciplines have not necessarily served to undermine the position and practice of social research. Nevertheless, the changing political economy of knowledge with its increased expectations for particular kinds of relevance and demands for epistemic permeability as defined above, places institutions under considerable pressure in terms of the prioritization of different knowledges and the provision of conditions for their production. While views of science are increasingly mediated by economic conditions (Fuller 2000), institutions also mediate, translate, transform or even transcend external values in ways that reposition different forms of knowledge.

Shifting Values, Shifting Sands

Against both continuity and change in the academic mode of production, we have witnessed, since the late 1970s, intensification in the climate of neo-liberal ideologies resulting in an ever-greater penetration into management thinking of practices whose power rests upon their supposed self-evidence. Of all these it is the idea and necessity for competition that has become the most naturalized of ideologies (Schoenberger 1997). From this basis, the pact with the state is under more pressure: critique may be readily dismissed as impractical, ideologically motivated, tolerated due to it not having any effect on practice, or even dangerous and anarchic.

Part of this has seen an increased incorporation of industry modes of organizational control. Ideas of 'corporate culture', informed by the dominance of knowledge as a commodified product, have translated into the need to control human service organizations with a resulting proliferation of bureaucratic measures and practices, leading to significant changes in forms of management (Pollitt and Bouckaert 2004). These transformations have witnessed an accompanying move towards concerns with what were once regarded as being 'outside' of the remit of management. As 'scientific' approaches, inspired by Taylorist principles (Brown R.K. 1992), found themselves under increasing question, practices have emerged encompassing employee emotions, values and motivations, along with attention to organizational culture in general. Total quality and human resource management, business process reengineering, the learning organization and knowledge management are symptomatic of these general developments (Knights and McCabe 2003; Knights and Willmott 2000).

In this changing climate strategies are sold as solutions to problems of organizational performance as part of the management of identities and relations that accompany 'the capitalization of the meaning of life' (Gordon 1991: 44). In order to monitor external environments to produce appropriate internal responses, it then becomes necessary to have whole armies of statisticians and evaluation units so that no apparent deviation from optimum performance is permitted. These processes are ably assisted by evaluations via appraisal systems where opportunities are afforded for individuals to consider and act upon their own lack of zeal in the pursuit of the organizational mission.

Public sector organizations are critical cases as their primary goals have always been recognized as being the provision of services to correct for the inefficiencies of the market system. Nonetheless, those universities conforming to this form of funding have become the targets of transformation for representing practices that are inefficient, ineffective and uneconomic in comparison to the private sector with its apparent efficiencies and unquestioned contributions to economic well-being. The essence of the private sector firm is taken to be 'its ability to create, transfer, assemble, integrate, and exploit knowledge assets. Knowledge assets underpin competences, and competences in turn underpin the firm's product and service offerings to the market' (Teece 1998: 75). The idea of 'capturing value' from knowledge assets within public sector organizations is, in contrast, seen as significant in its absence. Instead, knowledges informing and arising from practice are subject to modes of control that aim at conformity to expectations that are born in the shadow of the market.

Assumptions regarding the superiority of commodified knowledge translate into increasing levels of bureaucracy. While this creates anomalies, tensions and contradictions, it also ends up creating de-politicized views of processes and practices. The result is to bracket a history whose values are rooted in the provision of political checks upon the market system. What then arises are spaces of ambiguity in which administrative-technical discourses produce rationalizations for organizational existence that ignore the relationship between knowledge and practice at the front line of service provision. The result is to bracket political-allocative issues concerning the overall volume of budgetary allocation in relation to the quality of services through the production of narrowly defined objectives and targets. Strategic visions become informed by knowledges derived from the private sector and individualistic views of people or units within those organizations then predominate because they are separated from its history, the context of their actions, as well as the knowledges that inform those actions and communications at an interactional level with clients (read 'customers').

What we see is a triumph of method over purpose in a movement of these organizations away from a problem-solving to performance mode of operation (Mintzberg 1983), with clear effects upon the distinctiveness of the university as a site of knowledge production. A public service ethos, however broadly defined, has found itself the target of transformatory practices as judgement and discretion, with its power and partiality, gives way to audit as an expression of the power of indifference. While interpreted and altered in the process of implementation with different professional groups being more successful than others in ignoring or resisting administrative edicts, it tends to produce individualized cultures within increasing bureaucratic environments with clear implications for the development of forms of reflexivity.

A continual and unfounded celebration of the private over the public sphere or the market over any notion of civil society heralds a shift in the values attached to different forms of knowledge and the institution of the university. As outlined in Chapter 6, this informs the dance between excellence and relevance and their conflation in the clamour for competitive advantage. In the search for position in international league tables and for additional relevance-related finance, particular forms of knowledge have become prioritized. The articulation of a more utilitarian or instrumental discourse on knowledge, accompanied by the categorization of states and places according to their scientific and technological output and rankings of excellence, has very real effects for the positioning of different types of research in the popular consciousness and in terms of resource allocation.

There have been many critiques of attempts to improve the public understanding of science that emphasize the limits of a deficit model and the need for a two-way process of communication between science and society (S. Harding 2006; Irwin and Michael 2003). Yet despite this background, these knowledge-producing communities remain black boxes for many societal actors which, over time, have been populated by assumptions that contrast strongly with those made for social science. A 'mutually tolerable ignorance' (Fuller 2000: 8) persists in which neither science nor society is equipped to evaluate the claims of the other. Science is seen as difficult, hard and therefore an expert activity around its own set of justifications and social science provides understanding in application. Science can then remain the preserve of scientists, whether within universities or industrial laboratories, while social scientific sites of knowledge production see consultancies that proclaim to offer understanding and analysis but may do little more than provide that which is already known, or confirm existing prejudices. One is seen as expensive and time-consuming, while the other is cheaper and able to be performed at speed.

The media has a key role in influencing the perceived status of different work within the cultural consciousness. Despite a strong unified message from different disciplines that there are no easy answers to contemporary dilemmas, the big issues tend to be couched in scientific black and white terms. Science is portrayed as both remedy and cause, while it is the shocking, unusual or controversial that courts attention, rather than contributions to understanding or meaning. Given the normative orientations which take 'Big Science' as the standard against which other forms of enquiry is judged (Fuller 2000), other forms of knowledge sit in its wake.

Some do emphasize the extent of integration of science, in general, into the fabric of modern societies and economies (de la Mothe 2001: 3), lying at the heart of decisions about the environment, health, welfare and security (Stehr 2004). Michel Foucault tended to see the human sciences as implicated in power-knowledge in this way but the role of institutions, which we have emphasized, is not evident in these formulations. It is said that knowledge societies 'run on expert processes and expert systems that are epitomized by science but are structured into all areas of social life' (Knorr-Cetina 1999: 1). Science is seen to be transforming the nature of democracy from a politics of sovereign citizens to a politics of diffused experts in which electoral struggle is replaced by expert bodies and specialized technical discourse threatens democratic discussion (S. Turner 2003). While we can have justifiable claims for our beliefs, there is no knowledge that can justify the absence of social value in the assessment of their implications. Yet such is the effort made to avoid recognition of this, the value attributed to scientism has fundamentally altered the nature of democratic society and is seen to provide disinterested technocratic 'solutions' to multiple areas of public policy.

We should also recognize the role of scepticism, trust and risk in these processes. Science is visible precisely because of the potential negative consequences of its practice. Here it is not so much science itself that is under scrutiny, but its application. We no longer taste the 'delicious savour of useless knowledge' (Russell 2004: 25), but have moved from a situation of lamenting a deficiency of relevance of scientific knowledge towards a surplus of effects (Stehr 2004). Now we face a fear 'that we know too much and are about to assume the role of God' and this can replace 'the concern that we are to a large degree poorly informed' (Stehr 2004: xi). The result is an increasing attempt to regulate, manage, control and direct science in a new form of knowledge politics where we have a surplus of information, but a deficit of intelligence.

Opportunities now arise for social research. The contemporary knowledge era, as described in Chapter 6, has undermined the 'privileged' position of social research vis-à-vis the conditions of relative autonomy under which it has traditionally been produced. There is no immunity to global forces across disciplines. However, the debate on relevance has been couched in very particular terms. Two positions seem to predominate. First, social research acts as a form of consciousness in the provision of ethics to the ('real') work of scientific and technological discovery. Second, it is a tool to enhance the effectiveness of dialogue with the public about (rather than public understanding of) science via new forms of engagement. Yet it is an end-game additionality, rather than transformation of practices, that dominates. Social research then validates existing epistemological hierarchies, or eases the passage of application of particular forms of knowledge. It becomes a problem if it calls into question 'a scientific hagiography which scientists often take part in and which they need in order to believe in what they do' (Bourdieu 1993: 9).

Attributed value arises from the conflation between forms of epistemic permeability. There remains a question over whether new discipline formation in areas such as biotechnology is a causal effect of knowledge-based transitions or a stage in the natural evolution of disciplines. Indeed, an imperative for cross-disciplinary working stems from within knowledge organizations themselves in the recognition that the exciting areas to work in, and often more risky ones, are at the edges of disciplines. Innovation within disciplines then becomes desirable from a supply-side point of view, through borrowing from elsewhere to answer the next question in the chain of discovery. To this extent, we can see pull-factors to blur or fragment the disciplines, as much as those that push: internal content-based dynamics accompany external context-driven ones.

While curiosity-driven, discipline-hopping exists, it is not the case that such innovations within and between disciplines necessarily have any relationship with innovation as defined by policy-makers as relating to economic benefit. Thus, we may see interdisciplinarity but not necessarily as a result of, response to, or contributing factor within, the knowledge-based economy. A flawed relationship is presumed to exist between interdisciplinarity and innovation that mirrors the assumptions made about excellence and relevance: that there is any automatic connection between academic excellence and economic and social benefit. The exemplars of biotechnology or synthetic biology are held up to demonstrate close working relationships with industry, application-oriented approaches and innovation in interdisciplinary research. Here we see continual variations in the divide between public and private economies of knowledge whose divisions and interdependencies are argued to generate 'new forms, new experimentations with epistemic practice and economic organization' (M. Harvey and McMeekin 2007: 185). Yet understandings of 'science' are vague enough to allow particular assumptions to flow into neighbouring areas, whether the methodologies and contexts bear any similarity or not. Similarly, collaborations between science and the arts are seen as innovative by virtue of their interdisciplinarity, but may have no transformative outcome in terms of how meanings are generated and attributed to different forms of practice.

The coexistence of positive and negative views of the status and role of science finds parallels with alternate views of the university. Universities have been characterized as being to the 'information economy what coal mines were to the industrial economy' (Castells and Hall 1994: 231). They are seen as key to providing competitive advantage in the knowledge economy (Etzkowitz and Leydesdorff 2000), to learning and development processes (Archibugi and Lundvall 2001) and as the basis for visioning a future resting on ideas or creative places (Florida 2002). Alternatively, universities are seen as barriers to change, problems to be managed rather than solutions to be harnessed, in the search for knowledge-based futures. Value is attributed to science, at the same time as a devaluation of scientific knowledge and expertise is occurring. The university is both a beneficiary and site of ambiguity over current socio-economic policy paradigms. Such distinctions map broadly onto a similar divide between policy doctrine ('science as saviour') and public attitudes ('the sceptics of science'), with academic literatures being used in support of divergent positions. The reasons for this apparent conflict lie in a paradox of values where debate over science frequently takes place in a normative vacuum (Perry 2006).

Value is being attributed to particular conceptions of market potential. This not only results from assumptions concerning relative economic potential, but also relates to how different disciplines are constituted as 'expert' or 'accessible' fields. In the process interdisciplinarity is often taken to be a sufficient condition for wealth generation. Commodification and relevance, combined with the symbolic power of excellence, then work to shape predispositions to favour and support diverse forms of knowledge production. Yet it is the institutional translation and mediation of pressures that more directly inform the practices of research, by constituting varying degrees of epistemic permeability.

Responses: Translation, Insulation and Mediation

The contemporary climate, defined both by the hegemony of the free market and its penetration into knowledge-based discourses, has led to shifts in values. These have been exemplified in corporate rebranding, institutional form and strategic orientation, as well as attribution of values in policy and funding streams to particular forms of knowledge. Such shifts have the potential to remould what we have traditionally recognized as the university. However, just as there is no single history of the university, there can be no single present. A variety of university responses which refract and mediate external values that are informed by degrees of institutional power, lead to tendential effects for the work that is performed within them.

If we imagine a continuum in which universities mobilize differential resources that lead to an embrace or absorption of external value shifts, the end points of the spectrum can be seen as translation or insulation. In their wholesale translation, in common with other public sector organizations as outlined above, we see higher education institutions becoming increasingly subjected to industry modes of organizational control: by the late 1990s it was estimated that approximately 30 per cent of a UK academic's time was spent on administration and bureaucracy (Court 1996). Through the adoption of quasi-market systems and processes, echoed more widely in the public sector, universities are increasingly judged in terms of their business performance through extended regulatory systems, performance indicators and so forth, not by the traditional reference to a public service ethic or their own professional values. A shift from a public service to entrepreneurial ethos is one from accountability based on trust and mutuality to auditable accountability based on formal contracts.

What results is a distinction between knowledge and context via a whole series of attempts to determine the 'how' of practice through new modes of supervision, surveillance and appraisals. The overall result is that the 'why' and 'how' of knowledge is subsumed within the narrow confines of the measurability of 'what' (May 2001): for example, external income generation, citation indexes, staff–student ratios, league tables and publications. A culture in which an understanding of differences, along with negotiations, discussions, deliberations and decisions that are things to be encouraged, rather than avoided, diminishes.

Due to such effects it has been argued that universities are engaged in a process of 'creative destruction' (Fuller 2000), or that they are architects of their own demise by virtue of their own success as a result of massification in higher education (Gibbons et al. 1994). To this we can also add a 'hollowing out' of their distinctiveness through retreat to increasing forms of managerialism and professionalization without any reference to the value of their own roles and responsibilities in society (Delanty 2001; Ziman 1994). Managerialism has aligned with professional ideologies to enable the targeting of the exercise of discretionary knowledge as if it unproblematically informed, as opposed to interacted with, the conditions under which actions take place. Moreover, there is no automatic connection between the importation of market principles and subsequent market advantage, as the search for innovation implies freedom and risk, incompatible with too great a focus on efficiency, public sector auditing requirements, user engagement and identifiable outputs.

With full-scale translation we see universities increasingly modelling themselves in the image of the market, seeing themselves as businesses and significant economic actors in their own right. It is not just the case that universities, industry and government are increasingly blurring roles and responsibilities, but that universities are seeking to become all-in-one as they seek to meet disparate expectations. Their estates are managed with profit and optimization in mind, rather than the provision of spaces and places to furnish and support the institution's cognitive requirements. In this way estate management is seen to be a more neutral endeavour represented in the physicality of buildings without accompanying discussion of, say, multiple use or access to different groups. The external generation of finance becomes a tool to supplement internal resources, replacing any notion of civic responsibility, while economic output is translated into intellectual property and commodified through new organizational units, designed to undertake activities called 'knowledge transfer' and 'public engagement'. In this way, whole new knowledge practices are created that have only an indirect bearing upon the core activities of these institutions as represented by teaching and research.

A resulting information politics then results whereby that which can be readily understood and codified as a precursor to commercialization, or proof of engagement with varying 'stakeholders', is seen to produce value. External values can be reproduced internally, rather than mediated according to a clear sense of purpose, resulting in the prioritization of very different forms of knowledge within the same institution. Markets are both economic, in terms of commercial value, as well as being academic, in terms of ranking in hierarchies and league tables. Strategic management then easily becomes the reproduction of these differences, driven by supposed grounds of necessity (being higher up the league table attracts a greater number of rich, national and international students), rather than a more general consideration of the need to examine the distinctiveness of the university as a site of knowledge production and transmission.

An analysis of whether such values are in tension or contradiction would require a degree of institutional reflexivity that is rare and a form of leadership that is confident in its critical capacity. Instead, academics assume scholars of international repute may be better able to run their institutions in a visible collusion between excellence and globalization, or those from the private sector are beamed in as if the work of translation of opportunities into occupational cultures were secondary to the practice of public, rhetorical flourishes. Specialization ensues in which survival of the fittest, clustering and developing centres of excellence are characteristic of inter- and intra-institutional strategies. The casualty is an understanding of the extent to which these institutions exhibit a diversity of practices across the range of research and teaching.

For some, translation is absolute. These observations lead some authors to speak of a postmodern university or a 'university in ruins' (Maskell and Robinson 2001; Readings 1996; A. Smith and Webster 1997). Here 'insulation' would be the preferred option in which universities seek shelter from external pressures and protect traditional academic values and methodologies. Such an option would clearly be contingent on absolute autonomy, which would be possible only under conditions of obtaining independent private and discretionary finance, but still reliant upon the academic market for its international standing to reproduce itself. Given the evident problems in such a strategy, neither translation nor insulation can be viable or indeed are visible responses.

What we see is widespread mediation of external forces leading to a series of inter- and intra-institutional variations. At one level, this mediation may be part of a deliberate strategy of universities to obtain and maintain positions in local, national and global hierarchies or to represent themselves with academic, governmental, industrial or societal groupings in particular ways. So for instance, University A might engage with a range of external organizations at the level of strategic managers through participation in relevant intermediary groups, while the practice of research carries on as usual across disciplines. In such a case, we see the external acting as a buffer to the internal. It is the representation of research and its prioritization externally that alters and is not necessarily reflected in a shift in internal practices. University B might see its very survival as tied to the successful exploitation of new funding opportunities for engagement, but place the burden for response on particular sub-units, thus similarly offering shelter to particular groups whose work is seen as requiring that degree of insulation or protection from external contaminants. University C might seek wholesale change within the university in terms of forms of engagement, without necessarily prioritizing particular areas of research. In this case, the emphasis is on new ways of working across all academic fields, rather than systematic prioritization of specific fields.

The issue in each case is the relationship between external orientation and internal reform; in other words, the extent to which external values are prioritized strategically and then subsequently internalized within the university with implications for the position of different forms of knowledge. More often, however, mediation occurs in ways that do not always accord with the notion of deliberate strategy, even though positive effects may be attributed to such practices. That is, the extent to which external forces reshape the university as an institution and the knowledge produced within it is dependent on the implicit, unacknowledged and unintended effects of structural, governance and informal arrangements.

A link between external positioning and representation of the institution in relation to shifting values is the relationship between stated position, recognition, reward, incentivization and promotion criteria. While strategic managers seek to position universities via criteria of economic or social relevance according to shifting environmental expectations, these dictates from on high are destined to remain so without a clear understanding of how strategic documents, texts or calls to engagement are to be incentivized and with what effect upon occupational cultures. In practice, there is a disjuncture between the demands for application and the messages communicated internally linked to particular sources of funding. Strategic posturing with significant, external others, serves little point if publication in peer-reviewed journals is valued above other forms of academic activity. Values in knowledge practices accorded to different activities are echoed in promotion criteria. A university may badge itself as an innovative and enterprising university, yet promotion criteria fail to take these into account and when they do they are disconnected from other activities and so allowed to become free-floating discourses in view of the absence of internal work at understanding.

Career trajectories may then be limited to those who play the normal academic game and adhere to strict hierarchies and ways of working that have traditionally furthered academic reputations. Relevance at both an institutional and individual level then becomes about the justification of research in order to access funding and produce particular outputs. Here the issue is not the relative importance of either relevance or excellence, but the point in the research process where they become applicable, with real effects for reward, recognition and organizational culture. A resulting gap is also apparent in relation to funding streams that claim to encourage academics to be innovative at the point of applying for funding, yet assess end products according to a narrow set of academic or user-defined metrics.

At this point the fundamental issue of governance structures comes into play (for example, see Braun and Merrion 1999; Hedmo and Wedlin 2008; Sporn 1999). University structures protect, shelter, mediate or magnify external pressures. Universities are multifaceted organizations that encompass elements associated with the characteristics that Max Weber found in bureaucracies – regarding the organization as an end in itself, rather than a means to an end – as well as those associated with a professionalism that regards autonomy as essential to knowledge production. These, in themselves, make for a tension and, without a sufficient understanding of these dynamics, recasting these institutions in the image of an environment which cannot be read as self-evidently possessing clear lessons for internal transformation, leads to ever greater anomalies. Such a situation is not helped by university managers speaking of the environment as if it possessed self-evident properties, rather than contestable claims.

Here we pick up on earlier points regarding the nature of the university as a Fordist organization in a post-Fordist era. Universities, for the most part, remain top-down, disconnected, hierarchical, siloed institutions, in which disciplines are divided through faculties, schools and research groups without effective cross-institutional coordination mechanisms and often subject to cost-centre budgeting that does little for imaginative collaborations. The reasons for such ossification also lie in the nature of scientific activity as a result of the tendency to enable deep specialization (Lohmann 2004). Structures mediate the relationship between the external and the internal and create the possibilities for the forms of epistemic permeability outlined earlier. The university is hardly unique in these respects. According to contingency theory the adoption of organizational forms will depend upon a relationship between structure and function (Mintzberg 1983). While conceptually neat, abstraction from societal influences, together with a simplification of complexity and the neglect of strategic choice, diminishes the levels of understanding when it comes to the direction of universities.

Taken to its extreme, interpretations at the level of boundaries between an organization and its environment can not only lead to the tendency towards necessity without choice, but also provide a set of reasons to undermine hierarchy: that is, if the organization is only a reflection of its environment, the role of strategy as having any effect rapidly departs and with that the justification for differential pay according to the assumption that those in strategic positions make any positive difference to outcomes. It is very rare for those in such positions to reason to this conclusion. More likely than this there is a lot of talk of configuring environments in the name of attracting excellence to institutions, or reconfiguring in the name of the pursuit of relevance. Balance and working hard at achieving understanding between different partners is, of course, another route, but a more modest and difficult practice whose visibility is not so great in the face of the attractions of hyperbole.

The traditional centralized and bureaucratic mode of organization of the university is challenged by the need to respond flexibly to increasingly unpredictable environmental changes, to engage with the varying needs of a locality and in the pursuit of funding streams beyond those normally associated with teaching and research. Concerted action does not simply require coherent policy frameworks, but also needs effective organization and consent. Internal coordination needs to be matched against external expectations, thereby providing a greater congruity between organizational design and the environment. Where the environment exhibits a sufficient degree of stability in its expectations, a more centralized and bureaucratic mode of organization would be exhibited. In less predictable situations, on the other hand, greater degrees of flexibility are required that enable interpretations of environmental changes to be rapidly implemented into organizational responses. In these instances, mechanical organizations would produce negative effects because of the centralization of their command and control functions; although this is not to recognize the importance of a particular ethos in a world whose demands are for change for its own sake (du Gay 2000).

As part of the changes outlined here and in Chapter 6, we might expect to see greater democratization and flexibility as universities seek to respond to new imperatives. The co-production of an administration occurs with clients due to the inability to fix, through objectification, what was once held to be a constant. As service organizations universities need to 'presuppose that clients are ready to engage in "productive interaction"' (Offe 1985: 311). Nevertheless, clients are not manifestly homogenous groups, nor are they located simply as students, but also as businesses, voluntary organizations, community groups and public sector organizations which are themselves varied and have different needs. What we see in this process is efficiency then moving from the bureaucratic mode which, according to the classic Weberian model, concerns following the rules, to also being defined as the causing of effects: for example, increased business efficiency through knowledge transfer and rates of participation among young adult populations.

Demands for flexibility now sit alongside those for standardization. Returning to an earlier point regarding ossification, it is now breadth (as a precursor for interdisciplinary working) and not just depth that is necessary. Universities rarely exhibit such flexible forms. Epistemic permeability between disciplines and between disciplines and institutions and the outside world is limited by structural and bureaucratic lines of accountability and management. Vertical and horizontal deadlock emerges that limits the capacity for innovations to emerge up and out or across and out of institutions, while preserving their sense of purpose and confidence in an otherwise fluid world.

We cannot presuppose the existence of a strategic position that is identifiable at the level of university management, as if utterances and actions were somehow reflected in institutional practices. Such a deceit allows chief executives to free float across sectors as if they were responsible for positive transformations in organizational functioning. It is not the case that a single and clearly communicated policy exists at strategic level that is subsequently impeded in its implementation by structures and cultures. Rather, sets of disparate and often conflicting strategies exist that internalize external ambiguities. Hence, it is perfectly possible for academics to receive communications from central management concerning the importance of engagement and knowledge transfer activities, while also being urged to target particular journals in ever more rapid timeframes in order to meet the next round of research evaluation exercises that have yet to be determined.

Communications become disjointed. Despite hierarchical structures, tensions dominate in the translation of strategic direction through faculty and institutional structures to individual researchers. From the bottom-up, similar problems emerge. How can the university collectively develop a position or understanding when there is no single point of intelligence – although there is a great deal of information – on what the university has to offer? Universities can be seen as hybrid organizations connected through multiple links between the internal and the external that are not, nor are we arguing should necessarily be even if it were possible, filtered through any central point. The result, for those wishing to engage with the university, is often the absence of a collective voice or understanding of what values different institutions represent, as if they themselves could translate such expectations into their own organizations.

We have said that the manifestation of such issues differs in national contexts. The infiltration of market values into US higher education has emphasized how the advancement and transmission of knowledge as a core university value has been ousted by the just-in-time, immediate gratification values of the marketplace (Kirp 2003). In such an analysis, translation is synonymous with capitulation to external forces. Isolated examples of insulation may be found in European contexts where universities have exploited environmental conditions and institutional power to turn their back, both physically and symbolically, on the outside world. During one of our interviews with a senior manager of a European university, its role was characterized as serving civilization by the very protection of the liberal arts and humanities that were under threat in contemporary politic-economic climates. Here, the role was seen to exist at the supra-societal level, better placed to speak on society's behalf than short-lived political administrations or vested social interests, with a role to protect the future from the present, or society from itself. While admittedly a very different view than that found in many institutions, such a characterization can stretch the relationship with democracy too far, with the few claiming to speak for the many (Fuller 2000).

There is no single typology that can account for the different forms of mediation visible between the external and the internal. We can gain insights by considering the relative degrees to which external economic or civic values are subsequently incorporated within either (or both) a university's strategic direction or internal value base. Important factors clearly relate to the warmth with which different governments at multiple scales embrace knowledge capitalist discourses, linked to greater or lesser degrees of neo-liberalism or social democracy; to the distinction between research-intensive, Ivy League or Russell Group universities and other institutional types and the extent to which they can mobilize institutional power in support of particular knowledges; to the nature of funding streams and governance regimes which offer greater or lesser degrees of bureaucracy and control over university policies and structures.

Taking on board the insights from previous chapters regarding the balance between generalized trends and context-specific manifestations, a gap can emerge between the external and internal, resulting in a structural and strategic mismatch at the level of the university. Even where clear institutional positions have been defined, external values are mediated in different and unanticipated ways through internal structures and policies. Mediation is then unpredictable, leaning either towards translation or insulation, with potential positive, but more often than not, negative results. Far from institutional shelter provided for in terms of clear and confident values capable of interpretation of consequences and adaptation to various pressures, we see a magnification of turbulence and an absence of a concerted challenge to dominant assumptions.

Conditions for Change

Conditions for the practice of research are variable and dependent not only on positions and dispositions of academics in occupational cultures, but also on the positions of their institutions themselves and the extent to which forms of reflexivity are enabled in complex political-economic environments. Within the above set of responses, research finds differential levels of commitment and varying conditions for its production. Translation may result in a sidelining in favour of more commercially relevant or internationally renowned areas of science, in line with society's expectations and views on the relative ease to which different forms of knowledge can be produced. A subsequent de-valuing may take place at the institutional level, but which may paradoxically provide the conditions in which business as usual can characterize its production. Alternatively, it may be through areas of social research that engagement is specifically sought: for instance, in relation to industry or community outreach. Here both increased *and* decreased prioritization can lead directly to shifts in conditions of production through new modes of working such as knowledge transfer partnerships, placements or secondments.

An alignment then occurs with the 'process-driven' view of knowledge-based development outlined earlier. Here knowledge tends to be broader, taking in the sciences, social sciences, humanities and arts. A product-driven view tends to be more economically driven and focused on exploitable products, in terms of new companies, patents and intellectual property. End-game additionality would also fall under this rubric in terms of activities relating to public engagement and communication. In process-driven, knowledge-based development, the researcher has joint or prime responsibility for dissemination or application, while product-driven, knowledge-based development allows for a clearer separation of roles and responsibilities, allowing the researcher to carry on regardless of external expectations while others take application forward. Most frequently, as already noted, it is acquisition-based development that is favoured in the search for excellent, 'science'-based futures, leaving scientists to carry on with independently defined agendas, while demands for relevance are to be met by other parts of the university.

Mediation results in nuanced positions and conditions for research. There is no necessary relationship between the prioritization and conditions of production for different forms of knowledge. Social research may be either insulated from or exposed to the requirements for referential reflexivity as a result of its relative importance in institutional hierarchies. This accounts for the differences in strongly held views about what is actually happening in higher education in relation to different subject areas and its ramifications for the practice of social science. Yet what is certain is that funding streams remain oriented towards external values and the search for the science-based, world-class university that assumes both excellence and relevance, leaving little scope or funding for the creation of productive conditions for alternative forms of knowledge production.

In seeking a more positive mediation between the external and the internal to create the conditions in which different forms of epistemic permeability at the individual and institutional level can emerge, there is one clear precondition: to link the 'what' with the 'how', underpinned by a shared understanding of different values attached to forms of knowledge and for what reasons in both contemporary and future scenarios. The missing middle between content, context and consequence results in a disconnection that renders impossible any meaningful discussion on the appropriate purpose, structure and governance of the university as a site of knowledge production.

The mismatch between external expectations and internal reform of the university has been noted widely in policy discourses. Yet responses are more often than not formulated in the absence of recognition of what universities have traditionally stood for and the reasons for particular conditions for knowledge production. Hence, we see the imposition of structural solutions from on high, aimed at reforming bureaucratic, slow and unwieldy institutions, in favour of a 'one-size-fits-the-market' solution.

The Bologna process aims to create a European Higher Education Area as a precursor for the harmonization of degree cycles and structures and systems of credits across Europe, as well as cooperation in quality assurance, to accord better with the market's need for fit and ready graduates (Corbett 2009). Such reforms may claim to be well intended and founded on recognition in theory of the core values of the university, for instance, through acknowledgement of the

1988 Magna Charta Universitatum. The implications of Bologna, however, are still being analysed in terms of the unintended effects on different institutional contexts and histories, in many cases exacerbating rather than alleviating internal issues of reform (see Witte et al. 2008). Similarly, in an account of the Austrian university system in transition, reforms which 'introduce new hierarchies into an already complex and pillarised system, destabilise that system by creating new forms of polarisation' (Burtscher et al. 2006: 243). Reforms then create new risks and inefficiencies that are insensitive to the institutional qualities necessary for specific organizational purposes (A. Scott 2006).

Changes impacting on the university cannot be seen as part of an active desire to destroy public universities, but may be characterized as: 'gradual erosion ... through a series of short-term, half-measures ... these individual, sequential and apparently practical choices are destroying a resource that, though far from perfect, is extremely valuable to the maintenance and further development of democratic society' (Levin and Greenwood 2006: 5). The issue is one of values; not necessarily their absence, but a conflation and layering of different values for what the university should do, how it should be structured and the importance of particular forms of knowledge. Values are unarticulated, hidden and assumed, yet have very real impacts in terms of the activities carried out within universities.

One way of defining the problem is the construction of a democratic science policy regime to specify the grounds on which a choice between competing proposals should be made in a resource-scarce environment. Finalization, cross-disciplinary relevance and epistemic fungibility then emerge as three responses (Fuller 2000). The latter is particularly demanding in terms of the requirements upon scientists to justify their own proposals and work in open fora in the presence of those from different fields. An institutionalized form of 'cognitive euthanasia' (Fuller 2000: 136) is designed to extend the principles governing science to society itself. Here we see concern to create the spaces for debate or 'agora' that we have argued is so clearly missing from contemporary political-economic environments.

There are those who have argued for a re-education of both society and the university itself as to its values via a form of pragmatic action research that links an understanding of needs with the environment in which researchers operate (Levin and Greenwood 2006). Echoes are found here with a call for a pragmatic social science and attention to the conditions that enable its production (Stehr 1992). The Gulbenkian Commission to 'Open the Social Sciences' (Wallerstein 1996) similarly drew attention to the responsibility of social scientists themselves for leading and defining the parameters of debate, as well as defining, through action, the types of activities that may characterize a revised relationship between social research and the outside world. Social scientists should 'take a hard look at their present structures and try to bring their revised intellectual perceptions of a useful division of labour into line with the organizational framework they necessarily construct' (Wallerstein 1996: 96). As Pierre Bourdieu reminds us, however, there are difficulties in positions that contradict received wisdom as it leaves one open to charges of 'ideological bias' or 'political axe-grinding'. The result is that the social sciences must work harder to provide 'infinitely more proof than is asked of the "spokesmen" of common sense' (Bourdieu 1993: 11).

Appeals for changes in behaviour from the bottom-up do miss the importance of institutional context. A match between purpose and structure, activities and incentivization is clearly needed, through a mixed economy of research that links excellence with relevance and production and application. Good leadership, combined with clear communications externally and internally within the university, is critical. In the absence of clarity in the external environment and an open debate about values, institutional contexts for social research remain varied and often structure knowledge production in ways that are not conducive for productive agonisms between forms of reflexivity and epistemic permeability.

Summary

In Part 1 of this book an understanding was developed concerning the content of different approaches to reflexivity. In Part 2, the consequence of this analysis was manifested in terms of the relations between position and disposition in the study of the social world and epistemic permeability. We have examined the dynamics of these issues as applied to the university in this chapter, building on Chapter 6 which examined the political economy of knowledge in terms of the changing relationship between excellence, relevance and reflexivity. It identified a particular set of issues concerning universities and their relationship to external demands and their often ambiguous roles in national and sub-national coalitions that seek to implement knowledge economy rhetorics in practice.

The institutional context of the university informs the production of social research. We have identified a generic shift towards the importation of private sector or corporate values. At the level of the university, as with many public sector organizations, the effect is to introduce modes of industrial control and organization incompatible with traditional conceptions of the university. Second, we see a set of often conflicting value shifts relating to the prioritization of different forms of knowledge. Assumptions regarding the relationship between a world-class, 'science'-based university and economic and social relevance predominate, with the demand for engagement and relevance being introduced across the sector.

In the case of knowledge production within universities, there are mediating factors that prevent the constitution of forms of reflexivity and instead enable the continued objectification of knowledge. Our evidence from interviews with senior managers, policy-makers and staff across different national and regional contexts points to greater complexity in accounting for particular university responses to external forces than simple mapping would allow. Translation of corporate values for the university is undoubtedly more acute in neo-liberal contexts, such as the United States and United Kingdom, while insulation appears an isolated example, possible only with the convergence of very particular political, economic, cultural and institutional contexts. More commonly, it is mediation that dominates, as universities act as buffer, mirror or magnifier of external forces.

Questions are raised about the capacity and desirability of the university to act at the front line for the knowledge economy. How can a mediating role be performed, either as an intended or unintended consequence, without undermining its own distinctiveness as a site of knowledge production? How can external forces be mediated, distilled and made intelligent in their effects prior to falling upon different institutional and sub-institutional contexts? Overall, to enable its fundamental role to respond without capitulation to short-termism and engage without losing its sense of purpose and value, there is a need for greater active intermediation between university and society, research and practice. We will return to the issue of active intermediaries in our final section. For now, we turn to a discussion of the last element in our inquiries concerning contexts of reflexivity: the occupational cultures that shape the practice of social research.

CULTURES OF RESEARCH PRODUCTION

8

We continue our journey of examining the dynamics through which research is constituted in universities by looking at cultures of production. In so doing we seek to avoid the backdrop of presuppositions that so often inform modes of knowledge production and speak of 'academic' as if it had no relevance to contemporary issues. Rather, we seek to populate an understanding of those places in which research is conducted, in order that it may become a more reflexive, supportive and supported practice. Such practices can and do exist in universities and there is good work undertaken in varying circumstances. While the pressures on universities and occupational cultures are clear, we hope to contribute to a more valued distinctiveness for the knowledge produced in these sites of production through an understanding of their contexts.

Only after the issues that inform academic production have been examined can any further potential be properly assessed. No claim to exhausting such possibilities is made here. Nevertheless, without an understanding of the dynamics of context – which implies context-sensitivity – in relation to what knowledge is produced, exchanged and disseminated – the consequences and possibilities that come with current challenges will not be fully understood nor acted upon. At present we find a variable response from commentators: from assumptions concerning the need for wholesale change, through implications for the engagement and development of universities, to acts of critique as detachment.

There are variations in the processes we will describe according to history, forms of governance, national traditions and political economy. Nevertheless, we have witnessed a heightened effort in the maintenance of what are assumed to be the self-evidential ideas that underpin policies. As part of this general trend we find a managerialism that expresses a faith in the ability of performance and evaluation measures to offer administrative solutions to political problems. What are produced are taxonomic devices that regulate particular sections of activity and produce indifference that does not understand, or respect, difference (Herzfeld 1992). Politics is then sealed within organizational sub-units through the supposition that it is sufficient to deal with revealed preferences within its confines. Particular consequences then follow for the exercise of reflexivity and varying degrees of epistemic permeability.

We have argued that calls for an enhanced and/or maintained civic role for the university sits in tension with the importance placed upon knowledge as a commodity in a 'knowledge transfer' model informed by the knowledge economy. For some commentators the most valued role of universities is held to be sites of knowledge diversity in a world in which legislators seek order (Bauman 1989). Running alongside this is a hypodermic model of knowledge transfer that judges the worth of what is produced according to a narrowly conceived economic instrumentality measured according to impact and outputs. Not surprisingly, these pressures have led to a series of organizational transformations within universities that not only have varying consequences, but also exhibit and produce tensions between these aims and aspirations.

Transformations in Occupational Cultures

While knowledge has always played an important role in human activities, it is 'the quantity of knowledge, the speed and acceleration of knowledge production and the complexity and permeation of knowledge into all spheres of life which mark the current economic "phase" more than in any preceding era' (De Weert 1999: 52). The consequences for academic production may be seen as indicative of a social, not political revolution because: 'Unlike a political revolution, a social revolution does not break out: it takes place' (Heller and Fehér 1991: 144). We are witnessing a reconstitution of the university as a terrain of not only variable, but also contradictory, expectations. Yet instead of having a public debate, the technicians of the state and economy tend to resort to catch-all phrases like 'engagement' to characterize a diversity of practices in universities that have different sets of purposes.

Having undertaken work on the socio-economic contribution of universities in society, examined innovation and 'science cities', designed processes that explore the future of the university and conducted research on governance, science and regional development, we have been able to develop a number of insights. Our work has led us to questions concerning the content and recognition of the knowledges produced within universities as a condition of their future survival. As we have suggested, questions of distinctiveness have to be linked with institutional conditions and changing environmental circumstances. Calls to reflexivity are empty without this reframing in place. Rapid changes are occurring and there is no use in denying their effects. Yet no necessary outcomes result from these changes in terms of having particular consequences, in general, for occupational cultures. We would agree with the proposal that imaginative adaption, with a confident and clear sense of possibilities, requires that intellectuals: 'undertake serious reflection designed to formulate a solid self-understanding of their purposes' (Graham 2002: 126).

Understanding the dynamics of occupational cultures, alongside institutional positions in knowledge production, are essential ingredients for this practical effort. The uncomfortable nature of such questions may be easily avoided in individualistic demonstrations of the triumph of expertise over the context in which it is enabled or constrained. Equally, aspirations may be united in the pursuit of the game of excellence as global league tables leave critical capacities in their wake and a narrowly constituted elitism is triumphant. It can also be ignored by not thinking of position in relation to belonging and how cultural support and effort is a part of both. Institutional positions and cultural aspirations interact and have effects on what can be achieved. As Ellen Messer-Davidow put it: 'we did what the self-reflexivity rule said we should do: we debated our positionalities and practices within feminist studies without acknowledging that they, too, were the effects of trying to operationalize our discourse within the academy's rule-governed routines' (Messer-Davidow 2002: 213).

The Effort Bargain and the Alignment of Ambiguity

Two factors provide for continuity across time in the study of work. First, employers and managers mobilize strategies to extract the maximum effort from employees in the name of productivity; whether that is defined in the name of output in terms of profitability or the most effective and efficient means of achieving organizational goals; around which there is contestation. Second, for employees, there is the need to balance the occupational and social costs associated with these strategies through the receipt of sufficient remuneration and/or recognition for their efforts.

In considering the dynamics of the effort bargain, a distinction can be made between 'occupational' and 'effort' controls (Baldamus 1961). The former refers to earned income in terms of the distribution of people in different occupations. From this point of view, those in certain occupations have costs associated with the acquisition of skills, education and experience that they seek compensation for in the form of wages and other rewards. Nevertheless, 'effort' possesses elements that render it problematic for the purposes of rigorous definition and measurement. The most common form of institutional control at work remains standardized conceptions of effort. In industry, they take the form of what are variously called production standards, job values, workloads, standards of application and effort. A gap exists in the determination of workplace performance with the result that managers and employers often resort to standardized institutional controls whose overall aim is to extract the maximum effort from occupations.

Outcome measures of organizational effort are expected to feed back into appraisal schemes in which practitioners, in 'reflexive' moments, focus upon their individual abilities to meet a set of targets. These practices and techniques carry with them a set of expectations that call a person into being within a specific form of enterprise (du Gay 2007). Yet what we see in performance appraisals is a replication of the separation between knowledge production and context. To express this another way, it is the separation between *ability*, in terms of monitoring and accounting for actions and *capability*, in terms of being positioned in order that one's actions can have a tangible effect upon given expectations.

Built into appraisal is an abstraction whereby the determination of performance is assumed to lie in the realm of individual discretion. There is an assumption that a person is somehow separate from the social domains they inhabit, leaving institutions and cultural conditions of actions to one side in a focus upon the abstract individual (Hollway 1998). A model of action is posited that is also accepted by professional groups who separate knowledge from the conditions under and through which it is realized. To admit of those conditions is seen to de-professionalize claims to exceptionality, based on divorcing effort from institutional context. Mobility and expertise then become synonymous in the international market for the knowledge worker.

The gap opened up by these alignments of assumptions, albeit from apparently different vantage points, allows for the targeting of the exercise of discretionary knowledge as if it directly informed, as opposed to interacted with, the conditions through which actions take place. In managerial terms, what results is a distinction between knowledge and context via a whole series of attempts to determine the 'how' of practice through modes of supervision, surveillance, appraisals and 'workload balancing' models. The modes for seeking to determine performance incorporate modes of surveillance that seek to traverse organizational space, but create tensions and contradictions which are played out at different levels. In professional terms, 'what' is produced is separated from 'how' as that would undermine the exceptionality of character as divorced from the context of production. These ambiguities are frequently seen in terms of differences between professional and managerial rationales. The problem, however, is that this assumes two worlds whose existence is based upon completely different criteria. In addition, it assumes not only a dichotomous knowledge base, but also one in the area of the personnel who occupy those positions.

Strategic managerial ranks within universities are occupied by those who were once, or who still claim to be, academics. Modes of incorporation into these organizational rationales have worked effectively as academics have found a place in the auditing culture informing the measurement and control of performance (Power 1999; Strathern 2000). Therefore, while some seek to distance themselves from the implications of these transformations, it is not those 'outside' an occupational culture who perpetuate the practices that are the objects of critique, thereby allowing a simple 'us' and 'them' mentality to predominate to inform the symbolic boundaries that enable epistemic impermeability, but those from 'within'. With these positions come allusions from their occupants to their

own cultural capital in terms of their past experiences. Because of this, there is
no privileged vantage point from which to base a critique of their practices, for
the target of those critiques are frequently those persons who have occupied the
same cultures from which they are launched. As a tactic in displacing and deflect-
ing resistance, derived from the privileged vantage point of occupational closure
and organizational power, it is most effective.

Among academics turned managers, there are those who are able to convert
external value into internal advantage. Occupants of these roles act as 'go-betweens'
(Goffman 1984) via the collection of information on the team's 'performance',
while also matching that against attributed value. The measurement of a team's
performance is indicative of a cognitive-instrumental rationality that carries
with it 'connotations of successful self-maintenance made possible by informed
disposition over, and intelligent adaptation to, conditions of a contingent environment' (Habermas 1984: 10). Disposition and position are combined to
produce an alignment between external attribution and internal modes of production so enabling justification and application to remain separate, with the
effort bargain exhibiting a less reflexive mode of operation. The content of
knowledge production continues because the consequences are assumed to be
of benefit. We have seen this occur in the mobilization of resources for the
biological sciences from national, international and regional agencies. Despite
the varying sources of funding and the aims and purpose of the organizations
that provide it, knowledge production may continue relatively unaffected by
different expectations.

Among university managers, cognitive dissonance and disappointment also
abounds. Many take on such roles with the assurance that they are only temporary and a sabbatical period and some additional remuneration will result as
compensation for a 'lapse' in career. It is also the case that those who once
represented such knowledges are the same who now, in their daily practices,
embody it as irrelevant to new situations. 'Critical' scholars, among whom
many pin their hopes for better management of universities, easily find themselves in situations for which they are ill prepared. Gate fever (the experience
that inmates have prior to ending their prison sentences) also plays its role: that
is, the assured sabbatical at the end of a term of office provides alleviation for
current suffering under mounds of paperwork and attendance at numerous
meetings.

Wholehearted embrace is another route. Along with a new modus operandi
come disparaging backward glances at those who do not understand the self-
evidence of new realities. We also find nostalgia for academic identity. As one
dean put it to us when describing an interaction with an academic about a
particular article they had both read: 'it was good, but I don't have many
opportunities to have interesting discussions'. What we are seeing here is a
clash in knowledge practices that lead to displacements, calculated adjust-
ments, forms of resistance that create spaces for alternative forms of practice,

but also what has been described as an embedded 'state of hostilities' (Prichard 2000), with one characterization being 'fields of conflict and competition between incompatible models living uneasily alongside each other' (Burtscher et al. 2006: 243).

A huge amount of effort goes into preventing an understanding of the reasons for this state of affairs and alternative possibilities. A great deal of this effort comes from the growing army of intermediaries in the effort bargain. These are the producers and reproducers of a culture informed by an administrative-technical discourse that can easily distance itself from the primary purposes of these institutions. People speak on behalf 'of' researchers, or 'to' them, but more rarely, 'with' them. Such practices replicate those within the business world in which 'corporate capitalism has not created a world of action where everyone works to fulfil an edifying mission. Countless businesses do not communicate with, and learn from, an empowered work force' (Johnson 1992: 203). These intermediaries are bolstered by information gathering units who perform two particular tasks. First, they devise the means of monitoring throughput and performance measures according to evaluation criteria, as well as devising ever-greater means of seeking quality via audits and processes of validation. Second, they feed back this information which has the power to structure organizational discourse.

These practices produce texts on organizational performance that constitute knowledge produced through particular descriptions of performance. Knowledge by acquaintance, which includes components of context-sensitivity and direct learning, may be dismissed as that which reproduces the professional discretion which is the target of transformation, as well as taking up too much time and effort – despite the enormous amounts of energy devoted to its avoidance. It challenges managerial prerogatives among those not comfortable in their position because it requires proximity. The producers of organizational documents and those who make decisions based upon them, are thereby relieved of engagement with the action knowledge within research cultures: that is, the knowledge generated, deployed and enacted in particular environments. Opportunities for reflexivity are diminished by institutional logics.

In this climate 'entrepreneurialism' has extended its reach into universities. On first glance this appears to cut across institutions characterized by managerialism and a defensive professionalism. In each of these latter cases effort tends to be directed towards self-evidence based upon a latent, assumed universality. Yet while offering a means through which to judge otherwise disparate practices and biographies, entrepreneurialism works upon and through those dispositions in particular ways, the result of which is to reproduce an individualism that categorizes people according to their ability to live up to its principles (du Gay 1996). Traditional boundaries, constituted within academic departments and sub-units that tend to represent the homogenization of knowledges, are blurred and rearticulated through its supposed self-evidence.

As a result of this blurring entrepreneurialism becomes, in practice, a two-dimensional process. First, it is held to offer an opportunity to those who might wish to reinvent themselves in the image of potentiality within the 'success culture'. Second, it works to regulate those who do not accord with its self-evident aspirations. Its power rests upon unexamined and unrealizable ends. Yet it is the absence of engaged challenge that allows for the continuation of its free play. Academics who are disparaging via their detachment enable the continuation of its unexamined presuppositions. It thus works both around and through academic cultures (Marginson and Considine 2000). Within the context of the university as a whole, the effect is to further uncertainty concerning its social, economic and cultural purpose.

In these environments there is a mixture of reactions on the part of academics: from resistance, via engagement, to indifference. In turn, this relates to degrees of recognition afforded to 'external' necessities within institutions, and also the positions of academics that enable or constrain their actual and potential courses of action. Natural scientists, for example, are argued to be more able to adapt their normative orientations to industrial links through the belief that this actually extends knowledge, while large companies now make the sort of long-term research investments once thought to be the province of university funding.

In terms of academic cultures, what about academic professionalism as a counter to those tendencies that are perceived to have an undesirable effect on modes of academic production? At one level we can see a reduced commitment to the organization in the name of free-floating ideals of academic freedom. Those who can play in the academic transfer market seek shelters that are more in line with their motivations and aspirations and so are rewarded accordingly. It may result from being employed in those institutions that are more resilient, but equally may arise from individually negotiated contracts that become the exceptions in less resilient institutional settings. Nevertheless, this is not a course of action open to the vast majority of academics. Individualized logics then meet one another with gaps being filled by varying rationalizations, expectations and performances.

The potential for the identification of difference and distinctiveness then diminishes. Forms of knowing through and in different practices emerge and clash. When they are apparent, they often rely upon attributed values that result in patents and spin-out opportunities, or the supposed self-evidence of organizational measures. Struggles for academic recognition take place in these terrains but they often misrecognize the content and forms through which it is realized. There is little active engagement that challenges pre-conceptions and it ends up being constituted in limited hierarchies of knowledge, or severs the understanding between character, context and culture. Learning is the casualty in the wake of these practices.

Cutting across the potential for learning is the supposition of the neutrality of organizational measures, ably assisted by the assumption that they are trans-local (D. Smith 1999). Applications of these forms of objectivism become their own justification. Criticism of the validity of such means falls upon deaf ears for they question the very presuppositions upon which decision-making processes are based. Opportunities to learn from a diversity of practices according to engagement with different groups evaporate. When all that fails, as it often does, there is never a questioning of the whole enterprise. On the contrary, the frenetic process goes in search of yet more measures. As Stan Cohen wrote of the difference between his conception of social control and the Orwellian image, we see meetings in which: 'Serious looking PhDs are sitting around a table. Each is studying the same computerized records ... The atmosphere is calm' (S. Cohen 1985: 185).

The effect is to gloss over the varying contributions that those who work within universities make to the development of their institutions, leaving one-dimensional views, administrative-technical 'solutions' and private sector consultants to occupy the space that is left through a plethora of reports about innovative practices and potentiality that take little account of the relations between context, content, capacity and opportunity. It works to downgrade the engagement of researchers with the environments of which they are a part at a local level, because it sits in the shadows of something called 'internationally recognized' in which professional and managerial rationales meet. Whatever happened to the dialectic between the global and local? What drives the changes in universities to be more relevant to the knowledge economy is very similar to the drivers for those scholars who seek international recognition on the conference circuits. In both cases production and reception of knowledge are severed, with the result that universities and their staff so often appear to be 'in' but not 'of' their localities.

Identity and Context – for Content

With the content of these organizational dynamics in play, what are the effects upon academic identity and belonging? Clear differences in orientation are constructed between those who lie within the boundaries of disciplines and share a common set of experiences and those who remain on the outside. A disciplinary orientation emerges which, when combined with an organizational context aligned to environmental expectations, creates positions and practices that stabilize sufficiently over time in order to turn subject into object. These spaces of practice or 'shelters' (Freidson 1994), are places of relative autonomy in which the macro realities of political economy are connected with micro experiences and activities to create particular kinds of culture.

What we find in these shelters are varying degrees of relative autonomy according to an occupational hierarchy, orientation to work and alignment with expectations of knowledge. We also find that: 'in addition to the requirements for personal integrity in general, individuals who practise or profess an academic subject are also constrained by the integrity of their subject' (Noble 1999: 173).

Yet while a reflexive orientation to processes of justification may emerge from time to time, those academic cultures that enjoy the most stability are, in the Kuhnian sense of the word, 'normal'. As long as the political-economic and cultural conditions remain relatively stable in their configurations, their power rests upon continuity and self-evidence. It is this relationship that go-betweens capitalize upon in performing boundary work.

In these segments practices emerge that constitute a distinction from practices in everyday life. Culturally speaking, we would expect reflections on practice to be shared among professionals in a supportive and developmental fashion that contributes to a clear understanding and justification of their role and value both in particular and in general. Without these cultural conditions in place, processes of justification easily become the province of those who lie outside of the profession. The result would be to undermine distinctiveness and a defence of practices whose legitimacy ultimately rests upon the perceived benefits of being made to work in the public realm. After all, if anyone can practise the inner workings of a discipline, its practitioners will find it difficult to claim a privileged position for their efforts.

If disciplinary positions are multiple and the forms of understanding generated are generally accessible, the authority for findings and the basis for practices will be considerably weakened. A situation would rapidly emerge in which the positions and cultures that enabled knowledge production in the first place become more tenuous and certainly not tenured! Against this background we would expect to see the emergence of other sites of knowledge production that provide career structures according to different cultures and political-economic conditions. We would also see a regurgitation of generated knowledge without due reference to its origins which, some may say, is a mark of its success. However, the consequence may well be to add to an undermining of the uniqueness and value of the knowledge produced in university cultures in the absence of such recognition.

At issue here is the extent to which an apprenticeship is required that sees a process of learning as a necessary precondition of entry and from there, the operation of occupation closure in order to regulate entry and control the modes through which practice occurs. That capability is related to the position that a discipline holds and that, in turn, to the institutional power that may be mobilized for its advantage. As we have argued, this relates to the value attributed to a discipline in the name of its relevance, either direct or indirect, to economic progress. However, the demand for disinterestedness in the pursuit of knowledge mixes with the one for relevance. At a disciplinary level, the pursuit of cultural capital through peer recognition is not assumed to be equal to the pursuit of money through redistribution. In other words, the institution may provide relative shelter for particular disciplines, but within the university itself, the distribution of resources can be skewed towards other disciplines. Sensitivity to intra-institutional as well as inter-institutional differences is thus required in an analysis of shelters or, in our terms, degrees of epistemic permeability.

The commitment that arises from within practice and provides for self-identifying narratives of professional experience and purpose becomes marginalized in these processes. The gendered components of professional knowledge may also be at their most apparent. Expressions of anger, born of this commitment and directed against the consequences and rationale of transformative practices that represent the supposed logic of the market, are readily dismissed as symptomatic of 'emotional outbursts'. Displays of episodic power (May 1999) are individualized and co-participants to these encounters are relieved of the need to consider the reasons *why* someone expressed such feelings in the first place. The contexts of practice that give rise to commitment are then bracketed via a concentration on the inappropriateness of behaviour in terms of *how* it is manifested by the individual concerned.

A process of professional denigration of inappropriate expressions of commitment to content or consequence has its parallels in the presuppositions of performance measures as the triumph of method over purpose. What we see here is the expression of a rationale that takes an understanding of the relationship between knowledge and the context of action as heightening professional discretion: that is, the very target of transformation. An alignment takes place with a professional rationale that has a limited understanding of commitment in relation to content, as well as the consequences of changes for working context. Misrecognition, combined within individualization, renders these contexts susceptible to poor management and cultures of support.

How often those charged with responsibilities, which they readily accept as part of their professional identities, are relieved of so doing through third party allusion. Here we are referring to what the system does, whose constitution is reproduced in the utterances, actions and also indifference of its participants. The peculiar disjuncture between what is good enough for an audience and one's professional identity in terms of critical knowledge, is suddenly suspended in the most extraordinary acts of institutional reproduction, leaving expertise to reside in the exceptionality of character as defined by outputs that become evident in long curricula vitae (CVs). The effort required in terms of desiring to bring about a particular outcome is suddenly halted through referral to the very thing that is known to bring about its likely demise. For this reason we hear utterances among academics such as: 'We have been advised that … '; 'according to administration we cannot … '; 'we tried that 20 years ago and it did not work then'.

In terms of positioning and the relations between trance and struggle, the field of academic life is constituted by distributions of capital that inform what takes place within them and are exemplified by particular expressions of inclusion and exclusion: for example, references to 'junior' and 'senior' colleagues by those who like to think they know about power and hierarchy and are critical of its effects. These terms exemplify the struggles for distinction that are part of the professional ethos in which a tacit knowledge of the mode of operation of the field, including its stakes and interests, is implied. Concerns then focus upon how the conservation or subversion of the structure of capital within the field should take place (Bourdieu 2000).

Those who benefit from current arrangements will seek to defend orthodoxy when it speaks in their name, with the overall aim being restoration of assent to normality. Yet if these strategies and tactics fail to take account of the reconstitution of fields according to the new forms of organizational control, they serve only to reproduce distinctions that are indifferent to the institutional conditions that enable them in the first place. Creativity separate from context may then be claimed in the struggles for recognition that inform academic production. When this is subject to examination, individualistic responses are common from occupational cultures, ably assisted by the assumption that anything else would be too political, idealistic or even unprofessional. Conflict exists, but is displaced and when manifest, as we suggested earlier, is met by techniques of individualization that refer not to the conditions under which people work, but the peculiarity of their individual characteristics (May 1999).

From an analysis of these relations, concern may then turn to a consideration of the potentiality for the university as a diverse site of knowledge production. All have a stake and a place within its relations and cannot but contribute to its reproduction at some level. However, to what degree and with what consequence? To return to an earlier point, those who castigate others for questioning what appears as self-evident and necessary will meet those for whom the limits of critical questioning arise when it comes to an examination of the positions from which their practices are based. What evaporate in practice are these relational dimensions. Knowledge is divorced from context and knowing and then repackaged for sale to a narrow group of users whether they be those who speak on behalf of the economy, government policy, or peers in the academy.

Sensitivity to variations in effects according to the position that a person occupies, which includes the power to be indifferent to consequence, is required. Nevertheless, a person is ill prepared to defend themselves upon a terrain that is so taken-for-granted. Engaging in battles whose stakes have long since changed can easily takes place with a negative effect upon cultures of inquiry: 'If the defenders of academic freedom only attend to its abrogations, they will not see the ways it is foreclosed' (Butler 2006: 16). Those whose careers predate new instruments of organizational control often resort to nostalgia that yearns for bygone days of supposed autonomy. On the other hand, those who have known no different and yet remain indifferent to the historical conditions that gave rise to their profession, can also reproduce the same misunderstandings as they clamour for occupational recognition.

In terms of formulating a position on changes and resistance within universities, in order to find the spaces of possibility for circumstances to be otherwise, we should 'doubt the reality of a resistance which ignores the resistance of reality' (Bourdieu 2000: 108). It is through the practices of individualization that are characteristic of academic cultures that universities can be managed in particular ways. The ambiguities of academic identity can, as suggested in Chapter 5, be seen in terms of a productive ambivalence born of a measured distinction between the self and the facticity of the world. In the absence of the recognition of such a relation in occupational cultures, however, disappointment, withdrawal and cynicism can easily result.

The idea of developing more collective cultures is often met with cries of indignation concerning its offence to individual autonomy. It is this dynamic that Pierre Bourdieu (2007) picks up on when reflecting on his experiences of forming a research group and being confronted with accusations of indoctrination:

> What is neither perceived nor understood, except as an object of fear or indignation, is the intense intellectual and affective fusion that, to different degrees and in different ways from one period to another, united the members of the group in participation in a mode of organization of the work of thought that was perfectly antinomic to the literary (and very Parisian) vision of 'creation' as the singular act of an isolated researcher (a vision which inclines so many ill-trained and intellectually ill-equipped researchers to prefer the sufferings, the doubts and, very often, the failures and the sterility of solitary labour to what they perceive as the depersonalizing alienation of collective understanding). (Bourdieu 2007: 19–20)

A defensive and protective posture towards academic autonomy is believed to have positive benefits. The context of knowledge production within the university, after all, is core to the means of providing a distance from necessity and thus the distinction of the knowledge that is produced. Here we have the occupation of an organizational position, disposition and gaze that is apparently denied to those immersed in the business of everyday life and the everyday life of business. To this extent the university is seen to provide a context in which a long-term exposure to a body of knowledge turns the subject of research into an object of analysis. This combination of gaze and position is the basis upon which the uniqueness and viability of the knowledge provided by the university is defended in contrast to other knowledge-based institutions such as consultancies and market research organizations.

To look towards academic positions as a basis for engaged critique is problematic if there is an expectation that others should change the practices that are reflected in their cultures, without an examination of those contexts from which the critique is constructed. Herein lays a limit to reflexivity noted in earlier chapters: that is, when critique gets close to the familiar, it activates a strong reaction that leads to preservation of the status quo. Those who are apparently critical of simplistic measures can suddenly become propelled into discussions that deploy such measures. How many times have the scores from the UK Research Assessment Exercise (RAE) been used to distinguish departments during informal conversations at conferences by the same persons who are apparently critical of crude performance indicators? Now this is to be replaced by 'metrics' where the focus is upon the process of measurement and the busy empiricists can, once again, find an outlet divorced from any general discussion of purpose.

At every moment these conversations occur, conversations concerning the practical activity that goes into support, development and recognition as the conditions for practice are less frequent. Instead we get a separation between expectation, context and culture. Thus the collective expectations of recruitment panel members lead to the idea that new researchers should have the CVs that those who are employing them never had at that stage of their careers. The opportunity to employ and develop people is easily lost according to allusions to necessity by those who write about contingency holding out possibilities. If such justifications are held to be a reflection of the real then, regardless of the theoretical and methodological differences between those assembled, finding other occupations where discretion is enhanced would certainly make more sense. The knowledge that is produced as being good enough for others is apparently redundant when it comes to one's own context and practice.

As frenetic activity continues and knowledge and context drift apart, how is expertise constituted? You may be comfortable if there was a line between your expertise in a particular department which has done well and has got a good research score, or you reside in an institution that has a high status in the global, hierarchical game. If you are so predisposed and prepared to regurgitate these ideologies, you can call yourself a 'four-star academic' and relieve yourself of further self-identification practices as if that granted a self-evidence to your excellence. Mostly, researchers do not think about the relationship between expertise and the context of their work except in a negative sense, or as the result of threats if they are not able to live up to the promise of international excellence. For those who do display a care for such matters, there is often little incentive from the occupational culture, or institutions, for the value of pursuing a relational understanding, while those who try may find themselves exhausted in the face of the efforts that are put into its avoidance.

Such things are routine in university life and may be seen best in promotions where commitment to help is rapidly dissolved into allusions to pre-ordained realities that have halted desired outcomes. Those who are critical of victim mentalities in other circumstances, suddenly revert to that in order to protect themselves from the consequences of places in which commitment to betterment appears to have faded. It is understandable that we then find actions ranging from situational withdrawal, to salvos of emails describing the degradation of academic life launched from computers behind doors that are closed to colleagues. A potentially productive space opened up in the effort bargain so readily disappears and fatalism takes its place. The critical thinking that is apparently good enough for dissemination to others now departs within the context of the culture of inquiry itself. A dynamic conservatism results in which the 'generative dance' (D. Cook and Brown 1999) between knowledge and knowing is one of studied avoidance.

The Effort of and for Representation

We have argued that the pursuit of excellence is an aspatial view of knowledge that is permitted to continue in a space produced by apparently disparate rationales. Equally, the place-based idea of relevant knowledge is assumed to operate unproblematically which allows a limited understanding of the relations between context and content. In this space calls for engagement reside. Overall, this affects the practice of representation and what then stands as 'legitimate' knowledge through invoking fixed ideas of space (Massey 2005). The results, however, fall upon institutions and those disciplines within them, in different ways. Limited and short-sighted ideas of competition prevail with a need to import internationally leading scholars on the back of trying to climb up the ladder of indicators of global excellence. Such persons are beamed into places in a celebration of the mobility of expertise over an understanding of the distinctiveness of existing contexts.

Talented teachers of research, those pursuing work that is regarded as less than international prominence, are left in the wake of these short-term cultures. Resulting tensions are assumed to be alleviated by invoking 'workload balancing models'. Spatial mobility is afforded for those individuals and groups who can play this game – in other words, for those whose personal circumstances permit mobility in the first instance – and the transfer market operates on this assumption with particular effects on the movement of knowledge workers (Ackers and Gill 2008). Institutions are internationally compared in extraordinary displays that relieve speakers of any burden of contextual understanding. New ways of measuring performance are always emerging, but the same hierarchies continue with the result that work of interest in research at scales of activity other than something called international, are afforded less recognition. Connectivity between institutions and their localities is important, but modes of academic production and what is regarded as a legitimate outlet for publications are not context-sensitive. It is not only institutions, but also researchers who may be in, but not of, the places where they work.

Here we see an alignment between apparently different rationales around the idea of excellence. Endogenous reflexivity within research cultures is organized, in its highest forms of recognition, through contributions to abstract knowledge. Canonic status is attributed to those who are not contaminated by contact with different expectations, but who engage in the single activity of research and spend their time in conferences networking with other like-minded persons. The engaged virtuoso, on the other hand, sees many different audiences and is thus committed to translation, the process of which places them in a frame of view that, by virtue of its activity, means the same knowledge is seen through different viewpoints. Audiences may then feel able to judge not only on the consequences, but also on the content of the knowledge deployed and represented. The occupational closure that affords endogenous reflexivity for the canonical is exposed to the referential dimension for the engaged virtuoso. Here we find a different ethos, way of being and commitment: 'This work of modifying one's own thought and that of others seems to me to be the intellectual's reason for being' (Foucault 1989a: 461).

Representing the above in spatial terms, the former ethos is concentric and turns in on itself to celebrate insularity as a precondition of knowledge generation. It serves to alleviate its practitioners of distractions, as in the case of nineteenth-century German universities that provided well-equipped facilities and attracted researchers (Pickstone 2000). Its outcomes are seen in terms of accepted outlets for ideas that are hierarchically constituted through the application of peer review. The latter way of being is more diffuse and deliberately so. To modify one's thought requires an alternative immersion, but one that is afforded by an occupational recognition in the first instance. In other words, it is necessary to succeed before one can risk diversification; assuming the disposition for translation is present along with the ability to move and translate and communicate between different audiences.

Here we see an isomorphism between an institution's clamour for a place in the global hierarchy and the forms of recognition exercised in academic cultures. Both invoke fixed ideas of space in which ambiguity is eradicated and certainties reign. Necessity and calculation come together in the fantasy that we are in total command of reality and the attributed logic of globalization finds its outlet in de-contextualized celebrations of rational individualism. What of the sustainability of these practices? Are those with the positions and power that result from these moves then predisposed and supported by their new institutions to build lasting cultures of inquiry with support and development, or is the door to the new office closed because it is business as usual? Or, if the individual is so predisposed, they are left to protect their professional space in the face of overwhelming expectations. Perhaps, quite simply, they are never there! It is surprising how little effort is made in understanding the work of colleagues.

There is no suggestion that these dynamics can be simply separated from environmental changes. We have mentioned the tensions, if not contradictions, in policies and practices and the expectations made upon universities to contribute to the economy according to limited understandings of their value and role. It is wrong, however, to simply allude to what is done 'to' universities. Here excellence can thrive on the attributed value given to relevance. Time for excellence may be given to certain disciplines in the promise of outcomes that are deemed relevant in the future. It may also be apparent in economics whose activity is given as value because of the thing called the 'economy' whose assumed dynamics are reflected in the limited models perpetuated in its endogenous domains. In terms of the lessons concerning the financial sector, the consciences of the profession may well find themselves trammelled by those who are already giving the models yet more variables.

A link can evaporate in research practice between textual production and reception that oscillates between two poles. At one end, pearls are said to be cast to swine as great works are produced for unreceptive audiences. At the other, validity is constituted according to the acceptability of findings for particular audiences. Both relieve parties of the need to engage with the complex relations between production and reception and credibility and applicability. These cultural manifestations cannot be simply blamed on the institution. The supposed hypodermic relation between text and action can act in the same way as that between bench and bedside in clinical trials. Similarly, to collapse credibility into acceptability denies the value of different forms of knowledge. The gap we now have is between assumptions informing practice and the effort required in reaching mutual understanding.

An enormous variability exists in the reflexive understandings that exist between the individual, their practice and institutional position. It is not simply that arrogance (as either reference to endogenous forms of credibility or ideas of unproblematic applicability) is bolstered by particular communities who never challenge such behaviour, it is also given by an assumed exceptionality that cannot admit of context. After all, to do so would be to admit of a relation between what is known and the place from which it is produced. It is something necessary for others, but in terms of the institutional conditions of knowledge production its reflexive limits lie in the perpetuation of an unrealistic individualism that allows particular identities to be claimed or drawn upon.

In terms of the results of effort, to absorb oneself in representation can mean to perform an apparent annihilation or, at least, a denial: that is, the expunging of biography in favour of that which stretches away from its starting point. As a counter to the denial of situatedness in the production of knowledge, we have also had its celebration. A resulting language of 'self-affiliation with its peculiar blending of the overaffirmative and the tentative or temporary' (Simpson 2002: 223), not only severs links with history, occupational culture and institutional position, but also forgets that research is ultimately interesting and important because of what is tells us about the world, not the person who performs it. Here is where occupational cultures so often fail to play a valuable role in denying support to individuals and being denied by individuals as necessary, at some level, to their work. At the intersections of biography and history many valuable insights are generated and learning from each other is an important process in constituting occupational cultures.

Whether through intensive or extensive empirical work, to absorb oneself in alternative forms of life which are reflected in representational endeavours, is not an aspatial activity. Not only is the author positioned as responsible in the eyes of the reader, but also they are located in an institution and occupation that has afforded this activity. That fate has not escaped the researcher in the age of the author's supposed death, for it is what makes research relevant to the present and work stands the test of time because it still resonates with contemporary issues. Max Weber saw this so beautifully, but his was ultimately a heroic and even romantic ideal in which context also evaporated.

The search for the place of passion from which is derived the affirmation 'here I stand' in knowledge production, mixes in an uneasy relationship to social research practice. Its professionalism accompanies uncertainties about commitment, leaving no place for caring and passion to be part of its practice:

> 'Commitment' is initially a lack of good manners: to intervene in the public space means exposing oneself to disappointment, or worse, shocking those in one's world who, choosing the virtuous facility of retreat into their ivory tower, see such commitment as a lack of the famous 'axiological neutrality' that they wrongly identify with scientific objectivity. (Bourdieu 2008: 386)

The ideal of autonomy still seems to reign in an age in which this is nothing more than a bygone yearning for one that, if it ever existed, was premised on an individualistic creativity which, for the vast majority, is not attainable and assumes a set of prerogatives reliant upon the persistence of institutions through time (Butler 2006). This is where the expressive and strategic provide for a rich mix which if not part of a culture that recognizes its place, strength and limitations in the world of which it is a part, leads to individualized frustration and even resentment towards unfulfilled promises that no discipline can provide. All this so easily becomes unproductive, as opposed to a productive tension that is taken forward in practice – together.

Sanctity is sought in neat theoretical schemas, refuges found in technicism and retreat in the production of texts on the futility of representation. Yet there is something that needs far more consideration, effort and joint action. Occupational cultures can exhibit a pernicious individualism whose continued existence depends on the institutions from which it originates, the same institutions which are nevertheless denied in allusions to an autonomy that is granted to the analyst, but apparently not to those who are analysed. How easy such limited understandings make those institutions to manage by utilizing a politics in ambiguous spaces, rather than an ambivalence that is an inevitable part of the vitality and relevance of knowledge production, transmission and reception in both dimensions of reflexivity.

In places where institutionalization undermines insight and provides for an indifference to conditions that enable actions, we may see bewildering and ultimately unproductive divisions of labour. We end up in places where it is better to dislike than commit and one can only commit when the conditions support and enable and even seek to prevent its repercussions as a chosen course of action. The existence is precarious and creates anxieties (Michael 2000) that are not conducive to the identified need for iconoclasm within higher education (Menand 2010). So we find consolations in individualism and abstract evasion. Yet where we work and practise and how others accord a value to that activity as a result, are essential ingredients for learning from the past and for the future.

There are no consolations in the recognition of contingency, only in infinitude, but that is not the reality of actually doing social research which, as a condition of its future, needs to be seen as a legitimate, expert and yet open, activity. If done well it is messy, complicated, uncertain, difficult, but no less insightful because of that. Out of its practice and interactions with social life comes greater insight which does not generate resolution, but makes an important contribution to clarification. That represents a real challenge because those in power rely upon obfuscation, as well as fatalism, to justify their practices. Social research needs supportive and successful places to work. For those reasons we need far better understandings of those conditions for the future.

Many courses of action serve to reproduce distinctions that are indifferent to an explanation of the institutional conditions that enable them in the first place. Any overall disjuncture within and between reflexive realms, rather than being objects of clarification that are taken forward in action to achieve degrees of resolution that have no end point, can be neutralized by the hierarchies and logics constituted by limited understandings of the changing conditions of knowledge production and unrealistic expectations of utility that serve to relieve of responsibility. In this sense we can learn from history and current practices and orientate ourselves to the future through an understanding of what makes sites of knowledge production distinctive in terms of both their strengths *and* limitations.

Social research now faces the demand for relevance; this has existed for a long time, but is now more intensive. These demands and the conditions of work mix with an attributed value given to relevance that provides for the absence of reflexive practice. Now, while a postmodern dance can move about effortlessly across the terrain of the spheres of economy, society, culture and nature, in practice it is policies, power, attributed values, institutions and occupational and organizational controls that are holding them sometimes apart, in tension or in states of collapse.

Allusions to the importance of knowledge production for its own sake, without due consideration for the context of its production, is characteristic of many responses to current changes. Here we find elitism according to the position of academics within more resilient institutions, as well as those within less resilient ones who are distanced from its everyday implications. Institutions are then ranked according to a set of indicators that are the classic replication of the 'black box' described by social studies of science and technology, in which process and context evaporate in a celebration of the products of work. Yet if the denial of context produces a skewed exceptionality around the cult of the individual academic and institutions go in pursuit of those with 'international reputations', to reduce all to context avoids an understanding of mezzo and macro influences, as well as the dispositions that individuals bring to their settings and how they interact with cultures and institutional positions.

What we then find is that academic cultures ascribe status to particular institutions in general and departments in particular, without a more general questioning about what makes a particular site of production of value, beyond what is the aggregate of narrowly defined professional standards. In a culture where displays of knowledge set each producer apart from one another and the success of particular groups or individuals constitute 'obligatory passage points' (Callon 1986) for those who wish to make their mark upon the field of endeavour, resultant texts add to the process of accumulation that, in turn, relates to degrees of recognition afforded by those positioned as the judges of worth. In the process connections and capacities can blur with the result that it is not what someone knows which is at stake, but equally who they know.

A process of 'departicularization' then occurs in which context is severed from product in what is held to be the universalization of ideas within academic communities. The effect is to add to the idea of the exceptionality of the individual divorced from the context of knowledge production. Equally, such a connection can be severed by cross field interpretations in order to constitute cultural capital: for example, as ideas are imported from other fields and disconnected from those that have emerged with their own particular histories, a novelty can be claimed for a body of work thereby adding to the process of accumulation and recognition for the researcher.

Summary

The bounded nature of professional knowledge production is variable according to discipline, institution and macro factors that attribute value to particular activities. To constitute a monopoly over an object of interest varies according to the capability to place limits on that which is, in different ways, open to contestation and negotiation. Recognition of this state of affairs and a willingness to move beyond existing ways of working has been argued to create more sustainable ways of working in scientific practice (Irwin and Michael 2003). Yet the university is a site of activity in which heterogeneous, open-ended and more dialogical approaches mix uneasily with those practices that are successful in claiming that they are context-free and generalized forms. Quite simply, in the latter case, if scholarly knowledge is produced in society then society, in all its myriad forms and uncertainties, becomes filtered out to constitute greater certainty.

In terms of transformations in universities, to provide for the relative stability that enables such certainties, we are now witnessing the clamour for elitism: 'world-class' status. The aspiration is to be found among politicians and managers alike, but there is a relative silence from those 'critical' academics that enjoy its privileges, thereby signalling evident limits to reflexive thought. What is absent is an understanding of what different sets of activities mean in terms of the culture of an organization, its practices and effects on individuals, their commitments, as well as overall value to society at different levels of scale – local, city-regional, regional, national and international. Purpose, process and product are severed at varying times and places to be pronounced upon and regurgitated, but never discussed, deliberated upon and taken forward into action.

Narrow claims to professionalism, based upon limited understandings of the changing conditions of knowledge production lead to arrogance and an absence of sustainable development for future generations of researchers. Professionalism as detachment, either explicitly or by default, bolsters the view that the production of scholarly knowledge takes place, for both administrative and technical purposes, according to the same abstractions that govern the pursuit of 'international excellence', thereby reducing the significance for understanding its place of origin (Bourdieu and Wacquant 2001). What this removes from the scholarly stage is an understanding of the relation of ideas to place, without reducing content to context and connections with lifeworlds allowing, among other things, the perpetuation of ideas that they are symptomatic of a degenerate culture (Habermas 1994). It removes from public gaze the fact that the university is a diverse community working at different levels, according to different logics – and it is this which makes it vibrant and distinctive. Oscillations between the revenge of instrumental positivism and the denial of position in relation to what is produced continue. In one we have the denouncement of doubt in the name of order and certainty and in the other, the abandonment of an understanding that leaves the terrain open to those who are not so reserved when it comes to speaking in the name of an unproblematic order. Both commit the fallacy of context-free knowledge production, but from different points of view.

Here we witness a discussion of these issues being reduced to the assumed peculiarities and pre-occupations of particular persons, often accompanied by the assumption that anything else would be too political, idealistic or even unprofessional. More generally, forms of lifeworld boundaries that are part of social life and provide for the conditions of production of knowledge about that life are not subject to an in-depth comparative investigation in order to analyse their implications for understanding. When everyday life oscillates between being caught in the headlights of routine (trance) and our actions as individuals who seek to shape it and be afforded recognition and redistribution as a result (struggle), the sites from which knowledge is produced are no different in terms of these dynamics.

We have argued that operating within these tensions we find an increasing number of intermediaries. They may enable the mediation of public recognition via redistribution into the laboratory situation where peer review and experimentation reigns. Intermediaries in this sense may be objects in terms of the products of research that lead to further investment due to the attributed value they are seen to possess: for example, patents. Intermediaries are also researchers who are particularly adept at capturing available monies through operating within domains outside of the laboratory: for example, in national and regional committees who allocate resources. What we see here is a combination of attributed relevance to particular activities in terms of their *potential* economic value, mediated through such persons into laboratory investment where endogenous forms of recognition lie. In this way different domains – the scientific and economic – do not de-differentiate, but retain a relative autonomy via the process of intermediation.

Whether relations between environmental, institutional and practice levels become positive or negative varies according to the following: the nature of the discipline; the type of institution in which it is performed; the scale of research activity; the value attributed to that activity and the relation of the state to the university and its personnel. Academics have shown themselves to be highly adaptive to continual changes in expectations. However, it is those in the most powerful institutions who have the greatest shelter from their implications (Henkel 2000). Given this, in terms of the relationship between position and a reflexive attitude towards such relationships, there are individuals who can invoke their position as the guarantor of distance from unwanted implications. Such positions within institutions which are the exception, rather than the rule, are not uncommon. Nevertheless, their capacity for generalization may be limited: for example, research-intensive posts in institutions whose overall political economy is reliant upon teaching large numbers of students.

In terms of academics-turned-managers in this climate, a common reaction is to assume that with a managerial position comes a capitulation to self-evidence driven by environmental imperatives – the 'inside' of the university as an institution, is reconfigured in the name of the 'outside' – there are no boundaries to defend, only external forces to reflect internally and remould them in the name of apparent imperatives. Choice evaporates in the face of this constructed fatalism and poor leadership results.

The assumption of mobility between inside and outside positions frequently assumes a basis in which the desire for flexibility ends up as a bureaucratic proceduralism that loses a sense of purpose for the place of higher education institutions within society as a whole. Academics-turned-managers find plenty of incentives in new positions to reinforce the message of change, yet often end up producing the very ossifications that were the target of the original transformations. Culturally speaking, what is argued to be at the level of second order justification as a critical, reflexive but supportive role for the institution in relation to the economy, ends up as a normalization of dominant assumptions. In practice, particular issues are focused upon to the exclusion of those that may lead to discomfort and questioning regarding possibilities, particularly when coming close to long-established beliefs.

Conflict results, or is avoided through less interaction via situational withdrawal or techniques of neutralization and, as noted in Chapter 5, denial is a frequent reaction. At an institutional level a combination of attitudes that obliterate the relationship between context and content leaves the place of activity to be the object of the attention of others outside of the cultures of academia. Overall, as Paul Rabinow puts it:

What we share as a condition of existence, heightened today by our ability, and at times our eagerness, to obliterate one another, is a specificity of historical experience and place, however complex and contestable they may be, and a worldwide macro-interdependency encompassing any local particularity. (Rabinow1996: 56)

These tensions, between the constitution of expertise as the disinterested pursuit of knowledge in an age of scepticism and the different expectations placed on universities, is manifested in frustrated ambitions and tensions played out at an individual level.

There is also the ability to attend to different practices at the same time in which forms of knowledge and effort ('organizational' and 'academic') are kept apart and yet ultimately rely upon one another. Snow's (1993) two cultures, in universities, are more informed by a tension between knowing and knowledge. These pressures create nostalgia for those who can remember a bygone era in which distinct domains of activity did not create fuzziness. As noted, this varies and there are cases in which communities continue to practice according to their capability to maintain boundaries. Knowledge, in terms of what is embodied and produced in textual products, is separated from knowing that comes to exist within dominant organizational practices as ways of seeking to measure the performance of production. Learning evaporates and with that, the opportunity to harness alternative futures for research beyond capitulation to narrow economic criteria. These courses of action serve to reproduce those distinctions that are indifferent to an explanation of the institutional conditions that enable them in the first place.

There are two important but related elements worthy of consideration when examining the uniqueness of the place of the university in society and the modes of research production that it contains. First, it is not only the culture, but also the political economy that constitutes practices. There are real limits to a celebration of the cultural as separate from the economic and instead it is the relation between the two which should be the topic of investigation (Thrift 2005). Second, in terms of public legitimacy, certain disciplines have to work harder than others to maintain a separation between the endogenous and referential realms of activity. It is the practice of presenting a normalized science that could be argued to constitute success when the political-economic conditions are in place. In other words, an absence of reflexivity in relation to cultural presentations of practice, as well as upon conditions of knowledge production, may explain why some practices in particular contexts are able to ignore these insights and so enable exogenous factors to remain at endogenous levels within knowledge communities. The limits to reflexivity then inhere in knowing how far to go in questioning the premises of one's own discipline or that of others. For if this takes place without due consideration of the wider factors we have charted, it misses its mark and can easily be written off as murmurings from the wilderness.

Rather than being objects of reflection that are taken forward in action, tensions can be displaced and neutralized by the hierarchies and logics constituted by limited understandings of the changing conditions and dynamics of research production. With occupational cultures continually emphasizing the production of cutting-edge research over, for example, the value of integrating existing knowledges according to the differing needs of varying communities, forms of organizational knowing abound, leaving this product-based mentality amenable to crude sets of understanding. Hierarchies then continue around a mutually agreed de-contextualization in which 'diversity with dignity' (Boyer 1990) suffers.

Currently we see an inability to analyse the relations between the present and the past, in terms of the constitution of academic fields, in order to explore alternative futures. Instead we find 'ruptures', 'breaks' and changes in modes and contexts of production. Organizational change is not something with purpose, but becomes focused on process matters as if they were a reasonable demonstration of action in the name of necessity. At the same time academic production is indifferent to context as that appears to undermine exceptionality and when it comes to entrepreneurialism, forgetting seems more important than memory (Bauman 1997) in the name of what is called 'innovation'. What is lost is the potential to 'free thought from the constraints exerted on it'. Instead, we see a surrender 'to the routines of the automaton' and a treating of 'reified historical constructs as things' (Bourdieu 2000: 182). The knowledge economy and the university are two 'things'.

We have suggested that sensitivity to context (which does not imply context-dependence) is precisely the key element missing in discussions. While networks of individuals, working together around particular issues, can bolster activity according to resources and contacts at their disposal, the sustainability of such activities is dependent upon the level and durability of cultures and resources. This is informed by more intensive ideas of the relevance of knowledge from frequently unstated and unexamined points of view. Context can be pushed to its limits in an analysis of modes of production of knowledge and an understanding of content and forms of culture can easily be eradicated. The result is that the potential to understand the relations between institutional conditions and cultures of production is diminished and with that, what is distinctive about particular sites of research in terms of what is produced. Overall, there is relative silence around these issues and as a result, learning and control is, by default, given over to other terrains of activity, rather than considered within occupational cultures. Quite simply, research is too important to be left to these terrains of continual misunderstanding.

A WAY FORWARD:
ACTIVE INTERMEDIARIES

The aim of this book has been to inform a more reflexive, engaged and confident social research through an interrogation of the content of reflexive calls, the consequences for understanding and practice, the dynamics of the contexts in which it is produced and the varying expectations that are placed upon its processes and products. While there is no doubt that social research does contribute to human betterment, issues remain over the forms of recognition of such work and the ambiguities and unrealistic expectations that so often surround its place in society. Our journey has meant going into terrains of investigation that are frequently overlooked in calls to reflexivity. As with many matters, the closer one gets to home, the more uncomfortable can be the reading.

There have been no blueprints in our journey. Dimensions of reflexive practice and degrees of epistemic permeability have been introduced to avoid, among other issues, conflating clarification with resolution in practice. An orientation to our work, in terms of its processes, purpose and potential is needed, but it should not spill over into assumptions of how it may then automatically inform what is to be done. We have suggested that too many frustrated ambitions and expectations have been sacrificed on such altars and expectations from within politics, policy, university management and occupational cultures do not help this situation. Any shelter that may be afforded by working in particular institutions, therefore, should not be conflated with other spaces of activity as if there were some simple relationship between the production and reception of knowledge and any subsequent action.

Those outside of the confines of professional research communities need to be more involved in this process and that means engaging in different fields of activity and those persons being positioned accordingly. In practice this necessitates high degrees of effort from all those concerned: to make this the sole task of researchers who are subject to different capacities and operate within cultures whose efforts are directed in other ways is unrealistic. All too often the difficulties inherent in making these expectations work in practice are displaced by narrow measures that confuse, rather than clarify, what needs to be done, with whom, using what resources and according to what assumed outcomes.

In our age of climate change, resource constraint, income and wealth inequality, knowledge needs to be owned and understood in order that it is sustainable in its applicability for how we live now and in the future. Findings will be contestable and uncomfortable for many. They will meet with denial or a refusal to recognize, let alone seek to understand, the content of what is produced and its implications. Active translation is needed that enables research to resonate with experiences and issues in order that they are intelligible. There are no quick fixes to this process and models are moved across contexts as if they were a panacea for social and environmental problems, thereby relieving their recipients of the efforts needed to reach understanding, let alone coordinate their actions. We face different and common challenges. They may be common in their origin, but contestable in their effects and consequences. Placing this at the feet of those who have different capacities and capabilities to respond is not only ineffective, it is unjust.

The two domains of reflexivity we have discussed will oscillate when reflecting upon research as a collective endeavour. A resulting ambivalence is a necessary feature to learn from the past and orientate towards the future and is part of the effect of collapsing these domains of activity. Too often our idea of expertise constitutes individuals as beyond reproach and allows for a celebration of knowledge within a limited sphere of activity. Part of this is to recognize newer divisions of labour and being willing to admit of ignorance, not just celebrate expertise and yet being confident enough in what we do to engage with publics. Academia is not set up for that and current trends place unrealistic burdens upon science in general which, in turn, should recognize its limits (Latour 2004). The world is, after all, richer than acts of representation and this drives the need for engagement. Learning is a two-way process and it is something that communities, including those within research contexts, can improve.

We need more understanding of the relations between reflexivity within the lifeworld under study and that of the social research community. As suggested, this encompasses an examination of the social conditions under and through which both operate and how the objects of scientific curiosity are constructed and with what implications for knowing the world. Second and relatedly, how and under what conditions referential reflexivity is achieved both within the lifeworld under study, as well as the social scientific community and with what implications for current and subsequent practices. We will then be better able to see how societies organize their production of sciences and from there better 'understand how sciences organize societies' (S. Harding 1996: 506).

Dominant ways of constructing the role of knowledge in society produce a missing middle in which the significance of this activity is diminished or impeded, or is taken up by new armies of intermediaries whose understandings are limited and whose efforts add to current processes, but are not actively translational, let alone transformational. They can act to keep cultures of enquiry and reception apart, reinforcing in the process the importance of their own function through allusion to different parties who never meet. They may have funding, but little, if any, effect on understanding and this is evident in the perpetuation of a project and grant mentality, with success being judged by narrow measures and indicators that are limited in their conception.

These forms of working overwhelm innovative practice and learning. Allusions to ignorant and resistant publics or academic obfuscation are not helpful in this process. There is no substitute for continual efforts that are aimed at coherent, consistent, coordinated and well-communicated under-standings between parties. Such work is not an annoying distraction, but a necessary pre-condition for facing contemporary challenges. A licence to think outside of the box is needed for all parties in order to learn, imagine and act. That means creating spaces in which it is acceptable to combine knowledge and imagination free from immediate consequence and also a preparedness to admit of and learn from failures.

The need for new ideas and the integration of what is already known is now greater than ever. In the search for the new, we must not forget the past. Disparate knowledges can be integrated, seen alongside each other and recontextualized. Sharing individual understandings can generate new social learning. Only then does it become possible to know when and how knowledge has had particular outcomes that are seen, by different parties, to have had benefits or contain potentials. Considerable effort is needed in order to learn from imaginative and effective processes and there are no quick routes towards this end. This implies a willingness to learn from the past and share an understanding of orientations according to working in different contexts and what is valuable and what are the limits of those places.

To remain within the confines of institutions whose distinctiveness arises from their different contributions to society, as well as the degrees of shelter they may offer to their inhabitants, despite the numerous attempts to flatten those in the name of narrow and unimaginative outputs, means giving up cer-tain expectations, while also recognizing the ways in which position and belonging enable and constrain courses of action. As we have said, certain expectations regarding the relationship between knowledge and action may be better afforded in other places. Issues of public concern are a condition of the topicality and vibrancy of social research, but that is not the same as meaning it has the attention of the public as a whole. Being asked to speak about par-ticular issues in the media as they arise is not the same as being asked to com-ment on many issues and be positioned as someone to whom the public can turn for general illumination.

The conditions under and through which social research generated in universi-ties can or cannot be taken forward, as well as having a sense of the consequences of that knowledge for subsequent action and possessing the capability to do so, can easily be bracketed out in assumptions informing connections between knowledge and action. Saying that one has a wish to learn is not the same as learning, while the timeframes in which knowledge may or may not have applicability vary, as do scales of activity and their consequences for localities and general policies. Occupational cultures in all organizations can place learning at a low premium and governments, universities and research councils fund work in allusions to something called the global and competitive knowledge economy – as if the work of cooperation and the effort needed for learning were not a necessary part of the reality of knowledge production itself, as well as what is done with that knowledge.

There is so much to celebrate about how communities share and develop their knowledge, including within social research communities, but this is easily denigrated in the name of particular constructs of knowledge production and reception. In addition, practices also result from informal networks that pass under institutional radars and yet add a great deal to our understanding and actions. The effort needed to develop trust and the building of effective practices that run counter to dominant ways of working are vulnerable to eradication in the name of narrow forms of expectation and unrealistic timeframes.

We have argued that different rationales align to produce a space where we find a lot of talk about excellence and global competition, as well as knowledge transfer and enterprise activities. Spin-outs and patents, or the 'dull thud' of the research report on the desk of the funders, or being 'user friendly', is usually what is meant by these terms. Charting different excellence-relevance dimensions and their confusion in political discourse, policy and practice, we turned to three alternative ways of seeing knowledge-based development: process-driven, product-driven and acquisition-driven, each with different implications for the role of universities as sites of knowledge production and for the disciplines within them.

In the face of confusion and the absence of clarification, researchers can avoid commitment through withdrawal and capitulation (Bourdieu 2008). Other consequences then follow: political choices are justified according to scientific 'fact' which enables accountability to collapse into the domain of the supposed self-evidence of technical allusion, or science is seen as the savoir of the political. Neither the responsibility that comes with political choice and its accompanying accountability, nor the integrity of scientific practice, escapes unscathed in these types of encounter. The power of attribution, which rests upon its narrow constitution via exclusionary practices, enables this to continue. Yielding additional income – which is what is often meant by relevance – is one outcome. The point is not that such an outcome is necessarily problematic in itself, but that it overlooks the importance of knowledge as a whole and perpetuates the idea that only particular knowledges 'add value'.

So much of what is known and practised is not amenable to frameworks that constitute knowledge in this way. With all the talk about knowledge transfer, little understanding populates the processes and contexts through which it can happen, as well as those conditions that stop it happening, in ways that are mutually engaged, supportive and helpful. Institutional contexts are ignored as if individuals can simply rise above them. While alternative practices do occur, it is despite, not because of, the institutions in which people find themselves. However, there are high negative costs and this perpetuates the idea that they are associated with exceptional characters, divorced from their cultures and contexts. Apparently the how of knowledge is secondary to what results from production. If the latter is good enough, it is assumed it will take care of the former. Simplistic and unhelpful understandings are permitted their space and ways of knowing and practical efforts are denigrated and excluded.

We seem to have a greater recognition of this through the deployment of the term knowledge 'exchange'. Yet the occupational and institutional arrangements for this to take place are rarely discussed, but exist as expectations that produce a vacuum to be filled by success at playing information politics. No one, despite all the talk of 'innovation', will risk blowing this apart and so we get enterprise in institutions being constituted as separate from research, along with knowledge transfer divisions and offices whose very existence is taken as evidence of success. It is real in its effects: monies are distributed to particular institutions as if the production of knowledge (property) and knowing (taking forward in practice), were synonymous.

The role of universities as knowledge producers is increasingly valued in particular ways, with an emphasis upon their relationships with businesses, governments and society in general. As we have suggested, priority is then given to social research that is 'robust', 'relevant' and exhibits 'user engagement' and 'knowledge transfer'. At the same time the roles and functions of the university in the knowledge economy are diverse and act at different levels of scale. On the one hand, social research is taken to be conducted at an international level in order to meet criteria of world-class excellence. On the other hand, it also needs to be embedded in local and regional contexts if the kinds of economic, social and environmental benefits expected from knowledge are to be realized. This rests upon particular assumptions and expectations that create ambiguities with a resulting diminishing of effectiveness.

While universities are places of these different expectations, this gives rise to a need to establish their distinctiveness in order to avoid becoming sites of activities that could take place in other contexts. Without this distinctiveness in place, what is their future and why would people wish to work there? A balance between the short and the long term is required. At present there is little evidence of a consistent and coherent approach to this issue and we have argued that this is reflected in institutional and occupational practices. The absence of a call for immediate application, combined with particular professional cultures and an emphasis on providing spaces for reflection, leads to a different – and unique – form of knowledge being produced within universities.

Valuing this function is of central importance if the place and role of the university in society and the research that is conducted within it, is not to give way to a short-term instrumentalism – just the type of practice that causes so many problems for so many, as perpetuated by so few. We live in a world where 'quick hits' drive criteria of relevance. Universities are now seeing themselves as significant economic actors in their own right and their role in the production of public goods – whose benefits are not be reducible to narrow economic calculation – is diminishing.

The challenge needs to be directed at the ambiguity perpetuated by environmental expectations of particular forms of knowledge (Box 1). We have also argued that for reflexivity to flourish, institutional and occupational practices can be improved to enable a diversity of roles within supportive cultures. If pushed too far, however, the results will be counterproductive. Reducing everything to its utility in terms of performing an operation on the world undermines the importance of the status of knowledge produced in a distance from that world. It is for this and other reasons that the distinction of what is produced in universities, in diverse ways, is so important for their future and that of societies as a whole. The issue is not to collapse them, nor to assume that they are unproblematically separated through sealed boundaries. As we have said, a great deal of boundary work goes on, consciously and otherwise, to create this distance from particular forces. How forms of knowledge interact and learn from one another, how we learn in terms of taking our background assumptions into an object for our contemplation and seeing how things and people are connected is central to a general understanding of ourselves through others and in the environments we inhabit.

A tension exists between modes of knowledge production and the goals of policy-makers and economic 'gurus'. More systematic programmes are needed, in collaborative endeavours with groups who are normally excluded from such processes that demonstrate the relevance of the university informing contemporary issues, without collapsing into a short-term instrumentalism. There is a need for more sustained and long-term programmes of work that systematically and productively take the knowledge produced by universities for socio-economic and environmental reasons, without undermining their civic and social value. Instead of ignoring the tensions that these issues raise and current trajectories ignore or characterize in limited ways, we wish to suggest a productive way forward that takes these important differences seriously for the benefit of us all.

As we noted in the Preface, within SURF we work at the interface between academic and policy worlds and research and practice. We have wrestled with issues associated with knowledge exchange, not only as a matter of organizational survival, but also on behalf of numerous clients in the public and private sectors, including universities. Our commitment to knowledge exchange, as we prefer the term, concerns the exchange of knowledge between different bodies to facilitate and strengthen links and improve practices for all concerned. We seek to avoid terms that imply a 'hypodermic' model in which grateful recipients receive the latest pearls of wisdom from those who are positioned as experts. Too much

Box 1
Knowledge and its Exchange

Production	Exchange
Knowledge is driven by individual and professional interests informed by institutional position and occupational cultures.	Problems are defined and set jointly through dialogue and negotiation with other interests.
Knowledge is produced and transferred in an output driven process subject to particular measures of performance.	Knowledges are integrated in continuous and interactive relationships between researchers and others that are non-linear.
Knowledge tends to be codified.	Forms of knowledge are translated and interact through recognition of being tacit, embedded and embodied.
Dominant methods of knowledge transfer tend to include report writing, articles, patents, spin-outs, etc.	Varied mechanisms for knowledge exchange include seminars, placements, informal gatherings, networking, job-sharing, workshops, use of media, etc.
Knowledge provided that can be stored, retrieved and referred to.	Knowledges may be stored, but subject to a process of translation leading to intelligence that may be incorporated into cultures and practices.
Knowledge transfer tends to be passive, contained and static and driven by narrow criteria of recognition.	Knowledge exchange is active, open, fluid and dynamic.

Knowledge Production

↓

Knowledge Transfer

↓

Knowledge Use

Knowledge Production

Knowing → Knowledge Production → Translation and Integration → Knowledge Reception → Knowing

(Drawing on Gibbons et al. (1994) *The New Production of Knowledge*)

emphasis is placed on the 'expert' who, for example, can end up modelling the economy in the name of particular and limited understandings. Knowledge exchange does not have a clear start or end point or fixed boundaries between funders, users and producers of research. It is about the active translation of work from information to intelligence according to the needs, in context, of particular groups of policy-makers, practitioners, researchers and the public at large.

A continuous and interactive relationship between research participants and users is required, in which differences in divisions of labour are recognized, negotiated, tolerated and acted upon for mutual benefit according to changes in the environments we occupy. This is far from an easy process. Active commitment, effort and institutional support to be effective are, at least, necessary. We have spoken at universities who want a centre such as SURF to be part of what they do. Yet it cannot be taken off the shelf, nor can it be generalized to universities as a whole without significant effects on the positive elements of their diverse cultures. There are no short-cuts or simple remedies and beware those peddling such wares!

Key to effective exchange is an understanding and recognition of different cultures of enquiry and reception, as well as the limitations to current understanding. Knowledge must be produced and communicated rather than simply transferred. Knowledge needs to be actively received, understood and interpreted and its processes of production informed by different groups. The reception of research requires more consideration than has been provided thus far. Without some understanding of use in context – which is not a one-way relation of research to practice, but also of practice informing research – exchange is an activity without substantial benefit. Knowledge exchange does not therefore take place between two separate spheres of activity, but is a space of communication where different cultures of enquiry and reception can engage, through drawing upon different forms of knowledge exchange (see Figure 1).

Take the representation of many contemporary urban issues as problems. There are different forms of knowledge, relating to a variety of motivations and understandings that together constitute distinct reactions to the 'same' sets of issues. To that end, the idea of transfer cannot adequately characterize the multiple negotiations that are required to develop effective responses to shared problems. A number of other issues act to prevent a simple problem-solution equation that policy-makers, politicians and academics reach for in their desire to apply knowledge. At this point technology often steps in. Technology can be used to access information quickly and efficiently, but explicit knowledge relates to tacit knowledge, so there are limits to codification as a solution. All too often technology is seen as a panacea to our collective problems. Context also matters. There are limits to deploying forms of communication that only accelerate information, but do little to add to intelligence. Understanding the context in which research is produced and received is critical in ensuring effective knowledge use in practice. Being context-sensitive is not the same as being context-dependent, for the former allows for revision in the process of learning.

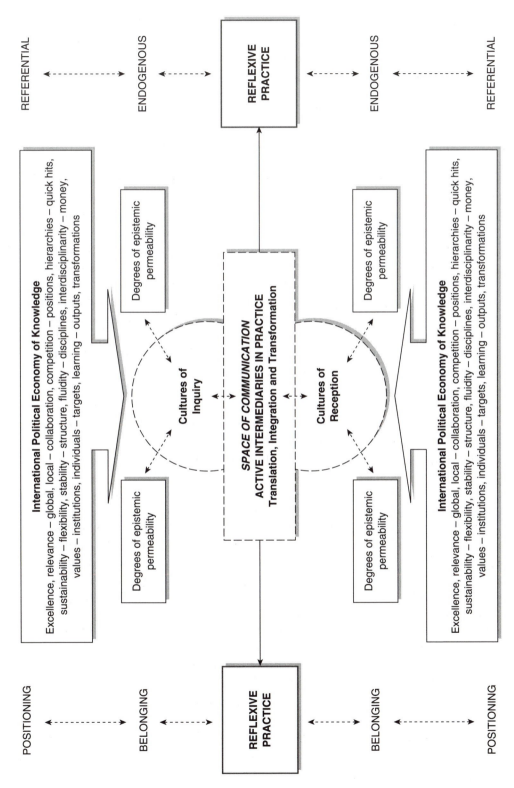

FIGURE 1   REFLEXIVE KNOWLEDGE PRODUCTION

Our research has found that spaces of communication between cultures of enquiry and cultures of reception do not exist in a systematic way. Populating what we have called the missing middle requires active intermediation between research and different social interests in order to mutually constitute a shared understanding of the need for knowledge exchange (see Box 2). We need a mode of operation in which knowledge is produced by interaction between parties, allowing the know-how of practice to inform the production of knowledge for practice. This is challenging not only to research funders and performers, but also to governments at multiple scales and to their policy-makers. The space of communication is frequently absent and we have found knowledge, context and action existing in a dynamic tension that is frequently unconnected. A missing middle, composed of the unarticulated and unrealistic expectations placed upon all in the research process, without a mutual understanding being developed, is apparent.

Across many different contexts, the landscape of social research in higher education raises complex sets of issues for those working in universities in respect to their roles and purpose. Questions are commonplace over what can be reasonably expected in relation to its positive impact upon the environment and social, political and economic issues. Translating opportunities into tangible realities poses a number of significant challenges. These need to be managed in ways that are not indifferent to the strengths, as well as weaknesses, of current practices. Issues of scale, forms of funding, academic research and working practices, university structures and governance and modes of knowledge production, are all part of this mix.

To be effective, knowledge exchange requires the building up of trust and commitment over time to joint working. It is a time-consuming mode of working and the drive for excellence in academia, through publication in journals upon which career progression is based, does not render itself amenable to these types of activity. It does have its place, but attempts to introduce novel and distinctive ways of approaching these issues hit conditions driven by particular values, expectations and measures of assumed effectiveness.

Effective coordination, communication and support between organizations, with sufficient funding and legitimacy, are essential to success. The appropriate scales of activity need to be considered without assuming all appropriate forms of expertise reside within a particular locality. Personnel, drawn from universities and other organizations, who are disciplinary specialists in their own right with the disposition to do something different, should not be disadvantaged by dominant forms of professional career structures. Working at inclusion within a well-developed framework of understanding what is trying to be achieved, how and why, takes time and a great deal of effort. Inter-institutional spaces, which not only move beyond current limits, but also recognize their strengths, would need a clear sense of purpose in acting as active intermediaries between sites of production and reception. In having the contexts to perform in this way, their cultures will produce the contents that have positive consequences for how we live together now and into the future.

Box 2
The Role of an Active Intermediary

- Map existing work in different institutions in terms of types of research activity and involvement of different personnel.
- Act as a bridge between organizations, institutions and groups, identifying gaps and strengths.
- Deploy personnel from different organizations and groups who understand not only the desired outcomes, but also the contexts in which personnel work.
- Take the need for staff mobility seriously in order to provide the necessary human resource through capability for success. That means understanding and even challenging institutional incentives and career structures and not placing the onus upon particular individuals to transcend those.
- Translate and disseminate the results of work by bringing together different expertise around a good understanding of the needs of disparate groups.
- Provide an integrative function to ensure that existing disparate information can be combined and reused for creating intelligence.
- Provide knowledge arenas for different groups to discuss and exchange ideas and knowing in practice without a concern for immediate consequence.
- Know when to admit of limits and find others to help with those.
- Provide a resource for identifying opportunities and add value through a more inclusive understanding of different processes and outcomes.
- Bring together otherwise disparate groups to work collaboratively for collective benefit within new partnerships by understanding the ways in which existing organizations and places work.
- Avoid duplication of effort.
- Bring together those from different areas of expertise to work on jointly defined issues according to a well-articulated understanding of expectations.
- Act, in partnership with others, as a resource for people in their daily practices and distinguish between information and knowledge – do not bombard people with information, but translate according to context-sensitivity.
- Deploy intelligence to inform groups and organizations to take best advantage of integrated, new and developing insights.
- Act and be supported through tangible financial and symbolic means to ask the uncomfortable questions.

REFERENCES

Ackers, L. and Gill, B. (2008) *Moving People and Knowledge: Scientific Mobility in an Enlarging European Union*. Cheltenham, UK: Edward Elgar.

Adorno, T. and Horkheimer, M. (1979) *Dialectic of Enlightenment*. Originally published 1944. Translated by J. Cumming. London: Verso.

Agger, B. (1991) *A Critical Theory of Public Life: Knowledge, Discourse and Politics in an Age of Decline*. London: Falmer.

Albrow, M. (1990) *Max Weber's Construction of Social Theory*. London: Macmillan.

Allen, J. (2000) 'Power/economic knowledge: Symbolic and spatial formations', in J. Bryson, P. Daniels, N. Henry and J. Pollard (eds), *Knowledge, Space, Economy*. London: Routledge.

Althusser, L. (1969) *For Marx*. Translated by B. Brewster. Harmondsworth, UK: Penguin.

Amit, V. (2000) 'The university as panopticon: Moral claims and attacks on academic freedom', in M. Strathern (ed.), *Audit Cultures: Anthropological Studies in Accountability, Ethics and the Academy*. London: Routledge.

Apel, Karl-Otto (1995) *Charles S. Peirce: From Pragmatism to Pragmaticism*. Translated by J.M. Krois. Originally published in 1967. Atlantic Highlands, NJ: Humanities Press.

Archer, M.S. (2007) *Making our Way through the World: Human Reflexivity and Social Mobility*. Cambridge: Cambridge University Press.

Archibugi, D. and Lundvall, B. (eds) (2001) *The Globalising Learning Economy*. Oxford: Oxford University Press.

Ashmore, M. (1989) *The Reflexive Thesis: Wrighting the Sociology of Scientific Knowledge*. Chicago, IL: University of Chicago Press.

Baldamus, W. (1961) *Efficiency and Effort: An Analysis of Industrial Administration*. London: Tavistock.

Barnes, B., Bloor, D. and Henry, J. (1996) *Scientific Knowledge: A Sociological Analysis*. Chicago, IL: University of Chicago Press.

Barnett, R. (1990) *The Idea of Higher Education*. Buckingham: Society for Research into Higher Education and Open University Press.

Barnett, R. (2000) *Realizing the University in an Age of Supercomplexity*. Buckingham: Open University Press.

Barrett, M. (1991) *The Politics of Truth: From Marx to Foucault*. Cambridge: Polity.

Baudrillard, J. (1988) *Selected Writings*. Edited by M. Poster. Cambridge: Polity.

Bauman, Z. (1976) *Towards a Critical Sociology: An Essay on Commonsense and Emancipation*. London: Routledge & Kegan Paul.

Bauman, Z. (1978) *Hermeneutics and Social Science: Approaches to Understanding*. London: Hutchinson.

Bauman, Z. (1989) *Legislators and Interpreters: On Modernity, Post-Modernity and Intellectuals*. Cambridge: Polity.

Bauman, Z. (1995) *Life in Fragments: Essays in Postmodern Morality*. Oxford: Blackwell.

Bauman, Z. (1997) *Postmodernity and its Discontents*. Cambridge: Polity.

Bauman, Z. (1999) *Culture as Praxis*. New edition. London: Sage.

Bauman, Z. (2000) *Liquid Modernity*. Cambridge: Polity.

Bauman, Z. (2007) 'Sociology, nostalgia, Utopia and mortality: A conversation with Zygmunt Bauman'. Interview by M.H. Jacobsen and K. Tester. *European Journal of Social Theory*, 10 (2): 305–25.

Becher, T. (1989) *Academic Tribes and Territories: Intellectual Enquiry and the Cultures of Disciplines*. Milton Keynes: Society for Research into Higher Education and Open University Press.

Beck, U. (1992) *Risk Society: Towards a New Modernity*. London: Sage.

Beck, U. and Beck-Gernsheim, E. (2002) *Individualization: Institutionalized Individualism and its Social and Political Consequences*. London: Sage.

Beck, U., Giddens, A. and Lash, S. (1994) *Reflexive Modernization: Politics, Tradition and Aesthetics in the Modern Social Order*. Cambridge: Polity.

Beilharz, P. (2000) *Zygmunt Bauman: Dialectic of Modernity*. London: Sage.

Bell, D. (1973) *The Coming of Post-Industrial Society*. New York: Basic Books.

Bénatouïl, T. (1999) 'A tale of two sociologies: The critical and the pragmatic stance in contemporary French sociology', *European Journal of Social Theory*, 2 (3): 381–98.

Benhabib, S. (1992) *Situating the Self: Gender, Community and Postmodernism in Contemporary Ethics*. Cambridge: Polity.

Benhabib, S., Butler, J., Cornell, D. and Fraser, N. (1995) *Feminist Contentions: A Philosophical Exchange*. London: Routledge.

Berger, P.L. and Luckmann, T. (1967) *The Social Construction of Reality: A Treatise in the Sociology of Knowledge*. New York: Anchor.

Bernstein, R. (1983) *Beyond Objectivism and Relativism: Science, Hermeneutics and Praxis*. Oxford: Blackwell.

Bernstein, R. (1992) *The New Constellation: The Ethical-Political Horizons of Modernity/Postmodernity*. Cambridge, MA: MIT Press.

Bhaskar, R. (1989) *Reclaiming Reality: A Critical Introduction to Contemporary Philosophy*. London: Verso.

Boix Mansilla, V., Gardner, H. and Miller, W. (1999) 'On disciplinary lenses and interdisciplinary work', in P. Grossman and S. Wineburg (eds), *Disciplinary Encounters*. New York: Teachers College Press.

Bonaccorsi, A. and Daraio, C. (eds) (2007) *Universities and Strategic Knowledge Creation: Specialization and Performance in Europe*. Cheltenham, UK: Edward Elgar.

Bourdieu, P. (1986) *Distinction: A Social Critique of the Judgement of Taste*. Translated by R. Nice. London: Routledge.

Bourdieu, P. (1989) 'Social space and symbolic power', *Sociological Theory*, 7 (1): 14–25.

Bourdieu, P. (1990) *In Other Words: Essays Towards a Reflexive Sociology*. Translated by M. Adamson. Cambridge: Polity.

Bourdieu, P. (1992a) *The Logic of Practice*. Translated by R. Nice. Originally published in 1980 as *Le Sens Pratique*. Cambridge: Polity.

Bourdieu, P. (1992b) *Language and Symbolic Power*. Edited and introduced by J. Thompson. Translated by G. Raymond and M. Adamson. Cambridge: Polity.

Bourdieu, P. (1993) *Sociology in Question*. Translated by R. Nice. London: Sage.

Bourdieu, P. (1998a) *Practical Reason: On the Theory of Action*. Cambridge: Polity.

Bourdieu, P. (1998b) *Acts of Resistance: Against the New Myths of Our Time*. Translated by R. Nice. Cambridge: Polity.

Bourdieu, P. (1999) 'The social conditions of the international circulation of ideas', in R. Shusterman (ed.), *Bourdieu: A Critical Reader*. Oxford: Blackwell.

Bourdieu, P. (2000) *Pascalian Meditations*. Translated by R. Nice. Cambridge: Polity.

Bourdieu, P. (2004) *Science of Science and Reflexivity*. Translated by R. Nice. Cambridge: Polity.

Bourdieu, P. (2007) *Sketch for a Self Analysis*. Translated by R. Nice. Originally published in 2004 as *Esquisse pour une auto-analyse*. Cambridge: Polity.

Bourdieu, P. (2008) *Political Interventions: Social Science and Political Action*. Texts selected and introduced by F. Poupeau and T. Discepolo. Translated by D. Fernbach. London: Verso.

Bourdieu, P. and Wacquant, L.J. (1992) *An Invitation to Reflexive Sociology*. Cambridge: Polity.

Bourdieu, P. and Wacquant, L.J. (2001) 'New Liberal speak: Notes on the new planetary Vulgate', *Radical Philosophy*, 105: 2–5.

Bourdieu, P., Chamboredon, Jean-Claude and Passeron, Jean-Claude (1991) *The Craft of Sociology: Epistemological Preliminaries*. Edited by B. Krais. Translated by R. Nice. New York: Walter de Gruyter.

Bowker, G.C. and Star, S.L. (2002) *Sorting Things Out: Classification and its Consequences*. Cambridge, MA: MIT Press.

Boyer, E.L. (1990) *Scholarship Reconsidered: Priorities of the Professoriate*. Carnegie Foundation for the Advancement of Teaching. San Francisco, CA: Jossey-Bass.

Boyne, R. (1990) *Foucault and Derrida: The Other Side of Reason*. London: Unwin Hyman.

Braun, D. and Merrien, F-X. (eds) (1999) *Towards a New Model of Governance for Universities? A Comparative View*. London: Jessica Kingsley.

Brown, R.H. (1992) 'Social science and society as discourse: Towards a sociology for civic competence', in S. Seidman and D.G. Wagner (eds), *Postmodernism and Social Theory*. Oxford: Blackwell.

Brown, R.K. (1992) *Understanding Industrial Organisations: Theoretical Perspectives in Industrial Sociology*. London: Routledge.

Brunkhorst, H. (1996) 'Critical theory and empirical research', in D. Rasmussen (ed.), *Handbook of Critical Theory*. Oxford: Blackwell.

Bryson, J. (2000) 'Introduction', in J. Bryson, P. Daniels, N. Henry and J. Pollard (eds), *Knowledge, Space, Economy*. London: Routledge.

Bryson, J., Daniels, P., Henry, N. and Pollard, J. (eds) (2000) *Knowledge, Space, Economy*. London: Routledge.

Burchell, G., Gordon, C. and Miller, P. (eds) (1991) *The Foucault Effect: Studies in Governmentality*. London: Harvester Wheatsheaf.

Burkitt, I. (1992) 'Beyond the "Iron Cage": Anthony Giddens on modernity and the self', Special issue on 'Politics and Modernity', *History of the Human Sciences*, 5 (3): pp. 71–9.

Burkitt, I. (1997) 'The situated social scientist: Reflexivity and perspective in the sociology of knowledge', *Social Epistemology*, 11 (2): 193–202.

Burtscher, C., Pasqualoni, P. and Scott, A. (2006) 'Universities and the regulatory framework: The Austrian university system in transition', in T. May and B. Perry. Special issue on 'Universities in the Knowledge Economy: Places of Expectation/ Spaces for Reflection?', *Social Epistemology*, 20 (3–4): 241–58.

Butler, J. (1994) 'Gender as performance: An interview with Judith Butler'. Conducted by P. Osborne and L. Segal. *Radical Philosophy*, 67: 32– 9.

Butler, J. (1995) 'For a careful reading', in S. Benhabib, J. Butler, D. Cornell and N. Fraser, *Feminist Contentions: A Philosophical Exchange*. London: Routledge.

Butler, J. (1999) 'Revisiting bodies and pleasures', in V. Bell (ed.), *Performativity and Belonging*. London: Sage.

Butler, J. (2002) 'Bodies and power, revisited', *Radical Philosophy*, 114: 13–19.

Butler, J. (2006) 'Israel/Palestine and the paradoxes of academic freedom', *Radical Philosophy*, 135: 8–17.

Byrne, D. (1998) *Complexity Theory and the Social Sciences*. London: Routledge.

Calhoun, C. (1995) *Critical Social Theory: Culture, History and the Challenge of Difference*. Oxford: Blackwell.

Callon, M. (1986) 'Some elements of a sociology of translation: Domestication of the scallops and fishermen of St Brieuc Bay', in J. Law (ed.), *Power, Action and Belief: A New Sociology of Knowledge?* Sociological Review Monograph 32. London: Routledge & Kegan Paul.

Cameron, A. and Palan, R. (2004) *The Imagined Economics of Globalization*. London: Sage.

Canguilhem, G. (2007) *The Normal and the Pathological*. With an introduction by M. Foucault. Translated by C.R. Fawcett with R.S. Cohen. Originally published in 1966. New York: Zone Books.

Canon, T., Nathan, M. and Westwood, A. (2003) *Welcome to the Ideopolis*. The Work Foundation Working Paper. London: The Work Foundation.

Castells, M. (1996) *The Rise of the Network Society*. Oxford: Blackwell.

Castells, M. and Hall, P. (1994) *Technopoles of the World*. London: Routledge.

Castoriadis, C. (1991) *Philosophy, Politics, Autonomy: Essays in Political Philosophy*. Edited by D.A. Curtis. Oxford: Oxford University Press.

Charles, D.R. (2006) 'Universities as key knowledge infrastructures in regional innovation systems', *Innovation: The European Journal of Social Science Research*, 19: 117–30.

Cicourel, A.V. (1993) 'Aspects of structural and processual theories of knowledge', in C. Calhoun, E. LiPuma and M. Postone (eds), *Bourdieu: Critical Perspectives*. Cambridge: Polity.

Clark, B. (1998) *Creating Entrepreneurial Universities: Organizational Pathways of Transformation*. New York: Pergamon.

Clifford, J. (1986) 'On ethnographic self-fashioning: Conrad and Malinowski', in T. Heller, M. Sosna and D. Wellbery D. with A. Davidson, A. Swidler and I. Watt (eds), *Reconstructing Individualism: Autonomy, Individuality, and the Self in Western Thought*. Stanford, CA: Stanford University Press.

Clifford, J. and Marcus, G. (eds) (1986) *Writing Culture: The Poetics and Politics of Ethnography*. Berkeley, CA: University of California Press.

Cohen, A.P. (1994) *Self Consciousness: An Alternative Anthropology of Identity*. London: Routledge.

Cohen, S. (1985) *Visions of Social Control*. Cambridge: Polity.

Cohen, S. (2001) *States of Denial: Knowing about Atrocities and Suffering*. Cambridge: Polity.

Collier, A. (1994) *Critical Realism: An Introduction to Roy Bhaskar's Philosophy*. London: Verso.

Cook, D.N. and Brown, J.S. (1999) 'Bridging epistemologies: The generative dance between organizational knowledge and organizational knowing', *Organizational Science*, 10 (4): 381–400.

Cook, J. and Fonow, M. (1990) *Knowledge and Women's Interests: Issues of Epistemology and Methodology in Sociological Research*, in J. McCarl Nielsen (ed.), *Feminist Research Methods: Exemplary Readings in the Social Sciences*. London: Westview Press.

Corbett, A. (2009) 'In the right place and for a long time: Policy entrepreneurship in the construction of the European Higher Education Area'. Paper given at University of Michigan Conference on European Integration, 6–7 March.

Coulter, J. (1979) *The Social Construction of Mind: Studies in Ethnomethodology and Linguistic Philosophy*. London: Macmillan.

Court, S. (1996) 'The use of time by academic and relation staff', *Higher Education Quarterly*, 50 (4): 237–60.

Craib, I. (1994) *The Importance of Disappointment*. London: Routledge.

Craib, I. (1998) *Experiencing Identity*. London: Sage.

Crespy, C., Heraud, J-A. and Perry, B. (2007) 'Multi-level governance, regions and science in France: Between competition and equality', *Regional Studies*, 41 (8): 1069–84.

Crouch, C. and Streeck, W. (eds) (1997) *Political Economy of Modern Capitalism: Mapping Convergence and Diversity*. London: Sage.

Czyzewski, M. (1994) 'Reflexivity of actors versus reflexivity of accounts', *Theory, Culture and Society*, 11 (4): 161–8.

Dahl, G. (1999) 'The anti-reflexivist revolution: On the affirmation of the New Right', in M. Featherstone and S. Lash (eds), *Spaces of Culture: City, Nation, World*. London: Sage.

Dawe, A. (1970) 'The two sociologies', *British Journal of Sociology*, 21 (2): 207–18.

Dawe, A. (1973) 'The role of experience in the construction of social theory: An essay in reflexive sociology', *Sociological Review*, 21 (1): 25–55.

Dawe, A. (1979) 'Theories of social action', in T. Bottomore and R. Nisbet R. (eds), *A History of Sociological Analysis*. London: Heinemann.

De la Mothe, J. (2001) 'Knowledge, politics and governance', in J. de la Mothe (ed.) *Science, Technology and Governance*. London: Continuum.

Delanty, G. (2001) *Challenging Knowledge: The University in the Knowledge Society*. Buckingham: Society for Research into Higher Education and Open University Press.

Deleuze, G. and Guattari, F. (1994) *What is Philosophy?* Translated by H. Tomlinson and G. Burchell. London: Verso.

Department for Education and Skills (2006) *Reform of Higher Education Research Assessment and Funding*. London: HMSO.

Derrida, J. (1996) 'Remarks on deconstruction and pragmatism', in C. Mouffe (ed.), *Deconstruction and Pragmatism* with Simon Critchley, Jacques Derrida, Ernesto Laclau and Richard Rorty. London: Routledge.

De Weert, E. (1999) 'Contours of the emergent knowledge society: Theoretical debate and implications for higher education research', *Higher Education,* 38: 49–69.

Dews, P. (1995) *The Limits of Disenchantment: Essays on Contemporary European Philosophy.* London: Verso.

Dresner, S. (2001) 'A comparison of RTD structures in EU Member States', in S. Dresner and N. Gilbert (eds), *The Dynamics of European Science and Technology Policies.* Aldershot, UK: Ashgate.

Dreyfus, H. and Rabinow, P. (1982) *Michel Foucault: Beyond Structuralism and Hermeneutics.* Chicago, IL: University of Chicago Press.

Dreyfus, H. and Rabinow, P. (1993) 'Can there be a science of existential structure and social meaning?', in C. Calhoun, E. LiPuma and M. Postone (eds), *Bourdieu: Critical Perspectives.* Cambridge: Polity.

du Gay, P. (1996) *Consumption and Identity at Work.* London: Sage.

du Gay, P. (2000) *In Praise of Bureaucracy: Weber – Organization – Ethics.* London: Sage.

du Gay, P. (2007) *Organizing Identity.* London: Sage.

Eggins, H. (ed.) (2003) *Globalization and Reform in Higher Education.* Maidenhead, UK: Open University Press.

Elliott, G. (1993) 'The Lonely Hour of the Last Instance: Louis Pierre Althusser, 1918–1990', in E.A Kaplan and M. Sprinker (eds), *The Althusserian Legacy.* London: Verso.

Etzkowitz, H. and Leydesdorff, L. (2000) 'The dynamics of innovation: From national systems and "Mode 2" to a triple helix of university-industry-government relations', *Research Policy,* 29: 109–23.

European Commission (2001) *Communication from the Commission: The Regional Dimension of the European Research Area.* COM (2001) 549 final. Luxembourg: Commission of the European Communities.

European Commission (2003) *Communication from the Commission on the Role of the Universities in the Europe of Knowledge.* COM (2003) 58 final. Luxembourg: Commission of the European Communities.

European Commission (2005) *Frontier Research: The European Challenge, High-level Expert Group Report.* Luxembourg: European Commission.

Falzon, C. (1998) *Foucault and Social Dialogue: Beyond Fragmentation.* London: Routledge.

Fay, B. (2009) 'For science in the social sciences', *Philosophy of the Social Sciences,* 36 (2): 227–40.

Ferrara, A. (1998) *Reflective Authenticity: Rethinking the Project of Modernity.* London: Routledge.

Feyerabend, P. (1978) *Against Method.* London: Verso.

Fichte, J.G. (1994) *Introductions to the Wissenschaftslehre and Other Writings (1797–1800).* Edited and translated by D. Breazeale. Indianapolis, IN: Hackett.

Fielding, N. (1982) 'Observational research on the National Front', in M. Bulmer (ed.), *Social Research Ethics: An Examination of the Merits of Covert Participant Observation.* London: Macmillan.

Flax, J. (1991) *Thinking Fragments: Psychoanalysis, Feminism, and Postmodernism in the Contemporary West.* Berkeley, CA: University of California Press.

Florida, R. (2002) *The Rise of the Creative Class and How It's Transforming Work, Leisure, Community and Everyday Life.* New York: Basic Books.

Foucault, M. (1982a) 'Is it really important to think? An interview translated by Thomas Keenan', *Philosophy and Social Criticism*, 9 (1): 29–40.

Foucault, M. (1982b) 'The subject and power', in H. Dreyfus and P. Rabinow, *Michel Foucault: Beyond Structuralism and Hermeneutics.* Chicago, IL: University of Chicago Press.

Foucault, M. (1984) *The Foucault Reader.* Edited by P. Rabinow. Harmondsworth, UK: Penguin.

Foucault, M. (1988) 'Truth, power, self: an interview', in L.H. Martin, H. Gutman and P.H. Hutton (eds), *Technologies of the Self: A Seminar with Michel Foucault.* London: Tavistock.

Foucault, M. (1989a) *Foucault Live: Collected Interviews 1961–1984.* Edited by E. Lotringer. Translated by J. Johnston. New York: Semiotext(e).

Foucault, M. (1989b) *The Archaeology of Knowledge.* Originally published in 1969. Translated by A.M. Sheridan Smith. London: Routledge.

Foucault, M. (1991a) *Remarks on Marx: Conversations with Duccio Trombadori.* Translated by R.J. Goldstein and J. Cascaito. New York: Semiotext(e).

Foucault, M. (1991b) 'Questions of method', in G. Burchell, C. Gordon and P. Miller (eds), *The Foucault Effect: Studies in Governmentality.* London: Harvester Wheatsheaf.

Foucault, M. (1991c) 'The ethic of care for the self as a practice of freedom: An interview with Fornet-Betancourt, R., Becker, H. and Gomez-Müller, A.', translated by J.D. Gauthier Snr, in J. Bernauer and D. Rasmussen (eds), *The Final Foucault.* Cambridge, MA: MIT Press.

Foucault, M. (1992) *The Order of Things: An Archaeology of the Human Sciences.* Originally published in 1970. London: Routledge.

Foucault, M. (1997) *Aesthetics, Method, and Epistemology. The Essential Works, Volume 2.* Edited by J. Faubion. Translated by R. Hurley et al. London: Allen Lane.

Fowler, B. (1997) *Pierre Bourdieu and Cultural Theory: Critical Investigations.* London: Sage.

Fraser, N. (1989) *Unruly Practices: Power, Discourse and Gender in Contemporary Social Theory.* Cambridge: Polity.

Fraser, N. and Honneth, A. (2003) *Redistribution or Recognition: A Political-Philosophical Exchange.* London: Verso.

Freidson, E. (1994) *Professionalism Reborn: Theory, Prophecy and Policy.* Chicago, IL: University of Chicago Press.

Fuller, S. (2000) *The Governance of Science.* Buckingham: Open University Press.

Gadamer, H.G. (1977) *Philosophical Hermeneutics.* Translated and edited by D.E. Linge. Berkeley, CA: University of California Press.

Gadamer, H.G. (1981) *Reason in the Age of Science.* Translated by F.G. Lawrence. Cambridge, MA: MIT Press.

Galbraith, J.K. (1992) *The Culture of Contentment.* Harmondsworth, UK: Penguin.

Gane, M. (1990) 'Ironies of postmodernism: Fate of Baudrillard's fatalism', *Economy and Society*, 19 (3): 314–34.

Gane, M. (1991) *Baudrillard: Critical and Fatal Theory*. London: Routledge.

Garfinkel, H. (1967) *Studies in Ethnomethodology*. Englewood Cliffs, NJ: Prentice-Hall.

Garfinkel, H. (1991) 'Respecification: Evidence for locally produced, naturally accountable phenomena of order, logic, reason, meaning, method, etc. In and as of the essential haecceity of immortal ordinary society, (1) – an announcement of studies', in G. Button (ed.), *Ethnomethodology and the Human Sciences*. Cambridge: Cambridge University Press.

Garfinkel, H. and Sacks, H. (1986) 'On formal structures of practical actions', in H. Garfinkel (ed.), *Ethnomethodological Studies of Work*. London: Routledge & Kegan Paul.

Gerth, H. and Mills, C.W. (eds) (1970) *From Max Weber: Essays in Sociology*. London: Routledge & Kegan Paul.

Gibbons, M. (2001) 'Governance and the new production of knowledge', in J. de la Mothe (ed.), *Science, Technology and Governance*. London: Continuum.

Gibbons, M., Limoges, C., Nowotny, H., Schwartaman, S., Scott, P. and Trow, M. (1994) *The New Production of Knowledge: The Dynamics of Science and Research in Contemporary Societies*. London: Sage.

Gibson-Graham, J.K. (Julie Graham and Katherine Gibson) (1996) *The End of Capitalism (As We Knew It): A Feminist Critique of Political Economy*. Oxford: Blackwell.

Giddens, A. (1976) *New Rules of Sociological Method: A Positive Critique of Interpretive Sociologies*. London: Hutchinson.

Giddens, A. (1984) *The Constitution of Society: Outline of the Theory of Structuration*. Cambridge: Polity.

Giddens, A. (1987) *Social Theory and Modern Sociology*. Cambridge: Polity.

Giddens, A. (1989) 'A reply to my critics', in D. Held and J.B. Thompson (eds), *Social Theory of Modern Societies: Anthony Giddens and his Critics*. Cambridge: Cambridge University Press.

Giddens, A. (1990) *The Consequences of Modernity*. Cambridge: Polity.

Giddens, A. (1991) *Modernity and Self-Identity*. Cambridge: Polity.

Giddens, A. (1996) *In Defence of Sociology: Essays, Interpretations and Rejoinders*. Cambridge: Polity.

Giddens, A. (1999) 'An interview with Anthony Giddens', in M. O'Brien, S. Penna and C. Hay (eds), *Theorising Modernity: Reflexivity, Environment and Identity in Giddens' Social Theory*. London: Longman.

Giddens, A. (2009) *The Politics of Climate Change*. Cambridge: Polity.

Giddens, A. and Pierson, C. (1998) *Conversations with Anthony Giddens: Making Sense of Modernity*. Cambridge: Polity.

Gieryn, T. (1999) *Cultural Boundaries of Science: Credibility on the Line*. Chicago, IL: University of Chicago Press.

Goffman, E. (1974) *Frame Analysis: An Essay on the Organization of Experience*. New York: Harper & Row.

Goffman, E. (1984) *The Presentation of Self in Everyday Life*. Originally published in 1959. Harmondsworth, UK: Penguin.

Gordon, C. (1991) 'Governmental rationality: An introduction', in G. Burchell, C. Gordon and P. Miller (eds), *The Foucault Effect: Studies in Governmentality*. London: Harvester Wheatsheaf.

Gouldner, A. (1971) *The Coming Crisis of Western Sociology*. London: Heinemann.

Gouldner, A. (1975) *For Sociology: Renewal and Critique in Sociology Today*. Harmondsworth, UK: Penguin.

Graham, G. (2002) *Universities: The Recovery of an Idea*. Charlottesville, VA: Imprint Academic.

Graham, G. (2005) *The Institution of Intellectual Values*. Exeter, UK: Imprint Academic.

Green, V.H.H. (1969) *The Universities*. Harmondsworth, UK: Penguin.

Griffiths, M. (1995) *Feminisms and the Self: The Web of Identity*. London: Routledge.

Guston, D. (2000) *Between Politics and Science: Assuring the Integrity and Productivity of Research*. Cambridge: Cambridge University Press.

Habermas, J. (1984) *Theory of Communicative Action, Volume 1: Reason and the Rationalization of Society*. Translated by T. McCarthy. London: Heinemann.

Habermas, J. (1987) *Theory of Communicative Action, Volume 2: Lifeworld and System: A Critique of Functionalist Reason*. Translated by T. McCarthy. Cambridge: Polity.

Habermas, J. (1989) *Knowledge and Human Interests*. Originally published in 1968. Translated by J.J. Shapiro. Cambridge: Polity.

Habermas, J. (1990) *On the Logic of the Social Sciences*. Originally published in 1970. Translated by S.W. Nicholsen and J.A. Stark. Cambridge: Polity.

Habermas, J. (1992a) *The Philosophical Discourse of Modernity: Twelve Lectures*. Cambridge: Polity.

Habermas, J. (1992b) *Postmetaphysical Thinking: Philosophical Essays*. Translated by W.M. Hohengarten. Cambridge, MA: MIT Press.

Habermas, J. (1994) *The New Conservatism: Cultural Criticism and the Historians' Debate*. Translated by S.W. Nicholsen. Introduction by R. Wolin. Cambridge: Polity.

Habermas, J. (2003) *Truth and Justification*. Translated by B. Fultner. Cambridge: Polity.

Hacking, I. (1999) *The Social Construction of What?* Cambridge, MA: Harvard University Press.

Hacking, I. (2004) 'Between Michel Foucault and Erving Goffman: Between discourse in the abstract and face-to-face interaction', *Economy and Society*, 33 (3): 277–302.

Hall, J.R. (1999) *Cultures of Inquiry: From Epistemology to Discourse in Sociohistorical Research*. Cambridge: Cambridge University Press.

Haraway, D. (1991) *Simians, Cyborgs, and Women: The Reinvention of Nature*. New York: Routledge.

Harding, A. (1997) 'Urban regimes in a Europe of the cities?', *European Urban and Regional Studies*, 4 (4): 291–314.

Harding, S. (1986) *The Science Question in Feminism*. Milton Keynes: Open University Press.

Harding, S. (ed.) (1987) *Feminism and Methodology: Social Science Issues*. Milton Keynes: Open University Press.

Harding, S. (1991) *Whose Science? Whose Knowledge? Thinking from Women's Lives*. Milton Keynes: Open University Press.

Harding, S. (1996) 'European expansion and the organization of modern science: Isolated or linked historical processes?', *Organization*, 3 (4): 497–509.

Harding, S. (2006) *Science and Social Inequality: Feminist and Postcolonial Issues.* Urbana, IL: University of Illinois Press.

Harding, S. and Hintikka, M.B. (1983) 'Introduction', in S. Harding and M.B. Hintikka (eds), *Discovering Reality: Feminist Perspectives on Epistemology, Metaphysics, Methodology, and Philosophy of Science.* London: D. Reidel.

Harloe, M. and Perry, B. (2004) 'Universities, localities and regional development: The emergence of the Mode 2 university?', *International Journal of Urban and Regional Research*, 28 (1): 212–23.

Harré, R. (1998) *The Singular Self.* London: Sage.

Harré, R. and Slocum, N. (2003) 'Disputes as complex social events: On the uses of positioning theory', in R. Harré and F. Moghaddam (eds), *The Self and Others: Positioning Individuals in Personal, Political, and Cultural Contexts.* London: Praeger.

Harré, R. and van Langenhove, L. (1991) 'Varieties of positioning', *Journal for the Theory of Social Behaviour*, 21 (4): 393–407.

Hartsock, N. (1987) 'The feminist standpoint: Developing the ground for a specifically feminist historical materialism', in S. Harding (ed.), *Feminism and Methodology.* Milton Keynes: Open University Press.

Harvey, D. (2006) *Spaces of Global Capitalism.* London: Verso.

Harvey, M. and McMeekin, A. (2007) *Public or Private Economies of Knowledge? Turbulence in the Biological Sciences.* Cheltenham, UK: Edward Elgar.

Hedmo, T. and Wedlin, L. (2008) 'New modes of governance: The re-regulation of European higher education and research', in C. Mazza, P. Quattrone and A. Riccaboni (eds), *European Universities in Transition: Issues, Models and Cases.* Cheltenham, UK: Edward Elgar.

Held, D. and Thompson, J. (eds) (1989) *Social Theory of Modern Societies: Anthony Giddens and His Critics.* Cambridge: Cambridge University Press.

Heller, A. and Féhér, F. (1991) *The Postmodern Political Condition.* Cambridge: Polity.

Henkel, M. (2000) *Academic Identities and Policy Change in Higher Education.* London: Jessica Kingsley.

Heritage, J. (1984) *Garfinkel and Ethnomethodology.* Cambridge: Polity.

Hertz, R. (ed.) (1997) *Reflexivity and Voice.* London: Sage.

Herzfeld, M. (1992) *The Social Production of Indifference: Exploring the Symbolic Roots of Western Bureaucracy.* Chicago, IL: University of Chicago Press.

Hesse, M. (1974) *The Structure of Scientific Inference.* London: Macmillan.

Hirst, P. and Thompson, G. (1999) *Globalization in Question: The International Economy and the Possibilities of Governance.* Second edition. Cambridge: Polity.

Hollway, W. (1998) 'Fitting work: Psychological assessment in organizations', in J. Henriques, W. Hollway, C. Urwin, C. Venn and V. Walkerdine (eds), *Changing the Subject: Psychology, Social Regulation and Subjectivity.* Revised edition. London: Routledge.

Holmwood, J. (1996) *Founding Sociology? Talcott Parsons and the Idea of General Theory.* Harlow, UK: Longman.

Holton, R. and Turner, B. (1989) *Max Weber on Economy and Society.* London: Routledge.

Holub, R. (1991) *Jürgen Habermas: Critic in the Public Sphere*. London: Routledge.

Horkheimer, M. (1972) *Critical Theory: Selected Essays*. Translated by M.J. O'Connell and others. New York: Herder & Herder.

Horkheimer, M. (1993) *Between Philosophy and Social Science: Selected Early Writings*. Translated by G.F. Hunter, M.S. Kramer and J. Torpey. Cambridge, MA: MIT Press.

Hoy, D.C. (1998) 'Foucault and critical theory', in J. Moss (ed.), *The Later Foucault: Politics and Philosophy*. London: Sage.

Hoy, D.C. and McCarthy, T. (1994) *Critical Theory*. Oxford: Blackwell.

Hughes, H.S. (1979) *Consciousness and Society: The Reorientation of European Social Thought 1890–1930*. Brighton: Harvester.

Hutchinson, P., Read, R. and Sharrock, W. (2008) *There is No Such Thing as a Social Science: In Defence of Peter Winch*. Aldershot, UK: Ashgate.

Irwin, A. and Michael, M. (2003) *Science, Social Theory and Public Knowledge*. Maidenhead, UK: Open University Press.

Jansen, S. (2002) 'Mode 2 knowledge and institutional life: Taking Gibbons on a walk through a South African university', *Higher Education*, 43 (4): 507–21.

Jay, M. (1973) *The Dialectical Imagination: A History of the Frankfurt School and the Institute of Social Research 1923–1950*. London: Heinemann.

Jessop, B. (2000) 'The state and the contradictions of the knowledge-driven economy', in J. Bryson, P. Daniels, N. Henry and J. Pollard (eds), *Knowledge, Space, Economy*. London: Routledge.

Joas, H. (1998) 'The autonomy of the self: The median heritage and its postmodern challenge', *European Journal of Social Theory*, 1 (1): 7–18.

Johnson, H.T. (1992) *Relevance Regained: From Top-Down Control to Bottom-Up Empowerment*. New York: Free Press.

Kirp, D. (2003) *Shakespeare, Einstein and the Bottom Line: The Marketing of Higher Education*. Cambridge, MA: Harvard University Press.

Klein, J.T. (1996) *Crossing Boundaries: Knowledge, Disciplinarities, and Interdisciplinarities*. Charlottesville, VA: University Press of Virginia.

Klein, J.T., Grossenbacher-Mansuy, W., Haeberli, R., Bill, A., Scholz, R.W. and Welti, M. (eds) (2001) *Transdisciplinarity: Joint Problem Solving among Science, Technology, and Society*. Basel: Birkhäuser.

Knights, D. and McCabe, D. (2003) *Organization and Innovation: Guru Schemes and American Dreams*. Buckingham: Open University Press.

Knights, D. and Willmott, H. (eds) (2000) *The Reengineering Revolution: Critical Studies of Corporate Change*. London: Sage.

Knorr-Cetina, K. (1981) 'The micro-sociological challenge of macro-sociology: Towards a reconstruction of social theory and methodology', in K. Knorr-Cetina and A. Cicourel (eds), *Advances in Social Theory and Methodology: Towards an Integration of Micro and Macro Theories*. London: Routledge & Kegan Paul.

Knorr-Cetina, K. (1999) *Epistemic Cultures: How the Sciences Make Knowledge*. Cambridge, MA: Harvard University Press.

Kraak, Andre (ed.) (2000) *Changing Modes: New Knowledge Production and its Implications for Higher Education in South Africa*. Pretoria: HSRC Publishers.

Larrabee, M.J. (ed.) (1993) *An Ethic of Care: Feminist and Interdisciplinary Perspectives*. London: Routledge.

Lash, S. (1999) *Another Modernity, a Different Rationality*. Oxford: Blackwell.

Lash, S. and Urry, J. (1987) *The End of Organized Capitalism*. Cambridge: Polity.

Latour, B. (1988) 'The politics of explanation: An alternative', in S. Woolgar (ed.), *Knowledge and Reflexivity: New Frontiers in the Sociology of Knowledge*. London: Sage.

Latour, B. (2004) *Politics of Nature: How to Bring the Sciences into Democracy*. Translated by C. Porter. Cambridge, MA: Harvard University Press.

Law, J. (1994) *Organizing Modernity*. Oxford: Blackwell.

Lawson, H. (1986) *Reflexivity: The Postmodern Predicament*. London: Hutchinson.

Le Gales, P. (2005) 'Interesting times for urban sociology', in T. May and B. Perry (eds), 'Symposium on the Future of Urban Sociology', *Sociology*, 39 (2): 347–52.

Lemert, C. (1997) *Postmodernism Is Not What you Think*. Oxford: Blackwell.

Letherby, G., Scott, J. and Williams, M. (forthcoming) *Objectivity and Subjectivity in Social Research*. London: Sage.

Levin, M. and Greenwood, D. (2006) 'The future of public universities: Academic freedom, university autonomy and freedom of speech from an organisational perspective'. Informational Papers of the *Transatlantic Forum on the Future of Universities*, Danish University of Education, 28–9 June.

Leyshon, A., Lee, R. and Williams, C. (eds) (2003) *Alternative Economic Spaces*. London: Sage.

Lohmann, S. (2004) 'Darwinian medicine for the university', in R.G. Ehrenberg (ed.), *Governing Academia*. Ithaca, NY: Cornell University Press.

Longino, H. (1990) *Science as Social Knowledge: Values and Objectivity in Scientific Inquiry*. Princeton, NJ: Princeton University Press.

Lovell, T. (2000) 'Thinking feminism with and against Bourdieu', in B. Fowler (eds), *Reading Bourdieu on Society and Culture*. Oxford: Blackwell.

Luhmann, N. (1982) *The Differentiation of Society*. Translated by S. Holmes and C. Larmore. New York: Columbia University Press.

Lynch, M. (2000) 'Against reflexivity as an academic virtue and source of privileged knowledge', *Theory, Culture and Society*, 17 (3): 26–54.

Lyotard, J.F. (1993) 'Answering the question: What is postmodernism?', in T. Docherty (ed.), *Postmodernism: A Reader*. London: Harvester Wheatsheaf.

McKie, L. (2002) 'Engagement and evaluation in qualitative inquiry', in T. May (ed.), *Qualitative Research in Action*. London: Sage.

McNay, L. (2000) *Gender and Agency: Reconfiguring the Subject in Feminist and Social Theory*. Cambridge: Polity.

McNay, L. (2008) *Against Recognition*. Cambridge: Polity.

Madison, G.B. (1995) 'Ricoeur and the hermeneutics of the subject', in L.E. Hahn (ed.), *The Philosophy of Paul Ricoeur: The Library of Living Philosophers Volume XXII*. La Salle, IL: Open Court.

Mannheim, K. (1960) *Ideology and Utopia*. Preface by L. Wirth. Originally published in 1936. London: Routledge & Kegan Paul.

Mannheim, K. (1970) 'The sociology of knowledge', in J. Curtis and J. Petras (eds), *The Sociology of Knowledge: A Reader*. London: Duckworth.

March, J. and Olsen, J. (1989) *Rediscovering Institutions*. New York: Free Press.

Marcuse, H. (1968) *One Dimensional Man: The Ideology of Industrial Society*. London: Sphere.

Marcuse, P. and van Kempen, R. (eds) (2000) *Globalising Cities: A New Spatial Order?* Oxford: Blackwell.

Marginson, S. and Considine, M. (2000) *The Enterprise University: Power, Governance and Reinvention in Australia*. Cambridge: Cambridge University Press.

Marquand, D. (2004) *Decline of the Public: The Hollowing Out of Citizenship*. Cambridge: Polity.

Martin, E. (1999) *Changing Academic Work: Developing the Learning University*. Buckingham: Open University Press.

Martin, J.R. (1994) 'Methodological essentialism, false difference, and other dangerous traps', *Signs*, 19 (3): 630–57.

Marx, K. (1963) *Selected Writings in Sociology and Social Philosophy*. Edited by T.B. Bottomore and M. Rubel. Originally published in 1956. Harmondsworth, UK: Penguin.

Marx, K. (1981) *Economic and Philosophical Manuscripts of 1844*. London: Lawrence & Wishart.

Maskell, D. and Robinson, I. (2001) *The New Idea of the University*. London: Imprint.

Massey, D. (2005) *For Space*. London: Sage.

May, T. (1999) 'From banana time to just-in-time: Power and resistance at work', *Sociology*, 33 (4): 767–83.

May, T. (2001) 'Power, knowledge and organizational transformation: Administration as depoliticisation', *Social Epistemology*, 15 (3): 171–86.

May, T. (2006) 'Transformative power: A study in human service organization', in H. Beynon and T. Nichols (eds), *Patterns of Work in the Post-Fordist Era: Volume 2*. Cheltenham, UK: Edward Elgar.

May, T. and Perry, B. (eds) (2005) 'The future of urban sociology: A symposium', *Sociology*, 39 (2): 343–70.

May, T. and Perry, B. (2006) 'Cities, knowledge and universities: Transformations in the image of the intangible', in T. May and B. Perry (eds), Special issue on 'Universities in the Knowledge Economy: Places of Expectation/Spaces for Reflection?', *Social Epistemology*, 20 (3–4): 259–82.

May, T. and Powell, J.L. (2008) *Situating Social Theory*. Second edition. Maidenhead, UK: Open University Press.

Maynard, M. (1998) 'Feminists' knowledge and the knowledge of feminisms: Epistemology, theory, methodology and method', in T. May and M. Williams (eds), *Knowing the Social World*. Buckingham: Open University Press.

Mead, G.H. (1964) *Selected Writings: George Herbert Mead*. Edited by A.J. Reck. Chicago, IL: University of Chicago Press.

Menand, L. (2010) *The Marketplace of Ideas*. London: W.W. Norton and Company.

Merleau-Ponty, M. (1989) *Phenomenology of Perception*. Originally published in English 1962. Translated by C. Smith. London: Routledge.

Merton, R. (1976) *Sociological Ambivalence and Other Essays*. New York: Free Press.

Messer-Davidow, E. (2002) *Disciplining Feminism: From Social Activism to Academic Discourse*. Durham, NC: Duke University Press.

Mêstrović, S. (1998) *Anthony Giddens: The Last Modernist*. London: Routledge.

Michael, J. (2000) *Anxious Intellectuals: Academic Professionals, Public Intellectuals and Enlightenment Values*. Durham, NC: Duke University Press.

Mills, C.W. (1970) *The Sociological Imagination*. Originally published in 1959. Harmondsworth, UK: Penguin.

Mintzberg, H. (1983) *Structure in Fives: Designing Effective Organizations*. Englewood Cliffs, NJ: Prentice-Hall.

Morrow, R.A. with Brown, D.D. (1994) *Critical Theory and Methodology*. London: Sage.

Mounce, H.O. (1997) *The Two Pragmatisms: From Peirce to Rorty*. London: Routledge.

Murray, G. (1997) 'Agonize, don't organize: A critique of postfeminisms', *Current Sociology*, 45 (2): 37–47.

Newfield, C. (2003) *Ivy and Industry: Business and the Making of the American University: 1880–1980*. Durham, NC: Duke University Press.

Noble, D. (1999) 'Academic integrity', in A. Montefiore and D. Vines (eds), *Integrity in the Public and Private Domains*. London: Routledge.

Norris, C. (1993) *The Truth about Postmodernism*. Oxford: Blackwell.

Nowotny, H., Gibbons, M. and Scott, P. (2001) *Rethinking Science: Knowledge and the Public in Age of Uncertainty*. Cambridge: Polity.

Oatley, N. (ed.) (1998) *Cities, Economic Competition and Urban Policy*. London: Paul Chapman.

Odin, J.K. and Manicas, P.T. (eds) (2004) *Globalization and Higher Education*. Honolulu, HI: University of Hawaii Press.

Offe, C. (1985) *Disorganized Capitalism*. Edited by J. Keane. Cambridge: Polity.

O'Neill, J. (1972) *Sociology as a Skin Trade: Essays Towards a Reflexive Sociology*. London: Heinemann.

O'Neill, J. (1995) *The Poverty of Postmodernism*. London: Routledge.

Outhwaite, W. (1986) *Understanding Social Life: The Method Called Verstehen*. Second edition. Lewes, UK: Jean Stroud.

Outhwaite, W. (1991) *New Philosophies of Social Science: Realism, Hermeneutics and Critical Theory*. New York: St Martin's Press.

Øyen, E. (1990) 'The imperfection of comparisons', in E. Øyen (ed.), *Comparative Methodology*. London: Sage.

Pels, D. (2003) *Unhastening Science: Autonomy and Reflexivity in the Social Theory of Knowledge*. Liverpool: Liverpool University Press.

Perry, B. (2006) 'Science, society and the university: A paradox of values?', in T. May and B. Perry (eds), special issue on 'Universities in the Knowledge Economy: Places of Expectation/Spaces for Reflection?' *Social Epistemology*, 20 (3–4): 201–19.

Perry, B. (2007) 'The multi-level governance of science policy in England', *Regional Studies*, 41 (8): 1051–67.

Perry, B. and May, T. (eds) (2007) 'Governance, science policy and regions', special issue of *Regional Studies*, 41 (8).

Pickstone, J.V. (2000) *Ways of Knowing: A New History of Science, Technology and Medicine*. Manchester: Manchester University Press.

Platt, R. (1989) 'Reflexivity, recursion and social life: Elements for a postmodern sociology', *Sociological Review*, 37 (4): 636–67.

Polanyi, M. (1962) *Personal Knowledge: Towards a Post-Critical Philosophy*. London: Routledge.

Polanyi, M. (1966) *The Tacit Dimension*. Garden City, NY: Doubleday.

Pollitt, C. (1993) *Managerialism and the Public Services: Cuts or Cultural Change in the 1990s?* Second edition. Oxford: Blackwell.

Pollitt, C. and Bouckaert, G. (2004) *Public Management Reform: A Comparative Analysis.* Second edition. Oxford: Oxford University Press.

Pollner, M. (1991) 'Left of ethnomethodology: The rise and decline of radical reflexivity', *American Sociological Review*, 56 (3): 370–80.

Popper, K.R. (1968) *The Logic of Scientific Discovery.* Revised edition. First published in 1959. London: Hutchinson.

Power, M. (1999) *The Audit Society: Rituals of Verification.* Oxford: Oxford University Press.

Prichard, C. (2000) *Making Managers in Universities and Colleges.* Buckingham: Open University Press.

Rabinow, P. (1996) *Essays on the Anthropology of Reason.* Princeton, NJ: Princeton University Press.

Rasmussen, D. (1996) 'Rethinking subjectivity: Narrative identity and the self', in R. Kearney (ed.), *Paul Ricoeur: The Hermeneutics of Action.* London: Sage.

Readings, B. (1996) *The University in Ruins.* Cambridge, MA: Harvard University Press.

Ricoeur, P. (1981) *Hermeneutics and the Human Sciences: Essays on Language, Action and Interpretation.* Edited, translated and introduced by J.B. Thompson. Cambridge: Cambridge University Press.

Ricoeur, P. (1986) *The Rule of Metaphor: Multi-Disciplinary Studies of the Creation of Meaning in Language.* Translated by R. Czerny with K. McLaughlin and J. Costello. London: Routledge.

Ricoeur, P. (1994) *Oneself as Another.* Translated by K. Blamey. Chicago, IL: University of Chicago Press.

Robbins, D. (2000) *Bourdieu and Culture.* London: Sage.

Romanos, G.D. (1994) 'Reflexive predictions'. In M. Martin and L.C. McIntyre (eds), *Readings in the Philosophy of Social Science.* Cambridge, MA: MIT Press.

Rorty, R. (1979) *Philosophy and the Mirror of Nature.* Princeton, NJ: Princeton University Press.

Rorty, R. (1982) *Consequences of Pragmatism: Essays 1972–1980.* Minneapolis, MN: University of Minneapolis Press.

Rorty, R. (1992) 'We anti-representationalists', *Radical Philosophy*, 60: 40–2.

Rorty, R. (1998) *Achieving Our Country: Leftist Thought in Twentieth-century America.* Cambridge, MA: Harvard University Press.

Ruivo, B. (1994) '"Phases" or "paradigms" of science policy?', *Science and Public Policy*, 21 (3): 157–64.

Russell, B. (2004) *In Praise of Idleness.* Originally published in 1935. Abingdon: Routledge.

Ryle, G. (1990) *The Concept of Mind.* Originally published in 1949. London: Penguin.

Sacks, H. (1974) 'On the analysability of stories by children', in R. Turner (ed.), *Ethnomethodology.* Harmondsworth, Penguin.

Salet, W., Kreukels, A. and Thornley, A. (eds) (2003) *Metropolitan Governance and Spatial Planning: Comparative Case Studies of European City-regions.* Aldershot, UK: E & FN Spon.

Sandywell, B. (1996) *Reflexivity and the Crisis and Western Reason: Logological Investigations, Volume 1*. London: Routledge.

Sassen, S. (2005) 'Cities as strategic sites', in T. May and B. Perry (eds) 'Symposium on the Future of Urban Sociology', *Sociology*, 39 (2): 352–7.

Scarborough, H. (2001) 'Knowledge a la mode: The rise of knowledge management and its implications for views of knowledge production', *Social Epistemology*, 15 (3): 201–13.

Schoenberger, E. (1997) *The Cultural Crisis of the Firm*. Oxford: Blackwell.

Schutz, A. (1970) *Alfred Schutz On Phenomenology and Social Relations: Selected Writings*. Edited and introduced by H.R. Wagner. Chicago, IL: University of Chicago Press.

Schutz, A. (1973) 'Problems of interpretative sociology', in A. Ryan (ed.), *The Philosophy of Social Explanation*. Oxford: Oxford University Press.

Schutz, A. (1979) 'Concept and theory formation in the social sciences', in J. Bynner and K. Stribley (eds), *Social Research: Principles and Procedures*. Milton Keynes: Open University Press.

Scott, A. (1995) 'Value freedom and intellectual autonomy', *History of the Human Sciences*, 8 (3): 69–88.

Scott, A. (2006) 'Knowledge production, management and the academic role'. Informational Papers of the *Transatlantic Forum on the Future of Universities*, Danish University of Education, 28–9 June.

Scott, J. (1997) *Corporate Business and Capitalist Classes*. Oxford: Oxford University Press.

Scott, J. (1998) 'Relationism, Cubism, and reality: Beyond relativism', in T. May and M. Williams (eds), *Knowing the Social World*. Buckingham: Open University Press.

Segal, L. (1999) *Why Feminism? Gender, Psychology, Politics*. Cambridge: Polity.

Seidman, S. (2008) *Contested Knowledge: Social Theory Today*. Oxford: Wiley Blackwell.

Sen, A. (1997) *On Economic Inequality*. Revised edition. Oxford: Oxford University Press.

Senker, J. (2006) 'Reflections on the Transformation of European Public Research'. *Innovation: The European Journal of Social Science Research*, 19 (1):67–77.

Shotter, J. (1993) *Cultural Politics of Everyday Life: Social Constructionism, Rhetoric and Knowing of the Third Kind*. Buckingham: Open University Press.

Shusterman, R. (ed.) (1999) *Bourdieu: A Critical Reader*. Oxford: Blackwell.

Silverman, D. (1997) 'Towards an aesthetics of research', in D. Silverman (ed.), *Qualitative Research: Theory, Method and Practice*. London: Sage.

Simmel, G. (1964) *The Sociology of Georg Simmel*. Translated, edited and introduced by K.H. Wolff. Originally published in 1950. New York: Free Press.

Simmie, J. (2002) 'Trading places: Competitive cities in the global economy', *European Planning Studies*, 10 (2): 201–4.

Simpson, D. (2002) *Situatedness, or, Why We Keep Saying Where We're Coming From*. Durham, NC: Duke University Press.

Skeggs, B. (2004) *Class, Self, Culture*. London: Routledge.

Slaughter, S. and Leslie, L. (1997) *Academic Capitalism: Politics, Policies and the Entrepreneurial University*. Baltimore, MD: Johns Hopkins University Press.

Smith, A. and Webster, F. (eds) (1997) *The Postmodern University? Contested Visions of Higher Education in Society*. Buckingham: Society for Research into Higher Education and Open University Press.

Smith, D.E. (1988) *The Everyday World as Problematic: A Feminist Sociology*. Milton Keynes: Open University Press.

Smith, D.E. (1993) *Texts, Facts and Femininity: Exploring the Relations of Ruling*. London: Routledge.

Smith, D.E. (1999) *Writing the Social: Critique, Theory and Investigations*. Toronto: Toronto University Press.

Smith, D.E. (2002) 'Institutional ethnography', in T. May (ed.), *Qualitative Research in Action*. London: Sage.

Smith, N.H. (1997) *Strong Hermeneutics: Contingency and Moral Identity*. London: Routledge.

Snow, C.P. (1993) *The Two Cultures*. Introduction by S. Collini. Cambridge: Cambridge University Press.

Soper, K. (1997) 'Generations of feminism', *Radical Philosophy*, 83: 6–16.

Spelman, E.V. (1990) *Inessential Woman: Problems of Exclusion in Feminist Thought*. London: The Women's Press.

Sporn, B. (1999) *Adaptive University Structures: An Analysis of Adaptation to Socioeconomic Environments of US and European Universities*. London: Jessica Kingsley.

Stehr, N. (1992) *Practical Knowledge: Applying the Social Sciences*. London: Sage.

Stehr, N. (ed.) (2004) *The Governance of Knowledge*. New Brunswick, NJ: Transaction.

Stones, R. (1996) *Sociological Reasoning: Towards a Past-Modern Sociology*. London: Macmillan.

Strathern, M. (ed.) (2000) *Audit Cultures: Anthropological Studies in Accountability, Ethics and the Academy*. London: Routledge.

Strydom, P. (2000) *Discourse and Knowledge: The Making of Enlightenment Sociology*. Liverpool: Liverpool University Press.

Sztompka, P. (1991) *Society in Action: The Theory of Social Becoming*. Cambridge: Polity.

Taylor, C. (1986) 'Foucault on freedom and truth', in D.C. Hoy (ed.), *Foucault: A Critical Reader*. Oxford: Blackwell.

Taylor, C. (1992) *Sources of the Self: The Making of the Modern Identity*. Cambridge: Cambridge University Press.

Teece, D.J. (1998) 'Capturing value from knowledge assets: The new economy, markets for know-how and intangible assets', *California Management Review*, 40 (3): 55–79.

Thompson, E.P. (ed.) (1970) *Warwick University Ltd: Industry, Management and the Universities*. Harmondsworth, UK: Penguin.

Thompson, J.B. (1981) *Critical Hermeneutics: A Study in the Thought of Paul Ricoeur and Jürgen Habermas*. Cambridge: Cambridge University Press.

Thrift, N. (2005) *Knowing Capitalism*. London: Sage.

Toulmin, S. (1992) *Cosmopolis: The Hidden Agenda of Modernity*. Chicago, IL: Chicago University Press.

Tribe, K. (1994) 'Commerce, science and the modern university', in L. Ray and M. Reed (eds), *Organizing Modernity: New Weberian Perspectives on Work, Organization and Society*. London: Routledge.

Turner, C. (1990) 'Lyotard and Weber: Postmodern rules and Neo-Kantian values', in B.S. Turner (ed.), *Theories of Modernity and Postmodernity*. London: Sage.

Turner, S. (2003) *Liberal Democracy 3.0: Civil Society in an Age of Experts*. London: Sage.

Tyler, S.A. (1986) 'Post-modern ethnography: From document of the occult to occult document', in J. Clifford and G. Marcus (eds), *Writing Culture: The Poetics and Politics of Ethnography*. Berkeley, CA: University of California Press.

Unger, R.M. (1987) *Social Theory: Its Situation and its Tasks – A Critical Introduction to Politics, a Work in Constructive Social Theory*. Cambridge: Cambridge University Press.

Visker, R. (1995) *Michel Foucault: Genealogy as Critique*. Translated by C. Turner. London: Verso.

von Glasersfeld, E. (1991) 'Knowing without metaphysics: Some aspects of the radical constructivist position', in F. Steier (eds), *Research and Reflexivity*. London: Sage.

Wacquant, L. (1992) 'The structure and logic of Bourdieu's sociology', in P. Bourdieu and L. Wacquant. *An Invitation to Reflexive Sociology*. Cambridge: Polity.

Walby, S. (1997) *Gender Transformations*. London: Routledge.

Wallerstein, I. (1996) *Open the Social Sciences: Report of the Gulbenkian Commission on the Restructuring of the Social Sciences*. Stanford, CA: Stanford University Press.

Weber, M. (1949) *The Methodology of the Social Sciences*. Edited by E. Shils and H. Finch. Glencoe, IL: Free Press.

Wiggershaus, R. (1995) *The Frankfurt School: Its History, Theories and Political Significance*. Translated by M. Robertson. Cambridge: Polity.

Williams, B. (2002) *Truth and Truthfulness: An Essay in Genealogy*. Princeton, NJ: Princeton University Press.

Williams, M. (2005) 'Situated objectivity', *Journal for the Theory of Social Behaviour*, 35 (1): 99–120.

Williams, M. and May, T. (1996) *Introduction to the Philosophy of Social Research*. London: Routledge.

Winch, P. (1990) *The Idea of a Social Science and its Relation to Philosophy*. Second edition. Originally published in 1958. London: Routledge.

Witte, J., van der Wende, M. and Huisman, J. (2008) 'Blurring boundaries: How the Bologna process changes the relationship between university and non-university higher education in Germany, the Netherlands and France', *Studies in Higher Education*, 33 (3): 217–31.

Wolin, S. (2004) *Politics and Vision: Continuity and Innovation in Western Political Thought*. Expanded edition. Princeton, NJ: Princeton University Press.

Wynne, B. (1996) 'May the sheep safely graze? A reflexive view of the expert–lay knowledge divide', in S. Lash, B. Szerszynski and B. Wynne (eds), *Risk, Environment and Modernity: Towards a New Ecology*. London: Sage

Young, A. (1990) *Femininity in Dissent*. London: Routledge.

Ziman, J. (1994) *Prometheus Bound: Science in a Dynamic and Steady State*. Cambridge: Cambridge University Press.

Žižek, S. (2009) *First as Tragedy, Then as Farce*. London: Verso.

AUTHOR INDEX

SUBJECT INDEX

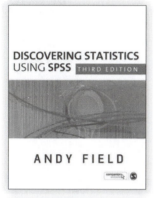
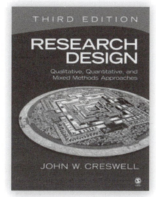

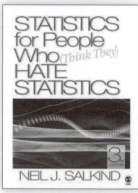

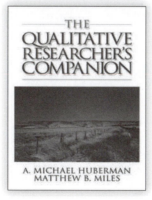

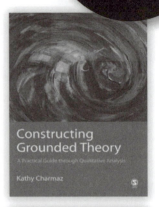

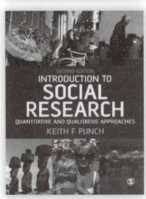
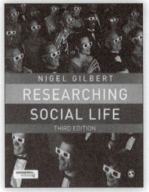
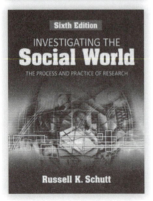